INVESTMENT ATLAS

FINANCIAL MAPS TO INVESTMENT SUCCESS

Kenneth G. Winans

KGW Publishing

Published by KGW Publishing, Novato, CA 94949 USA
www.winansintl.com
www.investmentatlas.com

See disclaimer on page 221.

ISBN: 978-0-9793014-4-5

Library of Congress Control Number: 2008926410

Author Portrait: © 2007 Jeanette Vonier
Book Angel: Renée Robinson, SG&A Productions, Inc., www.sgaprod.com
Copy Editor: John Maybury, www.goofbuster.com
Data Providers: Global Financial Data, Winans International
Designer: Rik Rice, mystrik@hotmail.com

Printed in the United States of America

TABLE OF CONTENTS

ACKNOWLEDGMENTS

No author ever writes a book by himself or herself, and with an illustrated reference book, it is especially true. A special "thank you" to the following:

Edward Brown

Warren Buffett

Karen Butler

Gary Hanauer

Bob Kerstein

John Maybury

Rik Rice

Jeanette Vonier

Debbie Wreyford

Global Financial Data

   Michelle Suzanne

   Bryan Taylor

Museum of American Finance

SG&A Productions, Inc.

   Renée Robinson

Winans International

   Karen Blair

   Sheila Cruise

   Justin Gularte

DEDICATION

This book marks a rare accomplishment—two books written and published by the same author in less than 20 months.

Hundreds of hours of intense work required to construct a book takes a toll on a person both physically and mentally. More important, it also requires sacrifices by the author's family.

This book is dedicated to my "lucky charm," my wife and soul mate Debbie Wreyford. Since we first met, great things have happened in my life!

Deb, while it would take me writing another book to express my gratitude for your encouragement as I accomplish my life's important tasks, I want to simply say "thank you" for supporting my ambitions and dreams.

Now, let's go on vacation!

Love, Ken

Ken and wife Debbie at the grand opening of the Museum of American Finance in New York City

ix

FOREWORD

Ken Winans has written a book that will fascinate anyone interested in the financial markets and their history, and will hopefully convince everyone else of the importance of studying our financial past.

Cable TV focuses our attention on what the market is doing this day, this hour, and this minute. If the market is up today, each person comes on and explains why the market is rallying, and tomorrow when the market declines, each person explains why the market is falling. You nearly forget they said the same things last week when the market rallied and fell. To get some perspective, it is important to step back and not get caught up in the mania of the moment.

I remember back in 1999, I read a survey of investors that asked them how much they expected the Dow Jones Industrials to go up each year for the next 10 years. The average answer was 35%. No doubt, they have been very disappointed.

I also remember an article that showed the performance of RCA stock during the 1920s, noting that its 90% decline in the 1930s was likely to be the fate of most Internet stocks. The person with the knowledge of RCA's history proved to be right and those caught up in the Internet mania were wrong.

If you're not a financial history expert, with 200 years of financial market history in the United States, where do you start? How do you get a handle on what was important in the past and what wasn't? Many investors have some understanding of the past, but the problem is how to put it all together.

Investment Atlas provides the perfect starting point. It is a comprehensive map to past financial markets, looking at many of the issues that have affected investors over the past 200 years. The book organizes the various factors that affect financial markets succinctly for quick reference. So next time someone comes out and proclaims, "This time, it's different," you can go to the investment atlas to find out that it probably isn't.

Though I love to analyze charts, the atlas is more than just a collection of charts. It's really more of a time capsule. Each chart is accompanied by pictures, cartoons, historical documents, old stock certificates, and other artifacts to give you the feel of what was going on in the past. It helps you see how people who lived through the events of the past viewed what was happening to them. Even those who aren't financial history buffs and technical analysts should enjoy the book for all the historical documents that are included.

Can't remember the details of the War of 1812? The charts document the history surrounding the stock market's movements. You can see how the stock market declined as Buffalo, then Washington, D.C., were destroyed. History and the stock market clash head-on in the charts as the primary events of the Civil War or World War II are documented. It's just a wonderful blast from the past.

One of the things I like about the book is that it goes beyond the traditional portfolio of stocks, bonds and bills, and includes real estate, commodities, collectibles, and other investments to show how they have performed over time. For most people, their home is the largest investment asset they own, and millions of people collect coins, stamps, art, or other non-financial items. Assessing the performance of real estate, collectibles, and other investments is difficult, and now you can get an idea of how these compare with traditional investments.

Like any atlas, the goal is to help the investor find out where they are going. The charts make me want to study the data in more detail and look at the real numbers, play around with them, test out my own hypotheses, and see what works and doesn't work in the market. Looking at the chart for Enron makes me wonder how similar the chart is to Bear Stearns.

In short, *Investment Atlas* is a fascinating book that helps you dive into the history of financial markets, and let's you live it as well. Enjoy!

Dr. Bryan Taylor, *President*
Global Financial Data

INTRODUCTION
IT'S DIFFERENT THIS TIME?

We have all heard the phrase "History repeats itself!" Yet very few people seriously apply long-term history to the art and science of investing.

There is no better example of this than how the majority of modern investors, the most knowledgeable and technologically advanced in history, mishandled the dot.com bull market and the prolonged bear market that followed. Throughout the 1990s, the phrase "It's different this time!" was repeated by Wall Street's elite analysts, and investors blindly kept buying stocks and mutual funds throughout 1999 and 2000, ignorant of the fact that they were playing long Las Vegas odds of success and not even taking a *Cliff Notes* glance at the behavior of past bull markets.

Does this sound familiar? "The Federal Reserve is much blamed because it made money easy, and that easy money help to start the current investment boom. The real fault is that too many people are eager to grab something for nothing."

No, it wasn't written in 1999 about technology stocks. It came out of a business publication in January 1929.

In the lunacy of this easy-money era, if the investing public had realized that the stock market's performance over the past 10 years had far exceeded the return of the great bull market of the Roaring 20s, would they have been so eager to buy another Internet stock IPO, with no earnings, and run by a whiz kid with limited business experience?

At the other end of the spectrum, the terrorist attacks of 2001 were publicly compared to the 1941 surprise assault on Pearl Harbor. Many panicked investors didn't even consider that the market would act in a similar "wartime" way as they dumped their stocks with no plans to reinvest.

The time-tested knowledge that stocks usually go up in war, not down, cost them dearly as the stocks posted a 25% rally over the next 3½ months.

This historical ignorance isn't limited to stock investors.

Today's real estate speculators recently bought overpriced investment properties with "nothing down" by using adjustable rate mortgages based on the myth that real estate never loses value. It might have been wise for them to study how rising interest rates and overdevelopment sent housing into a nosedive in the late 1960s and early 1980s.

Clearly, the constant barrage of news, earnings projections, economic reports, and advice from respected professionals streaming over media outlets 24 hours a day hasn't helped investors separate the forest from the trees and tackle the age-old problems of successful investing.

Cartoon—1882

1

HISTORY IS AN IMPORTANT KEY TO PROFITABILITY!

Though personal experience is an important teacher, learning to correctly interpret and apply history's lessons is a more important factor in successful investing. Remember, the names and faces are different, but the basic investment game hasn't changed in the past 150 years!

This reference book has been designed to help an investor build and maintain a strong foundation based on financial facts—a sort of investment history playbook—that an investor can refer to during a future calamity or to find out the performance record of a certain type of investment over the past 200 years.

This book is divided into five sections. The first section, "There's Gold in Them Financial Hills!" examines the amazing growth of the U.S. economy and key developments of investing in America.

The "Time-Tested Investments" section studies the basic characteristics of six different types of investments since 1800. Unlike many investment books that view only one type of investment in a vacuum, this section includes stocks, real estate, bonds, commodities, collectibles, and cash in combined studies. The reader will realize that each type of investment has a different personality, and just like dealing with people, investors either learn to deal with the different types or avoid the ones they can't get along with. Though investors don't have to invest in every type of investment studied in this book, it is important that they follow the historical trends and know the advantages and disadvantages of these investments to determine which are the best investments for them.

Section 3, "Market Cycles—From Easy Money to Crash Landings," examines the major bull and bear markets in stocks, and real estate since 1800, and demonstrates how some of the tools outlined in Section 2 can provide the reader with clues as to the market's overall health.

"Historical Events—Does Wall Street Care?" studies the reactions of stocks, housing, and interest rates to various factors and scenarios that have continuously confronted investors throughout history, such as wars, disasters (natural and man-made), and the never-ending government actions (i.e., interest rates, taxes, and regulations) in reaction to these situations.

The last section, "Investing the Historic Way," demonstrates ways to practically use historical information in establishing a disciplined investment strategy, which involves setting reasonable goals, dealing with taxes, and proper ways to monitor an investment portfolio's progress. This section demonstrates that a successful investor doesn't need to be a genius or well educated but needs to study major issues and events that have affected investments through the ages, and the discipline to stay the historical course and not emotionally follow the herd to the financial slaughterhouse during future bear markets in stocks, bonds, and real estate.

The knowledge in this book also serves as a good BS detector in screening investment professionals, and should help you find the elite investment advisors, financial planners, and brokers who are worth hiring. In other words, if they don't know the information in this book, don't waste your time and money working with them!

This book's emphasis is not to pick market tops and bottoms with a secret indicator, but rather to identify investment scenarios that have been historically good times to make money in, and warning signs to help preserve those hard-won profits as the investment climate becomes turbulent. In other words, this book helps you determine when you should be a "bull" or a "bear" for the right time-proven reasons. Simply put, only investors knowledgeable of history's trends can successfully navigate the investment world over time.

WHAT IS NEEDED TO STUDY INVESTMENT HISTORY?

Three items are required to conduct the proper historical analysis of investments:

RELIABLE INVESTMENT INDEXES

Invention of the Dow Jones Industrial Average (DJIA) marked an important milestone in the history of investing, because it provided a common reference point of current stock market activity as well as a means to track its past performance. The index has been so successful that it has spawned the development of other investment indexes and products such as index funds and market derivatives, just to name a few.

But not all areas of investing are as well indexed, and many investors have had to develop their own indexes. Take preferred stocks, one of the oldest and most reliable exchange-listed income investments in existence. Until the Winans International Preferred Stock Index™ (WIPSI™) was introduced in 2005, there hadn't been a reliable index tracking this investment medium since the early 1900s.

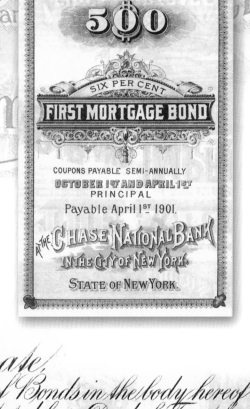

NEW YORK. MONDAY. JULY 8, 1889.

DJIA's First Day

Average Movement of Prices.

The bull market of 1885 began July 2, with the average price of 12 active stocks 61.49.

The rise culminated May 18, 1887, with the same twelve stocks selling at 93.27.

Prices gradually declined for about a year, reaching the next extreme low point April 2, 1888, the 12 stocks selling at 28. The movement since then, counting from one turning point to another, follows:

st low point	Apr. 2, 1888,	75.28
llied to	May 1, "	83.54
clined to	June 13, "	77.12
clined to	Aug. 8, "	85.95
llied to	Aug. 18, "	83.76
clined to	Oct. 1, "	88.10
llied to	Dec. 5, "	81.88
clined to	Feb. 18, 1889,	87.77
llied to	Mar. 18, "	83.59
clined to	June 12, "	91.38
sed Sat. night	July 6, "	87.71

The Market To-Day.

There is some reason for believing that operators identified h the bear party sent early orders to London to depress nericans in that market as a preparation for the opening These orders were faithfully executed, and London at quoted as opening weak and as having become very

Clearings Last Week.

Boston special—The Post's table of clearing, exchanges of 41 cities for the week ending Ju $1,127,114,523, against $883,993,314 last year, an in Outside of New York the inc. is 14.2%. New York Boston 27.9, Philadelphia 6.3, St Louis, 33.6, San 18, Cincinnati 7.2, Kansas City 27.5, New Orleans 3.1, 2, Omaha 39.5, Minneapolis 15.2, Detroit 2, Den Peoria 12.7, Indianapolis 3.9, Ft. Worth 90.3, Wich Chicago dec. 5%, Milwaukee 1.6, Duluth 44.6 and Top

For the month of June exchanges of 40 cities sho crease of 22.2%. Outside of New York increase 9.3 York increase 30.3%. Boston 18.8%, Philadelphia 12.1% 0.1%, St. Louis 18.9%, San Francisco 2.7%, Kansas Cit Paul 2.1%, Omaha 20.8%, Denver 26.6%, Peoria Worth 47%, Topeka 18.4%. Duluth decrease 45.5%

For 6 months gross exchanges of 40 cities show of 15.8%. Outside of New York increase 11.9% increase 18.2%. Boston 11.8%, Philadelphia 15.9% St. Louis 8.5%, San Francisco 1.9%, Kansas Cit 19.5%. Denver 38.9%, Peoria 17.3%, Duluth 31.8%, Topeka 31.4%.

Bankers Exerting Thei

Chicago special—It is stated on the Western presidents are getting York and Boston banking hous bles at the meeting to-morro

Charles Dow autograph—1891

FINANCIAL ARCHAEOLOGY

One of the greatest problems in conducting long-term investment analysis is getting reliable data. Because of this, most investors and Wall Street professionals don't take their studies far enough back in time to be useful for long-term historical comparisons.

A great amount of time and effort went into amassing and compiling data needed to construct studies for this book. In fact, many of the data are from hard-to-find sources or required physically going into the library stacks to find the information.

Furthermore, to have continuous, usable charts and tables over a long time frame, many different indexes' percentage movements had to be combined. In other words, the focus in constructing charts used in this book is on percentage change of various indexes, not the indexes' values. For example, U.S. common stock studies in this book came from many sources, such as S&P 500 Stock Index™ (1928-present), Dow Jones Industrial Average™ (1927-1887), Cowles Commission Studies (1871-1886), and Smith and Cole Studies (1800-1870), with volume figures from the New York Stock Exchange (1871-present).

CHARTS—THE "MAPS" OF INVESTMENT HISTORY

We have all heard the phrase "A picture tells a thousand words."

The "pictures" in this book are primarily charts of past investment activity. As you will see, these are an effective way to identify historical investment trends. Just as a traveler uses a road atlas to determine time and distance for a trip, charts of past market conditions help determine the overall direction and make historical comparisons with other types of investments.

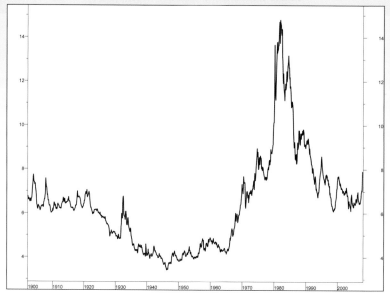

WIPSI™ Yield—1900 to 2007

WIPSI Price—1890 to 2007

Investment Table

Winans International Preferred Stock Index								
	Yield	Price		Yield	Price		Yield	Price
1900	7.90%	18.58%	1937	4.26%	-4.26%	1974	7.82%	-10.83%
1901	7.63%	22.33%	1938	4.45%	7.25%	1975	8.78%	4.42%
1902	6.81%	0.55%	1939	4.15%	0.95%	1976	8.50%	13.21%
1903	6.65%	-17.62%	1940	4.11%	4.34%	1977	7.65%	-4.26%
1904	7.60%	17.10%	1941	3.94%	-5.29%	1978	7.84%	-11.32%
1905	6.39%	5.61%	1942	4.15%	-0.95%	1979	8.91%	-13.43%
1906	6.17%	-7.71%	1943	4.19%	1.92%	1980	10.14%	-17.08%
1907	6.36%	-28.82%	1944	4.16%	7.06%	1981	13.78%	-6.56%
1908	7.37%	29.96%	1945	3.87%	8.14%	1982	14.78%	20.27%
1909	6.36%	7.17%	1946	3.57%	-5.08%	1983	12.36%	-0.04%
1910	6.06%	-6.51%	1947	3.75%	-8.30%	1984	12.46%	3.01%
1911	6.38%	0.37%	1948	4.04%	-0.99%	1985	12.18%	13.51%
1912	6.36%	-0.45%	1949	4.14%	7.02%	1986	10.65%	30.26%
1913	6.39%	-3.74%	1950	3.87%	-0.88%	1987	8.69%	-10.63%
1914	6.64%	0.19%	1951	3.90%	-9.95%	1988	9.76%	-0.96%
1915	6.62%	6.15%	1952	4.29%	5.00%	1989	9.76%	9.64%
1916	6.24%	1.61%	1953	4.11%	-1.94%	1990	8.96%	-2.04%
1917	6.14%	-12.20%	1954	4.22%	6.60%	1991	9.12%	12.42%
1918	6.99%	6.89%	1955	3.92%	-3.15%	1992	8.09%	4.80%
1919	6.54%	1.96%	1956	4.05%	-7.96%	1993	7.69%	9.88%
1920	6.42%	-8.98%	1957	4.62%	-0.13%	1994	6.97%	-16.43%
1921	7.05%	7.95%	1958	4.44%	-4.24%	1995	8.58%	16.06%
1922	6.53%	8.31%	1959	4.62%	-5.81%	1996	7.49%	-0.14%
1923	6.03%	-2.33%	1960	4.89%	2.11%	1997	7.49%	14.77%
1924	6.17%	3.26%	1961	4.85%	3.50%	1998	6.69%	9.87%
1925	5.98%	2.31%	1962	4.66%	5.17%	1999	6.23%	-14.74%
1926	5.84%	3.17%	1963	4.42%	1.64%	2000	7.43%	2.11%
1927	5.66%	4.93%	1964	4.32%	3.10%	2001	7.34%	11.54%
1928	5.40%	5.63%	1965	4.21%	-6.26%	2002	6.97%	6.90%
1929	5.11%	1.02%	1966	4.48%	-14.25%	2003	6.98%	9.78%
1930	5.06%	0.58%	1967	5.24%	-11.82%	2004	6.32%	4.76%
1931	5.03%	-15.88%	1968	6.00%	-1.27%	2005	6.32%	-4.35%
1932	5.98%	2.39%	1969	5.92%	-15.99%	2006	6.59%	1.98%
1933	5.84%	1.00%	1970	7.32%	3.58%	2007	7.90%	-17.46%
1934	5.78%	16.76%	1971	6.86%	1.88%			
1935	4.95%	12.02%	1972	6.83%	-2.04%			
1936	4.42%	3.72%	1973	6.89%	-12.28%			

As the examples show, it is much faster and easier to determine the overall direction of the market with a chart than with a table of numbers.

I started writing this book on a beach in Puerto Vallarta, Mexico. I was struck by how much the study of investment history resembles the movement of ocean waves. It was easy to see that the size and shape of no two waves were identical, yet the forces and factors that created them are the same.

Look at the front cover of this book. Isn't it amazing how much the stock market trends of the three great bull markets shown resemble one another? In other words, when charts of an investment, from the same scenario in two different time frames, are compared, the patterns are not usually identical and yet the direction of the trend is. This is because the economic forces that move the investment in a certain direction are the same in the long term.

Ultimately, people's emotions (i.e., greed and fear) about money and investing haven't changed much over time, and their actions typically resemble those of previous investors. The critics of this type of analysis will tell you that investment prices don't trend and instead move randomly through time. Their unrealistic answer to investing is to "buy all the time." As you study the following pages, it will soon become obvious that investment prices do trend over long periods of time.

This information, coupled with the tools outlined in the "Time-Proven Investments" section, can help investors make important investment decisions. As stated before, this book is not about attempting to pick market tops and bottoms with a magic formula, rather it uses history to keep you on the right side of the tracks in major bull or bear markets.

THE WINANS COLLECTION

Throughout my education and career, I have read many useful yet incredibly dull and boring books on economics, finance, and investing, whose important messages are lost on less-than-enthusiastic readers. To ensure this book does not fall into that infamous category, the best parts of investment, history, and art books are combined. Useful yet beautiful!

As a serious collector of antique financial documents, photographs and publications (many on display in the Museum of American Finance), I have used many pieces of this collection, some dating back to the 1600s, to decorate this book and help bring historical events back to life.

As a final note, I am a 12th-generation American whose Dutch family first arrived and established colonies in New York and New Jersey. They became some of this nation's first multimillionaires. My mother's Swedish family emigrated to California in the 1850s and soon became leaders in science, architecture, agriculture, and business.

An epiphany hit me as I began working on this book: "My ancestors experienced everything I'm writing about—the wars, depressions, natural disasters—all of it!" To honor their achievements, I also have accented their investment experiences throughout this text.

Enjoy the Journey!

Kenneth G. Winans

First edition of *The Wall Street Journal*—July 8, 1889
from the author's collection, on display at
the Museum of American Finance in New York City

6

Nieuw Amsterdam onlangs Nieuw Jorck genaemt. en nu hernomen by de Nederlanders op den 24 Aug 1673.

Eisen Family Crest—1600s

New York Stock Exchange during the panic of 1915

Winans Coat of Arms—1100s

Remember, successful investing is hard work!

WALL STREET, N.Y.
1847.

Town view of old "Dry Diggins" 1849 The beginnings of what would become Placerville, Ca. Large oak tree "middle left" was infamous "Hangmans' Tree" just behind the Jackass Inn.

Chinese miners, and partners, sluicing

TELEPHONE AND ORDER DEPARTMENT, HAIGHT & FREESE CO., N.Y.

THERE'S GOLD IN THEM FINANCIAL HILLS!

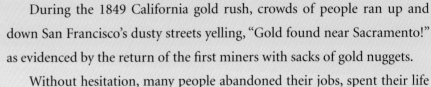

During the 1849 California gold rush, crowds of people ran up and down San Francisco's dusty streets yelling, "Gold found near Sacramento!" as evidenced by the return of the first miners with sacks of gold nuggets.

Without hesitation, many people abandoned their jobs, spent their life savings on mining tools, and headed into the wilderness with dreams of easy money. The plan was simple: just dig—something's bound to show up!

The outcome was predictable—only a handful of miners ever found enough gold to be rich. After a few years, many unsuccessful miners returned from the goldfields angry and bitter from the experience. Most blamed their misfortune on the businessmen who made their fortunes by selling equipment and supplies to them while filling their heads with fantasies that the easy riches were just another shovelful of dirt away.

Modern financial bull markets conjure up similar dreams of easy riches that are just a computer keystroke away for anybody and everybody with an Internet brokerage account!

Yet during the bear markets that follow, many novice investors blame the financial community for their economic demise, claiming the stock market is just another casino and that only Wall Street makes money through the fees and commissions they charge investors.

Is there really gold in them financial hills or is it a deception created by Wall Street to sell investment products?

In this section, it can be seen that the path to financial success has been, and continues to be, alive and well for disciplined, knowledgeable investors.

"Regardless of their professional standing, the vast majority of investors underperform the markets. Emotions easily overwhelmed reasoning when money is at stake. When times are good, investors take them for granted and do not prepare for risks."

Inside the Investor's Brain, Peterson—2007

U.S. ECONOMY

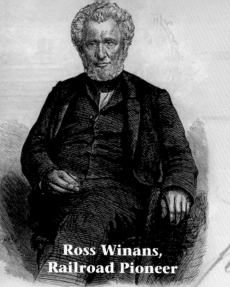

**Ross Winans,
Railroad Pioneer**

Long-term investing can be successful only within a healthy economic environment of solid growth and mild inflationary pressures.

As can be seen, the U.S. economy has grown to be $14.7 trillion in 2007. This is a 2.8 million percent increase since 1800!

The second chart shows that economic growth isn't a straight line. The cycle from a recession low point to the top of the following economic expansion has happened 38 times in the past 207 years, and averages 5½ years in duration, with future growth generally making up lost financial ground quickly.

U.S. Gross Domestic Product—1800 to 2007
Current Level—$14.7 Trillion

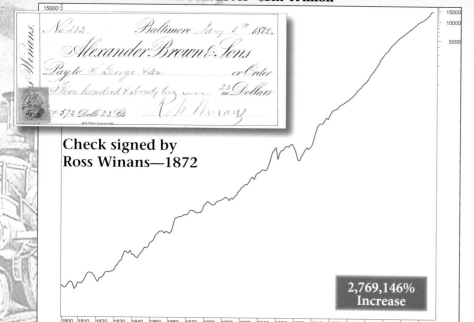

Check signed by
Ross Winans—1872

**2,769,146%
Increase**

The Stock Market
with Economic Expansions and Recessions—1800 to 2007

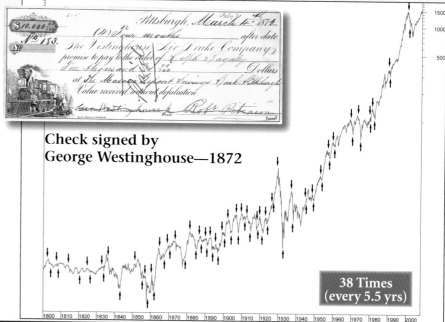

Check signed by
George Westinghouse—1872

**38 Times
(every 5.5 yrs)**

"From 1869 onward, the United States evolved from a preponderantly agricultural setting,
in which it depended on and was oriented toward foreign commerce,
into a growing industrial and service-oriented economy
with a vast and expanding domestic market at its disposal."
The American Economy, Spulber—1995

INFLATION

Inflation is the erosion in the value of money mainly caused by government policies that overproduce the amount of their currency held by the public in light of the limited availability of goods and services for consumption. Simply put, a dollar today doesn't buy the same goods and services as yesterday. History has repeatedly shown that unchecked inflation has led to worthless money and global conflicts.

As seen in this chart, over the past 207 years, the annual U.S. inflation rate has been as high as 25% (1864), deflation as low as –16% (1802), and has averaged 4.2%.

Inflation rates are significantly higher during wars than during peacetime. Since 1859, the average annual inflation rate has been 2.3%. During the seven wars since that time, the average inflation rate has been 7.3%, while the peacetime rate was only 1%.

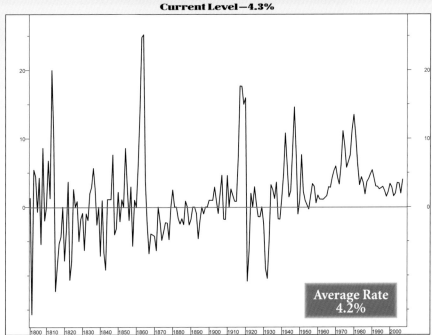

U.S. Inflation Rate—1800 to 2007
Current Level—4.3%

Average Rate
4.2%

"After World War II the Federal Reserve System continued to increase the quantity of money rapidly, thereby feeding the inflation."
Freedom to Choose, Friedman—1979

Article on Inflation—1934
The Magazine of Wall Street

"No Such Thing as Controlled Inflation"

We Must Abandon Our Complacent Indifference to Debt and Revive Our Fundamental Conceptions of Money or Face the Dire Consequences of Fiat Currency

ARTHUR H. VANDENBERG
U. S. Senator from Michigan

in an Interview with
THEODORE M. KNAPPEN

THERE is a very old saying that familiarity breeds contempt. We all know how true it is. There is now a perturbing national manifestation of deterioration of respect into contempt.

Since March, 1933, this nation has become so familiar with money in astronomic quantities that although most of us have less cash than we ever had before we share in a composite national contempt for money in any but the most imposing quantities. A million dollars has become small change to us, billions do not stir us; it is only when we get into the tens of billions that we begin to show a languid interest, even as the recipients. Even then we do not get wildly excited as taxpayers. When we read that the national debt, at more than $27,000,000,000, has reached a higher point than at the end of the World War, which was then looked upon as a record that would hold for all time, we are not shocked. We let Harry Hopkins pass the burden off lightly with the remark that we do not yet know what taxes are in this country, as he points admiringly at the higher taxes paid by the peoples of Great Britain, France and Germany.

expenditures, which presumab[ly] covered by the revenues, are five times as much as they w[ere] those relatively parsimonious [days].

Just as we look lightly upon which would have terrified other days we look indifferent[ly] money as an institution. It longer something interwoven the very warp and woof of [its] integrity and solidity. W[e] taken 40 per cent of the gold that abstraction, the standard dollar, and still call it a dolla[r] have made a fictitious profit Treasury of about three bil[lion] lars by taking away the gol[d] Reserve Banks and giving th[em] gold certificates according to [the] ered gold content. When school days we read about [the] basing the coinage with a thought of them as royal s[illy] Now, moreover, we are buy[ing] and issuing silver certificate[s] perhaps issuing each paper if the silver were worth ounce, whereas we begin [to] ounce for it. Here is inflation [by] 50 cents an ounce for it. [The] profit by a devious and dubious method. T[he] money and the bonds which were redeemable in lars at $20.67 to the ounce are now redeemab[le]

Wide World Photo
Senator Vandenberg

INVESTMENT LIQUIDITY

To effectively invest, you have to have systems of exchange to buy and sell investments efficiently. In world history, no country has done this better than the United States, where the financial industry has been able to keep pace with the ever-growing demand for stocks, bonds, and real estate.

NYSE Corporate Bond Volume—1900 to 2007
Current monthly level—30 billion bonds

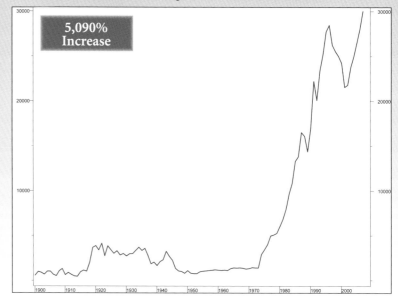

5,090% Increase

NYSE Share Volume—1874 to 2007
Current monthly level—26.3 billion shares

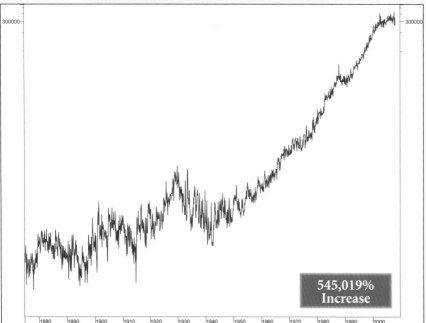

545,019% Increase

New Home Sales—1964 to 2007
Current monthly level—42,000 homes

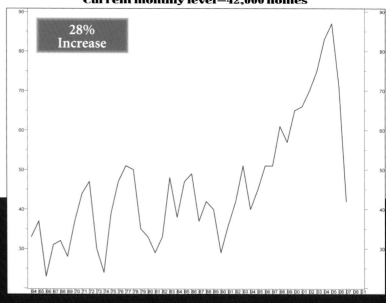

28% Increase

"The Stock Exchange or Bourse in its present use is a modern creation."
The ABC's of Stock Speculation, Nelson—1903

INVESTMENT INVENTIONS

Individual Retirement Accounts—1962 to 2007
Current Level—$457 billion

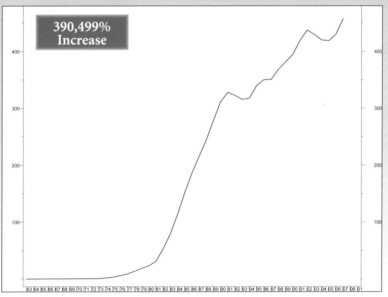

390,499%
Increase

Modern investors have a wide assortment of products that allow them to tax-effectively invest in stocks, real estate, bonds, commodities, collectibles, and cash-equivalent investments.

Two of Wall Street's most popular inventions are mutual funds and tax-deferred individual retirement accounts. In fact, both of these products have significantly increased the participation of smaller investors in stocks and bonds.

Summary

Yes, there is definitely still gold in them financial hills! The following sections of this book will show what is reasonable to expect from an investment in the next bull or bear market as well as how investors have typically reacted to historical events.

By learning history, you shouldn't end up like most miners of the 1800s, or the majority of investors today, who bank too much on luck and thus repeat the same financial mistakes that others have in the past.

Mutual Fund Assets ($ billions)—1940 to 2006

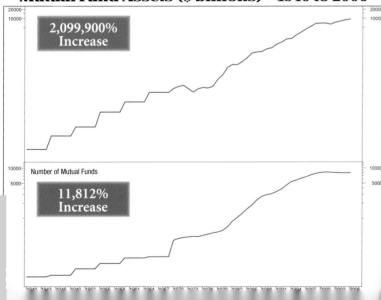

2,099,900%
Increase

Number of Mutual Funds

11,812%
Increase

Mutual Fund Article–1932

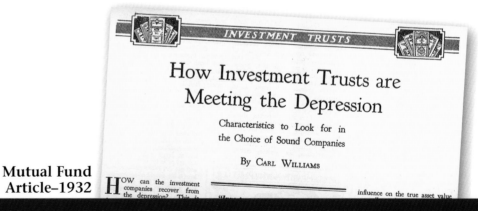

How Investment Trusts are Meeting the Depression

Characteristics to Look for in the Choice of Sound Companies

By CARL WILLIAMS

HOW can the investment companies recover from the depression? This is... influence on the true asset value

"There are over two hundred mutual funds, some of enormous size. Mutual funds are merely co-ops, and they can be started by anyone in any way."

TIME-TESTED INVESTMENTS

With all the colorful vocabulary produced by the financial community, it's interesting to note that all investments basically come down to two types. Investors either **own or loan,** and neither kind constitutes a "perfect" investment for everybody. Sorry, there is no holy grail of investments!

Undoubtedly, owning is the best way to create wealth over the long term (i.e., capital appreciation), but it can be volatile in the short term, and if done stupidly can cause significant, often devastating, losses.

On the other hand, loaning can provide a predictable rate of return and produce income to meet an investor's regular cash needs without the need to sell or borrow against investments. Unfortunately, many investors confuse low risk of default with market volatility that can cause surprising swings in market value throughout the life of income investments.

Simply put, every investment has its ups and downs!

This section examines the long-term characteristics of stocks, real estate, bonds, commodities, collectibles, and cash-equivalent investments.

Though the results might be a bit surprising and quite possibly contradict your own limited experiences, this long-term research should help investors better identify the best investments for their individual needs, and to know what is reasonable to expect, good and bad, from different types of investments over time.

WHY IS LONG-TERM INVESTMENT ANALYSIS IMPORTANT?

Investment analysis is often done backward, with an overemphasis on short-term results. Long-term statistics are commonly presented as un-important, curious facts. Ironically, most of the investing public consider themselves "long-term investors," yet they focus on the short-term value fluctuations of their investments.

We all enjoy pictures sent back from outer space that show the earth from a distance. They show us weather patterns and topographical forma-tions that seem random at ground level.

Long-range investment analysis can be seen in the same light. If an investor starts from a high or long historical vantage point, then the investor should gain a broader prospective of his/her investment's overall trends and performance characteristics. The wise investor hopes that when the next market panic erupts, he/she will be less likely to overreact to short-term events and the media's perspective on them.

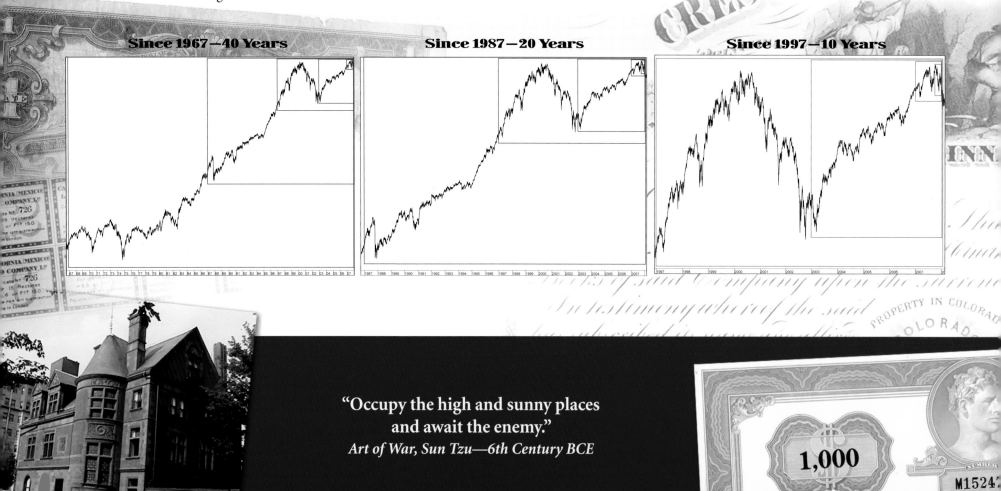

Since 1967—40 Years   **Since 1987—20 Years**   **Since 1997—10 Years**

"Occupy the high and sunny places
and await the enemy."
Art of War, Sun Tzu—6th Century BCE

Look at these charts of U.S. common stocks from different time frames:

1. Since 1967
2. Since 1987
3. Since 1997
4. Since 2003
5. 2007
6. Fourth Quarter, 2007

A picture (or chart) really does tell a thousand words! Though an investor focusing on volatility in the fourth quarter of 2007 could have been easily shaken out of solid stock investments, the longer-term charts show the market's overall trend is still advancing.

So let's ask the question again: Why is long-term investment analysis important?

Answer: If financial history repeats itself, how can investors take advantage of repeating conditions, if they haven't studied similar past situations and learned what to look for?

Since 2003—5 Years

2007—1 Year

4th Quarter—2007

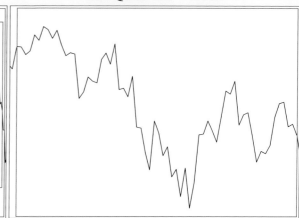

"We would not make a practice of studying these long-term charts every week or so, but say once a quarter it does make sense to review the long-term picture."
Technical Analysis Explained, Pring—2002

STOCK MARKET BARON

← DOW-JONES INDUSTRIAL AVERAGES

GROSS NATIONAL (in billions)

Bear Market

1929 1930 1931

EARNING

Mt. Eisen in California

READING

Dr. Eisen

Zadig & Co.

STOCK, BOND, OIL and GRAIN BROKER

No. 324 Bush Street

San Francisco, 6/4 190

To Mr. G. Eisen

We have this day **SOLD**
your account and risk as follows:

500 Laguna @ 1⁵

@

did will Kindly

bring in stock at

once @

@

Yours, etc.

Zadig & Co.

Mr. Gustav Eisen
1857 Pine St
City

**This stock transaction receipt from the
bear market of 1906 and 1907 belongs to
legendary collector and scientist Dr. Gustav Eisen
(the author's great-great-great uncle).**

STOCKS –

The invention of the corporation in the 1600s has transformed the world in ways that even Adam Smith, the father of modern economics, would have had trouble imagining. It is ironic that his classic work *Wealth of Nations* was written in 1776, the year America was born, because no country has embraced the corporation more passionately than the United States as it has amassed wealth at a rate never seen before in world history.

Every year, leading magazines list the richest people in America, and the vast majority of these individuals made the bulk of their fortune through various business (i.e., stock) investments, thus proving their value as the premier wealth producers.

But it is not "easy money" at the push of a button on a brokerage website. With billions of shares traded daily in the U.S. alone, stock investing is fast-moving and volatile, where strong companies can suddenly lose a year's worth of gain in seconds from events they did not necessarily cause. It's also worth noting that every single past generation has gone through serious multiyear stock bear markets (1906-1907, 1929-1932, 1973-1974, 2000-2002) where losses exceeded 40%, and the financial devastation is well remembered with fear and anger.

THE GREATEST SECURITIES MARKET IN THE WORLD.

"Distrust of stocks was the prevailing American attitude
throughout the 1950s and into the 1960s,
when the market tripled and then doubled again."
One Up on Wall Street, Lynch—1989

19

U.S. COMMON STOCKS

Below are charts showing the prices and dividends of U.S. common stocks since the early 1800s, as well as the total return (annual price change and dividends combined) adjusted for inflation since 1850.

SINCE 1850

Average Annual Total Return	11.1%
Inflation Adjusted Total Return	8.9%
Highest Total Return	87.5% in 1915
Worst Total Return	(42%) in 1931
Negative Returns	28% of the time
Consecutive Negative Returns	7% of the time

U.S. Common Stocks Prices
and Dividend Yield—1800 to 2007

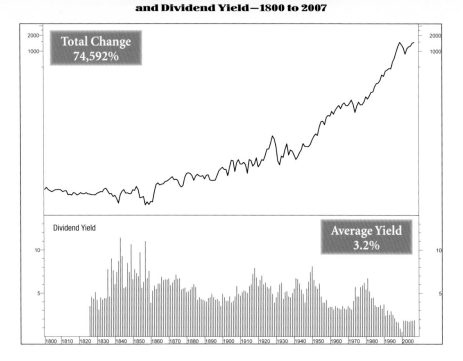

U.S. Common Stocks Total Return
and Inflation Adjusted Return 1850 to 2007

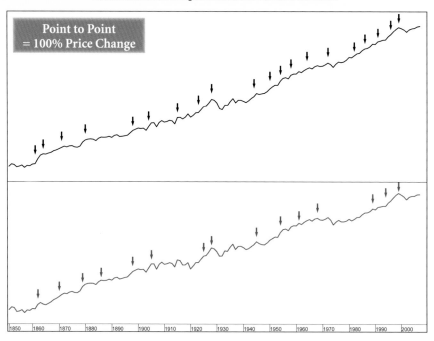

"Common stock is more often a speculative or semi-speculative security than preferred stocks or bonds.
In many cases common stocks have never received dividends and probably never will.
Their chief value is measured partly by their voting power and
partly by the fluctuating value of the equity in the property of which they are shares."
The Art of Wall Street Investing, Moody—1906

U.S. stocks come in many sizes. Wall Street has long indexed and evaluated their performance by the market capitalization of the companies within groups of similar-size corporations.

Which group performs best?

This chart shows large, medium, and small stock performance since 1927. They look nearly identical, and yet by far the best-performing group is mid-cap stocks. These securities have produced a higher cumulative return due to having fewer negative years than either small- or large-cap stocks.

Simply put, bigger does not mean better!

1927-2007	Total Returns	Negative Years	Consecutive Neg Years	Return Extremes < 20%	Return Extremes > -20%	Outperform U.S. Large-cap
U.S. Large-cap Stocks						
Cumulative Returns	195,704%	29%	10%	39%	6%	na
Average Annual Returns	12%					
Median	13%					
High	53%					
Low	-44%					
U.S. Small-cap Stocks						
Cumulative Returns	477,210%	34%	10%	43%	11%	58%
Average Annual Returns	15%					
Median	18%					
High	120%					
Low	-50%					
U.S. Mid-cap Stocks						
Cumulative Returns	1,071,395%	28%	10%	40%	8%	58%
Average Annual Returns	15%					
Median	16%					
High	102%					
Low	-46%					

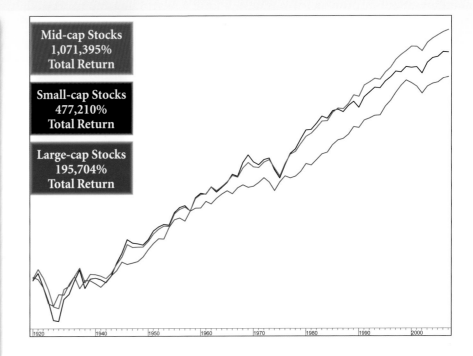

Mid-cap Stocks
1,071,395%
Total Return

Small-cap Stocks
477,210%
Total Return

Large-cap Stocks
195,704%
Total Return

"Higher returns are associated with higher risk.
If there is a trade-off between risk and reward, medium capitalization stocks
theoretically should track between the large-cap and the small-cap over the long run."
S&P MidCap 400 Directory—2006

GOING LONG

Besides its superior long-term performance, stock investing is multi-dimensional. Through the use of margin, short sales, and stock options, even a small investor can increase his or her gains during bull markets and make profits in bear markets.

Margin loans are backed by the assets held in a brokerage account. This allows investors to access their account equity by either withdrawing funds from the account or buying additional stocks without having to deposit more funds. It also allows aggressive investors to increase the return on investments in large, conservative companies whose shares are more liquid than smaller companies' shares.

Average Call Option Price—1989 to 2007

High	$19.46	2000
Low	$1.86	2003
Average	$5.37	

Current Level $8.38

NYSE Margin and Debt Limits—1918 to 2007

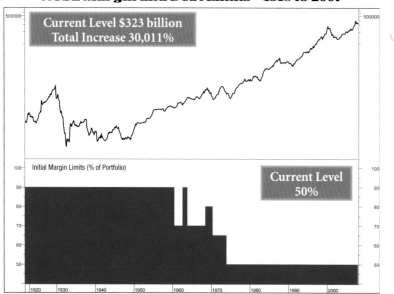

Current Level $323 billion
Total Increase 30,011%

Initial Margin Limits (% of Portfolio)

Current Level 50%

An investor can make money in stocks without even owning them. For a small price paid to the stock owner, a stock option gives its holder the right to buy (call) or sell (put) shares in the stock for a limited period of time at a set price. If the holder of the option has correctly judged the future direction of the stock's price within the option's limited life, then the option should greatly appreciate in price far more than the stock itself.

Remember that leverage is a two-edged sword and investment mistakes are very painful. Margin loans need to be paid back with after-tax dollars regardless of the account's current value, and options often expire worthless. Both add significant volatility to a stock portfolio in both bull and bear markets.

"Trading in put and call options is known to involve financial risks, but it is sometimes physically dangerous to trade options. Or at least it was in the 19th century, before organized option exchanges were developed. Before 1973, when the Chicago Board Options Exchange opened its doors, put and call options were primarily a matter between the buyer and the seller."
Financial History Magazine—Fall 2005

GOING SHORT

An aggressive stock investor can make money on stocks in bull markets by owning long for upward appreciation, and short selling during bear market declines.

This is done by borrowing another investor's stock held at a brokerage house with interest, selling the shares at the current price, with the objective of buying the shares back at a lower price in the future and returning the shares to the original owner. Remember, as with any margin loan, the shares borrowed for the short sale need to be paid back in the future at the brokerage house's discretion!

NYSE Short Interest Shares—1931 to 2007

Current Level 12.8 billion shares
Total Change 355,680%

Average Put Option Price—1989 to 2007

High	$18.30	2000
Low	$1.83	1990
Average	$4.49	

Current Level $5.84

"Short selling is not a short cut to fortune.
You might be right on the general market but go short on some stock
that rises against the trend and suffers enormous losses."
The Magazine of Wall Street—September 19, 1931

TIMELESS ADVICE

"Prudence suggests that investors have an adequate idea of stock-market history, in terms particularly of the major fluctuations in its price level and of the varying relationships between stock prices as a whole and their earnings and dividends."

The Intelligent Investor, Graham—1973

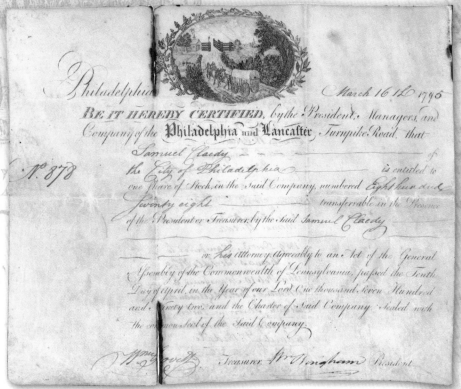

Philadelphia and Lancaster Turnpike Road—1795.
This is one of the first stock certificates to add artwork (vignettes) to the face of the certificate. The back of the certificate lists all its owners until its retirement in 1900.

"What has been done will be done again. Such examples fortify the doubts and misgivings which possess the mind during the first stages of a bull market, and stimulate the hardihood and pride that goeth before a fall."

Ten Years in Wall Street, Fowler—1870

THE ORACLE OF OMAHA

100 SHARES   100 SHARES

> "Buffett himself once said
> that growth investing
> and value investing
> are aspects of the same thing."
> *The Midas Touch, Train—1987*

100 Shares

No. TCA 35434

United Artists Theatre Circuit, Inc.
INCORPORATED UNDER THE LAWS OF THE STATE OF MARYLAND

COMMON STOCK

CANCELLED   NOV 13   CANCELLED

—WARREN E BUFFETT—

THIS CERTIFIES that..............
is the owner of ———— **ONE HUNDRED** ———— fully paid and
non-assessable shares, of the par value of One Dollar each, of the COMMON STOCK of
———— **UNITED ARTISTS THEATRE CIRCUIT, INC.** ————
(hereinafter called the Corporation), transferable on the books of the Corporation by said owner in person or by duly
authorized attorney upon surrender of this certificate properly endorsed.

A description and statement of the respective classes of the capital stock of the Corporation and of the preferences, voting powers, restrictions, limitations and qualifications thereof, as set forth at the date hereof in the Certificate of Incorporation of the Corporation, as amended, is printed on the back hereof. By the acceptance of this certificate and the shares represented hereby, the holder hereof thereby consents to, and agrees to be bound by, said
statement and all the provisions of said Certificate of Incorporation and all amendments thereto, copies of which are
on file with the Transfer Agent.

This certificate is not valid until countersigned by the Transfer Agent, and registered by the Registrar.

IN WITNESS WHEREOF the Corporation has caused this certificate to be signed
by its proper officers and to be sealed with its corporate seal.

Dated ....

UNITED ARTISTS THEATRE CIRCUIT, INC.,
by

A. H. Frisch
Secretary.

E. H. Crowley
Vice-President.

UNITED ARTISTS THEATRE CIRCUIT, INC. INCORPORATED 1926 MARYLAND

Registered: THE MARINE MIDLAND TRUST COMPANY OF NEW YORK, Registrar,
Authorized Officer.
by

Countersigned: THE CHASE MANHATTAN BANK, Transfer Agent,
Authorized Signature.
by

AMERICAN BANK NOTE COMPANY.

**This is a stock issued
to Mr. Buffett in 1961.**

The most successful stock investor of all time is Warren Buffett,
who has amassed $62 billion in assets since 1951 and is currently
ranked the richest man in the world.

Warren Buffett

> "The essence of Warren Buffett's thinking is that the business world is divided into
> a tiny number of wonderful businesses—well worth investing in at any price,
> and a huge number of bad or mediocre businesses that are not attractive as long-term investments...
> Bonds are often better investments than stocks of bad or mediocre businesses."
> *The Money Masters, Train—1980*

FOREIGN COMMON STOCKS

Investing in foreign equities is not new to Wall Street. Since colonial times, there has been active free flow of investments, with American investors buying foreign stocks and foreign investors buying American stocks. In fact, foreign stocks have been traded on U.S. stock exchanges since the late 1800s.

Below are charts listing foreign investment activity and prices since 1958, and they clearly show that as the post-World War II world economy expanded, so did the trading of stocks globally.

It is commonly believed that foreign stocks outperform domestic stocks and provide better protection against a bear market in U.S. stocks. This is not necessarily true. As can be seen in the charts and tables below, mid-cap U.S. stocks have outperformed world markets overall, and both mid-cap and small-cap U.S. stocks provide better diversification against a sell-off in large U.S. stocks than international stocks. It should also be noted that many investors confuse investment performance of a foreign stock with changes in the value of the U.S. dollar versus the home currency of the foreign company. This analysis was done in U.S. dollars.

Global Stock Transactions—1958 to 2007

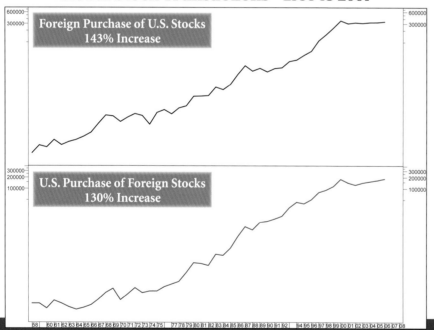

Foreign Purchase of U.S. Stocks
143% Increase

U.S. Purchase of Foreign Stocks
130% Increase

Foreign Stocks (returns in USD $)—1958 to 2007

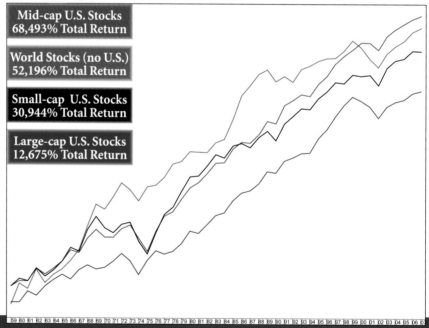

Mid-cap U.S. Stocks
68,493% Total Return

World Stocks (no U.S.)
52,196% Total Return

Small-cap U.S. Stocks
30,944% Total Return

Large-cap U.S. Stocks
12,675% Total Return

"From the standpoint of U.S. investors,
the benefits of global diversification tend to decline
just when they are needed most (in bear markets)."
International Monetary Fund Report—2007

"A lot of the world's financial markets
have been moving in the same direction
at the same time in recent years."
The Wall Street Journal—May 30, 2006

COMMON STOCK FACTS and OBSERVATIONS

SINCE 1850

Positives

- U.S. common stocks have produced a 772,599% cumulative gain (an 11.1% average annual return). In fact, $1 invested in stocks in December 1849 is worth $1,220,360 today ($34,560 after inflation)!

- They have been able to double in value 20 times (every 7.5 years on average).

- 44% of the total return was from dividend income.

- The best annual return was 87.5% in 1915!

Negatives

- U.S. common stocks have posted negative years 28% of the time (25% of these corrections were consecutive negative years).

- The average loss in a negative year was 12.2%, and the worst yearly loss was -42% in 1931.

SINCE 1927

When stocks are separated by size (i.e., market capitalization), U.S. mid-cap stocks have produced the best overall returns (1,071,395% cumulative, 15% average annual returns). They also have fewer negative years than large- and small-cap stocks.

SINCE 1958

When U.S. stocks are compared to world markets, U.S. mid-cap stocks have produced better overall returns and offer better diversification against a sell-off in large U.S. stocks than a basket of foreign markets in general.

1958-2007	Total Returns	Negative Years	Consecutive Neg Years	= Large Cap Neg Years	Return Extremes < 20%	Return Extremes > -20%	Outperform U.S. Large Cap
U.S. Large-cap Stocks							
Cumulative Returns	12,675%	22%	6%		35%	4%	
Average Annual Returns	12%						
Median	12%						
High	38%						
Low	-26%						
U.S. Small-cap Stocks							
Cumulative Returns	30,944%	29%	4%	36%	39%	10%	59%
Average Annual Returns	15%						
Median	18%						
High	64%						
Low	-34%						
U.S. Mid-cap Stocks							
Cumulative Returns	68,493%	22%	6%	36%	39%	4%	59%
Average Annual Returns	16%						
Median	16%						
High	57%						
Low	-26%						
World ex U.S. (in USD)							
Cumulative Returns	52,196%	24%	6%	64%	35%	4%	59%
Average Annual Returns	16%						
Median	13%						
High	70%						
Low	-26%						

Ads—1929

NYSE listed the Mexico Telephone Company—1899

U.S. PREFERRED STOCKS

These investments have been called "Wall Street Orphans," and are often overlooked for the high returns of common stocks and the promised interest payments of bonds. In reality, these income investments offer several key advantages: a high fixed-rate dividend paid indefinitely, unpaid dividends usually accumulate, many issues can be convertible at any time into the company's common stock, and they can qualify for lower taxes than bonds.

Most important, history has shown that preferred stocks have generally outperformed corporate and municipal bonds over the past 107 years, and that they could be included in investment portfolios for overall better returns. Simply put, they are Wall Street's best-kept secret in income investing!

Winans International Preferred Stock Index™ (WIPSI™) Price—1890 to 2007

Current Level $20.40

High	$28.48	1945
Low	$7.65	1981
Mean	$19.00	

Preferred Stock issued to Thomas A. Edison
The Edison Portland Cement Company—1906

"As between the comparatively low yields on good bonds and the uncertainty in connection with common stocks, investors are paying more attention to the attractive return and security obtainable in the preferred share market."
The Magazine of Wall Street—September 29, 1923

PREFERRED STOCK FACTS and OBSERVATIONS

SINCE 1900

Positives

- U.S. preferred stocks have produced a 104,854% cumulative gain (an 7.4% average annual return). In fact, $1 invested in stocks in December 1900 is worth $1,359 today!

- They have been able to double in value 10 times (every 10.6 years on average).

- 89% of the total return was from dividend income.

- The best annual return was 41% in 1986!

Negatives

- U.S. preferred stocks have posted negative years 24% of the time (27% of these corrections were consecutive negative years).

- The average loss in a negative year was -5.6%, and the worst yearly loss was −22.5% in 1907.

> "Investors are showing a renewed interest in, if not a preference for, preferred stock."
> *The Wall Street Journal—June 16, 2005*

WIPSI Yield—1890 to 2007

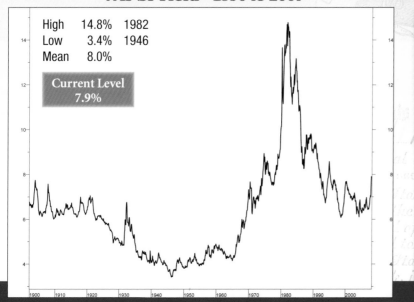

High	14.8%	1982
Low	3.4%	1946
Mean	8.0%	

Current Level 7.9%

> "While preferred shares are listed on major stock exchanges, they aren't widely followed or understood—so there's a chance to unlock hidden value."
> *The Wall Street Journal—August 6, 2006*

Preferred Stock issued by legendary stock speculator Russell Sage—1866

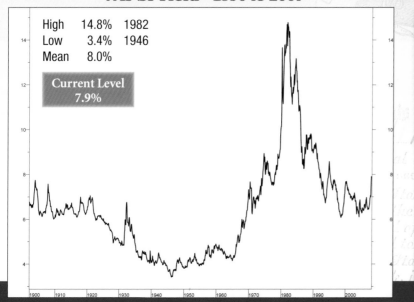

STOCK INVESTOR TOOLS
Some Things Never Change

Stock investing has always been a curious mixture of old and new. Every day, hundreds of billions of dollars in stock transactions travel the globe through electronic transfers by the marvels of modern technology, yet the basic tools used by earlier investors such as financial news, corporate annual reports, brokerage house statements, and charts of stock market barometers are as important today as they were in the 1800s.

As you review the following analysis, remember that successful stock investing is as much about identifying the overall stock market's trends (i.e., when to buy or sell) as it is selecting individual investments (i.e., what to buy or sell). Unfortunately, it is hard to conduct long-term analysis on individual stocks, because very few companies have continuously traded over a long time frame.

An almost infinite number of fundamental and technical tools are used by market analysts to determine market trend and to measure the market's strength. On the following pages are market indicators every stock investor should monitor.

Annual Report 1835

Brokerage Report—1837

Charts 1963

Charts 1963

The Wall Street Journal First Edition—July 8, 1869

Charts 1936

PROFITS : Rising in a Down Market

All but five of the 30 Dow Jones industrial stocks will earn more per share this year than last, according to even the lowest Wall Street estimates. But stock prices continue to fall, in part because investors believe that the earnings trend may soon turn down.

	1968 Earnings	1969 Estimates		1968 Earnings	1969 Estimates
ALLIED CHEMICAL	$1.46	$1.75-$2.20	INTERNATIONAL NICKEL	$1.93	$2.00-$2.35
ALCOA	4.75	5.00 - 5.60	INTERNATIONAL PAPER	2.27	2.50 - 2.70
AMERICAN CAN	4.25	4.35 - 4.70	JOHNS-MANVILLE	2.38	2.30 - 2.50
AT&T	3.75	3.90 - 4.13	OWENS-ILLINOIS	3.10	3.50 - 4.00
AMERICAN BRANDS	3.38	3.40 - 3.65	PROCTER & GAMBLE	4.30	4.50
ANACONDA	4.05	5.20 - 6.00	SEARS, ROEBUCK	2.73	2.90 - 3.00
BETHLEHEM STEEL	3.55	3.65 - 3.85	STANDARD OIL (CALIF.)	5.32	5.70 - 6.00
CHRYSLER	6.23	5.00 - 6.00	STANDARD OIL (N.J.)	5.93	6.35 - 6.60
DU PONT	7.82	8.10 - 8.40	SWIFT	1.12	1.25 - 1.75
EASTMAN KODAK	2.33	2.45 - 2.65	TEXACO	6.15	6.60 - 6.70
GENERAL ELECTRIC	3.95	4.20 - 4.50	UNION CARBIDE	2.60	2.75 - 3.00
GENERAL FOODS	4.16	4.35 - 4.50	UNITED AIRCRAFT	5.05	5.75 - 6.60
GENERAL MOTORS	6.02	5.10 - 6.05	U.S. STEEL	4.69	4.65 - 5.00
GOODYEAR	2.06	2.15 - 2.35	WESTINGHOUSE ELECTRIC	3.49	3.60 - 3.75
INT'L HARVESTER	2.69	2.35 - 3.00	WOOLWORTH	2.29	2.45 - 2.55

Earnings Projections—1969

"In 1904 there was begun the pioneering work of keeping investors informed on fundamental conditions and on specific issues in which they might be interested. The need was urgent, for too many people were making investments blindly, not really knowing whether a security fitted their needs, nor whether it was a proper time to buy or sell."

Investment Fundamentals, Babson—1930

The simple and effective way to use the following tools is to remember the **technical indicators should be moving in the same direction as market prices.** When these indicators are moving in the opposite direction to market price (called a divergence), there is a strong possibility of a change in market direction.

In the "Market Cycles" section later in this book, these tools will be further examined to show that they proved useful in past bull and bear markets in providing investors advanced warnings that things were changing for better or worse.

200-Day Moving Average of Market Indexes

Used as a filter to determine overall price trend. When price is above the moving average, the trend is up. When price is below the moving average, the trend is down. If a moving average is flat, the trend is sideways—better known as a trading market.

NYSE Advancing Volume/Declining Volume

Used to measure the strength of the market's price movement. Weaker levels of volume are usually present near bull market tops and bear market bottoms. It uses the 200-day moving average similar to the previous chart.

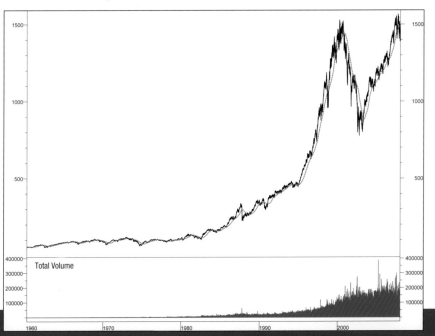

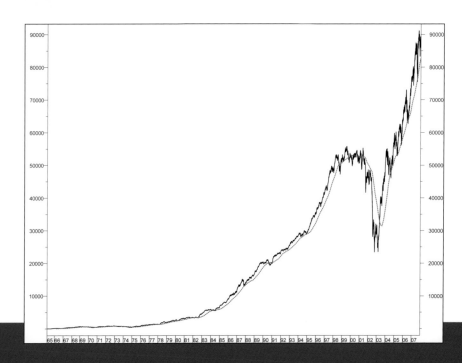

> "The moving average is one of the most versatile and widely used of all technical indicators."
> *Technical Analysis of the Financial Markets, Murphy—1993*

Technical Indicators

NYSE Advancing Issues/Declining Issues Line

This measures the number of individual stocks where prices are moving up versus down. It uses the 200-day moving average similar to the charts on page 31.

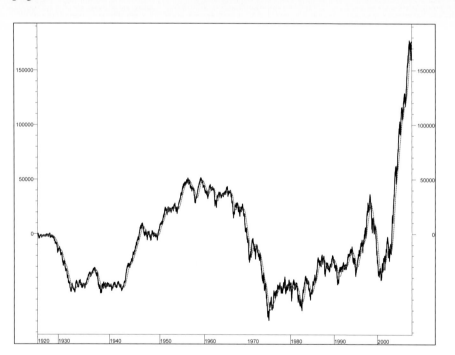

NYSE 12-Month
New High Prices/New Low Prices Line

This measures the number of individual stocks making 12-month highs versus 12-month lows. It uses the 200-day moving average similar to the charts on page 31.

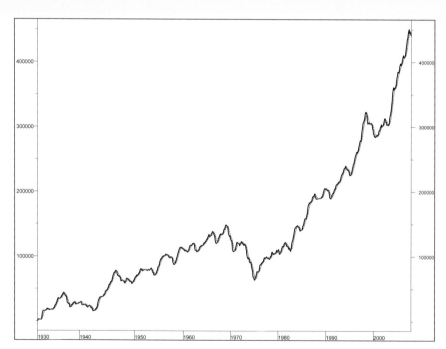

"The Trend is Your Friend!...
The Advance/Decline Indicator is one of two ingredients that,
when combined, have an outstanding record in calling bull market advances."
Winning on Wall Street, Zweig—1986

Fundamental Measures

NYSE Average Price to Earnings Ratio
(with regression line)—1870 to 2007

Measures common share price level in relation to corporate earnings: 30 and higher occur near major market peaks, and below 10 indicate a very undervalued market. The average level is 18.

NYSE Average Dividend Yield
(with regression line)—1825 to 2007

Measures common share price level in relation to cash dividends: 6% and higher indicate the market is very undervalued. The average level is 3%.

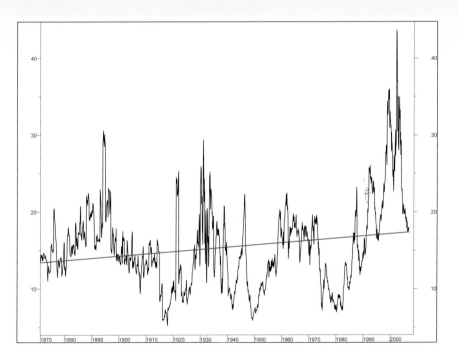

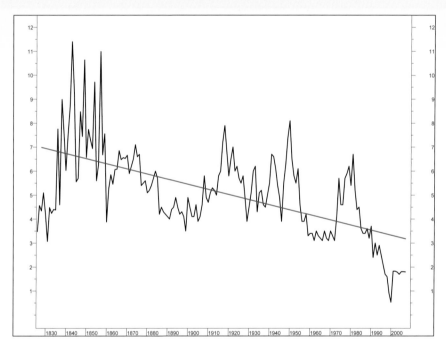

> "The security analyst should compare the price
> with earnings, dividends, asset value, and with sales."
> *Security Analysis, Graham/Dodd—1962*

REAL ESTATE
GRANDDADDY OF THEM ALL

British
Real Estate
Deed—1737

"Real estate itself is one of the oldest forms of investment and has come to be an absolute essential of life under the present established form of civilization. Real estate is also a form of investment which ordinarily does not become worthless in periods of drastic financial readjustments… One thing about real estate, however, is that it is not always readily saleable on short notice."

Investment Fundamentals, Babson—1930

House of Ross Winans (author's ancestor) as it appeared in
American Architect and Building News—April 30, 1887.
Maryland Historical Society

With shelter of primal concern to all people, real estate is one of
mankind's oldest types of investments and has been one of the
most effective ways to amass wealth and power in all past civilizations. Today, home ownership is called the "American Dream"
and is the largest asset owned by most investors.

Winans Mansion, Baltimore, Maryland—2006

"Many people who traditionally invest in real estate
didn't really understand—or trust—the stock market,
while most people who invest in stocks were uncomfortable with,
or had little understanding of, real estate."
Investing in REITS, Block—2006

U.S. RESIDENTIAL REAL ESTATE

Unlike the fast-paced world of stocks, where market values are accessed every second in organized exchanges worldwide, real estate's slower pace is conducted through loose networks of brokers centered on publications and websites that post listings of properties for sale. This decentralized transaction structure, where a typical sale takes 30-90 days to complete (due to the high amount of mortgage debt used in most purchases), makes it one of the hardest investments to analyze, and only a handful of indexes track home prices over the long term.

The Winans International Real Estate Index™ (WIREI™) shows the price of new U.S. homes since 1830. As can be seen in these charts, residential real estate was more volatile before 1950, with dramatic swings in value during the 1930s and the late 1800s. Even though home price appreciation since 1950 looks like endless profitability, there were rough times in the early 1970s, early 1980s, early 1990s, and early 2000s when excessive leverage wiped out many investors.

	SINCE 1850	
	Owner Equity	
	100%	40%
Cumulative Return	152%	438%
Average Total Return	4.9%	7.9%
Highest Return	107% in 1933	67%
Lowest Return	(70%) in 1932	(44%)
Negative Years	35% of time	
Consecutive Neg Years	15% of time	

WIREI™ U.S. New Home Prices—1830 to 2007

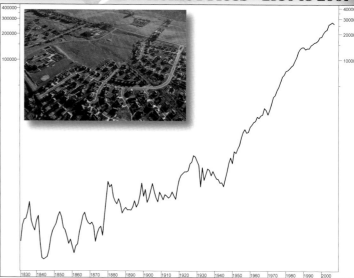

U.S. Home Prices Total Return—1850 to 2007

(60% Mortgage of Value)
(Point to Point = 100% Gain in Price)

Inflation Adjusted Total Return

"Since the Great Depression,
real estate values pursued a profitable upward bias,
notwithstanding a few potholes along the way."
Investing in REITs, Block—2006

U.S. REGIONAL REAL ESTATE

California Mexico Land Company—1888

This was a deed to Southern California property. It was printed in both English and French because France occupied Mexico in the 1860s.

Though it is important to follow the overall trend of the U.S. real estate market, an investor also needs to follow the regional differences of home values. U.S. real estate has long been divided into four regions for evaluation and comparisons: Northeast, South, Midwest, and West.

As can be seen below, the Western states have had the best overall performance over the past 33 years, followed closely by the Northeast.

But the steadiest performance came from the South, with negative years occurring only 3% of the time. This is especially astounding when you consider the substantial number of major hurricanes and tornado storms that have caused damage to this region over this time frame.

Regional Total Return

WEST—Alaska, Arizona, California, Colorado, Hawaii, Idaho, Montana, Nevada, New Mexico, Oregon, Utah, Washington, Wyoming

NORTHEAST—Connecticut, Maine, Massachusetts, New Hampshire, New Jersey, New York, Pennsylvania, Rhode Island, Vermont

SOUTH—Alabama, Arkansas, Delaware, District of Columbia, Florida, Georgia, Kentucky, Louisiana, Maryland, Mississippi, North Carolina, Oklahoma, South Carolina, Tennessee, Texas, Virginia, West Virginia

MIDWEST—Illinois, Indiana, Iowa, Kansas, Michigan, Minnesota, Missouri, Nebraska, North Dakota, Ohio, South Dakota, Wisconsin

New Home Prices

1974-2007		Total Returns	Negative Years	Consecutive Neg Years	Return Extremes > 10%	< (10%)	Outperformed U.S.
9 Northeast States							
	Current Price	$381,750	15%	5.9%	32%	0%	50%
	Cumulative	736%					
	Average	6.9%					
	Median	6.2%					
	High	25%					
	Low	-4%					
17 Southern States							
	Current Price	$230,650	3%	0%	15%	0%	53%
	Cumulative	518%					
	Average	5.8%					
	Median	6.8%					
	High	16%					
	Low	-2%					
12 Midwest States							
	Current Price	$219,750	21%	3%	24%	0%	41%
	Cumulative	455%					
	Average	5.6%					
	Median	6.7%					
	High	18%					
	Low	-9%					
13 Western States							
	Current Price	$343,600	18%	2.9%	35%	3%	59%
	Cumulative	750%					
	Average	7.1%					
	Median	7.6%					
	High	41%					
	Low	-11%					

"I heard countless times that what matters most in real estate is location, location, location. I don't dispute the validity of this mantra, but location in and of itself cannot protect an investor buying at the top of a cycle and taking a loss on the way down."

Timing the Real Estate Market, Hall—2004

OTHER WAYS TO OWN REAL ESTATE

*"Only ten REITs of any real size existed during the 1960s…
The 1970s were tumultuous times for the economy,
for the stock market, and for REITs."*
Investing in REITs, Block—2006

Which is the best way to own real estate: direct ownership in properties or exchange-traded investments that focus on real estate?

Traditional investors believe that owning "brick and mortar" is the best way to play the real estate game, and that the time spent dealing with the problems surrounding the "four T's" of investment property ownership (tenants, taxes, toilets, and termites) is the price paid for success.

But Wall Street offers investors another route to successful real estate investing: real estate investment trusts (REITs), pools of numerous residential, commercial, and industrial properties throughout the nation, and stocks in home-building companies.

All have produced impressive returns. Since 1974, REITs have risen 580% (not including dividends); home-building stocks have appreciated 4,060%; and the average 100% equity return for U.S. homes was 531%. Though direct ownership offers the use of higher levels of leverage (margin on stocks is limited to 50% of value), REITs and home-building stocks are more liquid and are cheaper to buy and sell because they trade on major stock exchanges.

Today's real estate investors could take advantage of both types of investments to maximize performance and liquidity while minimizing transaction costs.

Home Building Stocks—1965 to 2007

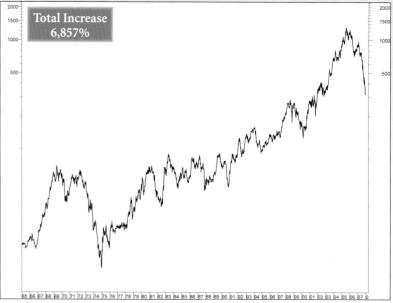

Total Increase
6,857%

Reale Estate Investment Trusts (REIT)—1969 to 2007

33-year Increase
580%

*"Builders of new homes also are tinkering
with their pricing formulas to generate sales."*
The Wall Street Journal—September 28, 2006

FOREIGN REAL ESTATE

French Real Estate—1957 to 2007

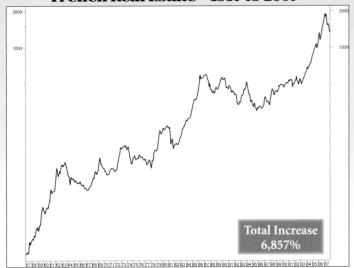

Total Increase 6,857%

Japanese Real Estate—1957 to 2007

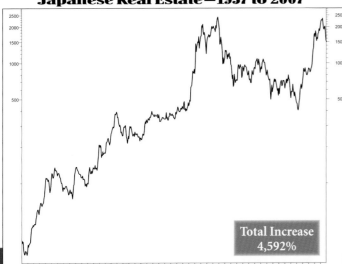

Total Increase 4,592%

As with most types of investments, there are opportunities outside the United States. As can be seen in the charts of real estate investments in Japan (4,592%) and France (6,857%), they have seen appreciation significantly better than U.S. homes (1,466%) since 1957. Yet Japan still has not reached the high price levels seen in 1988.

"The performance of real estate as a financial asset has been astounding."
Are You Missing the Real Estate Boom, Lereah—2005

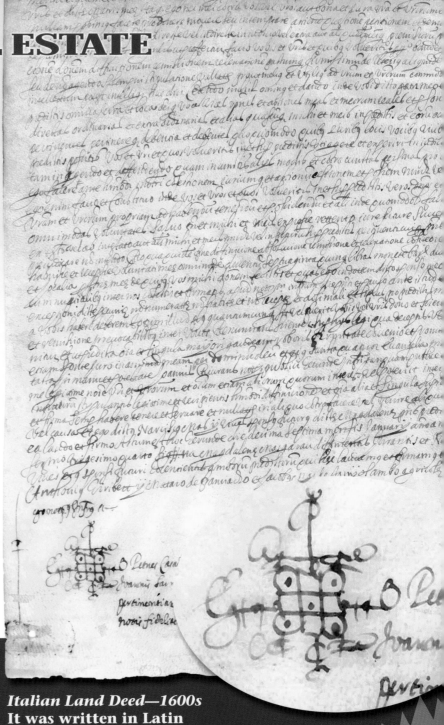

Italian Land Deed—1600s
It was written in Latin and had to be notarized.

REAL ESTATE TRUST DEEDS

Trust deeds are income investments made directly between an investor and a real estate owner. As can be seen in the charts, these illiquid, expensive notes are issues at yields significantly higher than exchange-traded corporate bonds of average quality. Like mortgages, these notes are secured by the value of the real estate itself, and if the trust deed goes into default, then the property can be sold to repay the trust deed investor.

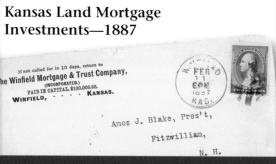

Kansas Land Mortgage Investments—1887

U.S. Corporate Bond Yield—1990 to 2007

High	11%	1990
Low	6%	2005
Current	6.5%	

First and Second Trust Deed Yields 1990 to 2007

High	17%	1994
Low	10%	2001
Current	12%	

"Speculators in real estate often borrowed of the United States Bank for speculative purposes, sums as high as $250,000."
Bull & Bear of New York, Smith—1875

REAL ESTATE INVESTOR TOOLS

Successful real estate investing is as much about identifying the overall real estate trends
(i.e., when to buy or sell) as it is selecting individual investments (i.e., what to buy or sell).
Listed are several tools that investors can use to monitor the real estate market.

25-month Moving Average of Indexes

Moving averages are effective in identifying the overall trend of a market. If
the index and sales levels are above the moving average, then the market is
in a bullish uptrend, and vice versa means real estate is in a bear market.

U.S. New Home Prices Adjusted for Square Feet

The size of the average U.S. home has increased 54% since 1974. To make
"apples to apples" price comparisons to new houses in the past, prices should
be adjusted to size.

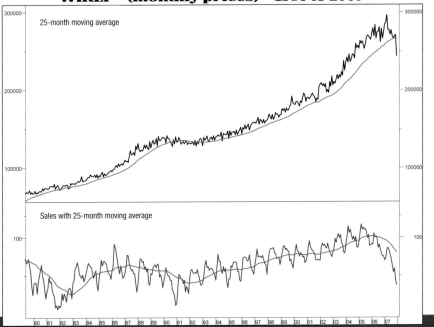

WIREI™ (monthly prices)—1980 to 2007

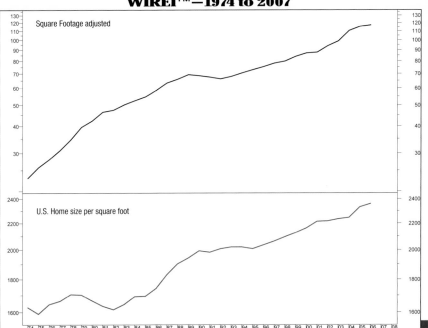

WIREI™—1974 to 2007

"Traditionally, brokers have set listing prices
by reviewing how much comparable homes sold for in a neighborhood."
The Wall Street Journal—September 28, 2006

New Homes Listed and Inventory (with regression line)

These indicators measure the number of new houses listed for sale and the number of months it would take to sell this at the current sales rate. Generally speaking, prices trend upward when the number of listings and inventory levels are low.

Sales and Months on Market (with regression line)

Similar to stock trading volume, these indicators measure the number of new houses sold and the number of months they were on the market. Generally speaking, declines in sales volume coincide with a dramatic rise in the time (from 4-8 months) it takes to sell a house.

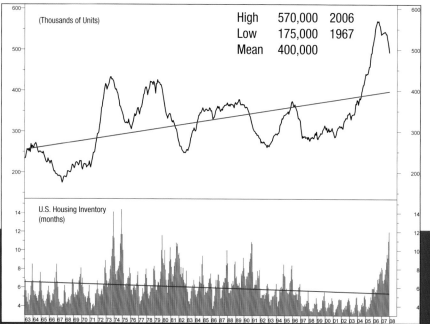

U.S. New Home Listings
(with regression line)—1963 to 2007
Current monthly level—494,000

(Thousands of Units)

	High	570,000	2006
	Low	175,000	1967
	Mean	400,000	

U.S. Housing Inventory (months)

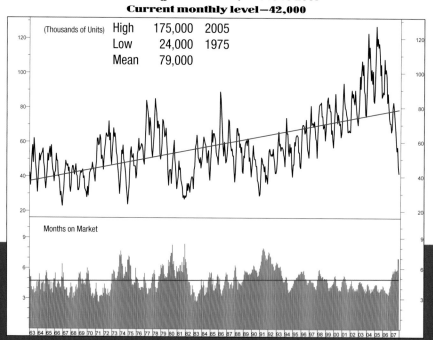

U.S. New Home Sales
(with regression line)—1963 to 2007
Current monthly level—42,000

(Thousands of Units)

	High	175,000	2005
	Low	24,000	1975
	Mean	79,000	

Months on Market

42

"Sausalito, California is a place of half a dozen houses, once 'destined' to be a great town; $150,000 lost there—city laid out, corner lots sold at enormous prices, 'water fronts' still higher—a big city was bound to grow up there. The old California story—everybody bought land to rise in value, but no one built, no city grew there. Corner lots and water fronts are alike worthless."

Journal of William Brewster—1862

Mortgage Rates

Because leverage is heavily used in real estate investing, the level and direction of interest rates are key to performance. Generally speaking, high or rising interest rates should be viewed with caution by real estate investors.

Mortgage Rate Spreads

Since 1981, the difference between a 30-year fixed-rate loan and a 1-year adjustable-rate mortgage has ranged between 3.5% and 0%. Real estate investors need to closely evaluate the differences between the rates on various types of loans that are available to find the best deal at the time.

U.S. Mortgage % Rate Spread—1981 to 2007
(30-yr Conventional minus 1-yr Adjustable)

High	3.3%	1994
Low	0.1%	2007
Mean	1.1%	

Current Level 0.1%

U.S. Mortgage % Rates
30-yr Conventional—1900 to 2007

High	18.5%	1981
Low	4.7%	1945
Mean	8.9%	

Current Level 6.1%

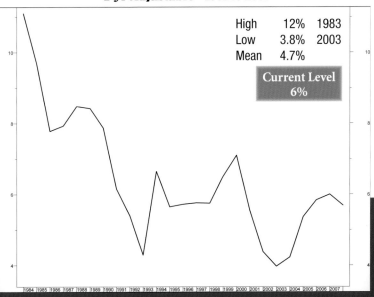

U.S. Mortgage % Rates
1-yr Adjustable—1981 to 2007

High	12%	1983
Low	3.8%	2003
Mean	4.7%	

Current Level 6%

REAL ESTATE FACTS and OBSERVATIONS

Since 1850

Positives

- With a mortgage of 60% of the value, residential real estate has produced 438% cumulative gain (a 7.9% average annual return). In fact, $1 invested in residential real estate in December 1850 is worth $694 today!
- New homes have been able to double in value 9 times (every 17 years on average).
- The best annual return was 100% in 1933 (in the middle of the Great Depression)!

Negatives

- New homes have posted negative years 35% of the time (15% of the time there were back-to-back negative years).
- 6% of the time losses exceeded -20%. The worst yearly loss of -70% was in 1932.

SINCE 1974

- The homes in the West and Northeast posted the best results.

"This was a market phenomenon characterized by 30 years of house price growth with very few defaults."
Financial Times—April 22, 2007

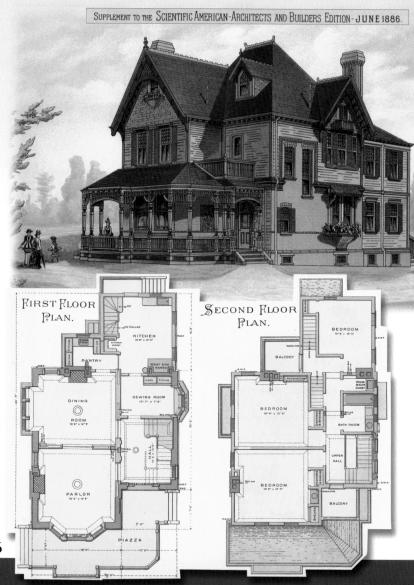

SUPPLEMENT TO THE SCIENTIFIC AMERICAN-ARCHITECTS AND BUILDERS EDITION · JUNE 1886.

1886

"(In 2001) even as stock prices tumbled and businesses faltered, the real estate market continued to soar, with home prices rising steadily in most areas of the country. For most homeowners, their house is far and away their biggest investment."
Are You Missing the Real Estate Boom, Lereah—2005

BONDS –
WHEN INCOME and SAFETY ARE WANTED

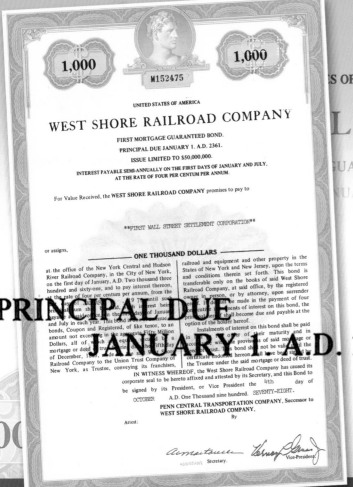

14¼% DEBENTURE DUE 2011

Many investors can't handle, or are wealthy enough that they don't need to deal with, the moderate to high level of investment risks associated with stocks and real estate. These investors value a greater certainty of return over the level of investment return, and or have income requirements that can't be met by common stock dividends.

Bonds are debts issued by corporations, governments, and state and local municipalities. Interest rates vary and maturities range from a few years to many decades. Because bonds provide a fixed income over a defined period of time, the near certainty of returns is their greatest advantage.

"Recently, record numbers of consumers have been buying these little-understood investments, which many past investors considered to be downright boring. Regrettably, many of these seasoned stock and real estate investors rushing into this sector of investing have failed to learn the time-proven rules of bond investing."
Preferreds: Wall Street's Best-Kept Income Secret, Winans—2007

U.S. CORPORATE BONDS

Below are charts showing the price and interest yields of U.S. corporate bonds and the total return (annual price change and interest earned combined) adjusted for inflation since 1862.

Unlike common stocks, where most profits are made through increases in the value of the shares, the price of bonds oscillates around the maturity value (or par value) of $1,000 per bond, thus showing only a small change in bond values over the past 145 years.

The real profit power of bonds comes through the regular interest paid to the investor by the company that issued the bond. This has averaged 6.7% since 1862 for a total interest return of 927%.

Traditional corporate bonds have been steady performers where returns have doubled 13 times since 1862 and have generally performed well against inflation.

U.S. Corporate Bonds—1862 to 2007

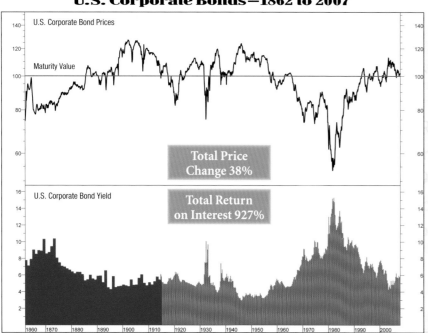

Total Price Change 38%

Total Return on Interest 927%

U.S. Corporate Bonds Total Return—1862 to 2007

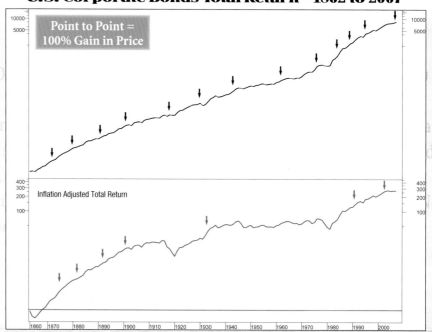

Point to Point = 100% Gain in Price

Inflation Adjusted Total Return

Corporate income investments can be divided into bonds of high-quality companies, bonds in companies of lower standing, and preferred stocks (a type of stock that pays a high level of income to its investors and usually doesn't have a maturity date).

As can be seen in the charts on this page, while the levels of yield are different, the three types of corporate income investments look nearly identical. In fact, all had record low yields in April 1946 and record high yields in late 1981.

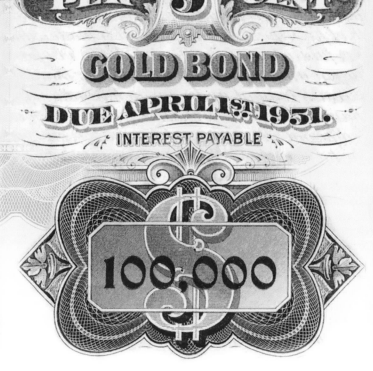

High-Quality Corporate Bond Yields—1900 to 2007

Low-Quality Corporate Bond Yields—1900 to 2007

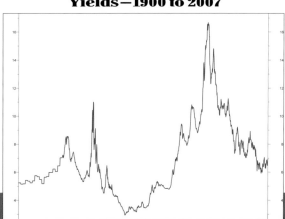

Preferred Stock Dividend Yields—1900 to 2007

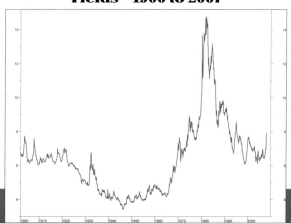

"Low grade bonds, long and short term, can be judged more like stocks. It is better to look at them frankly for their appreciation possibilities."
The Battle for Investment Survival, Loeb—1936

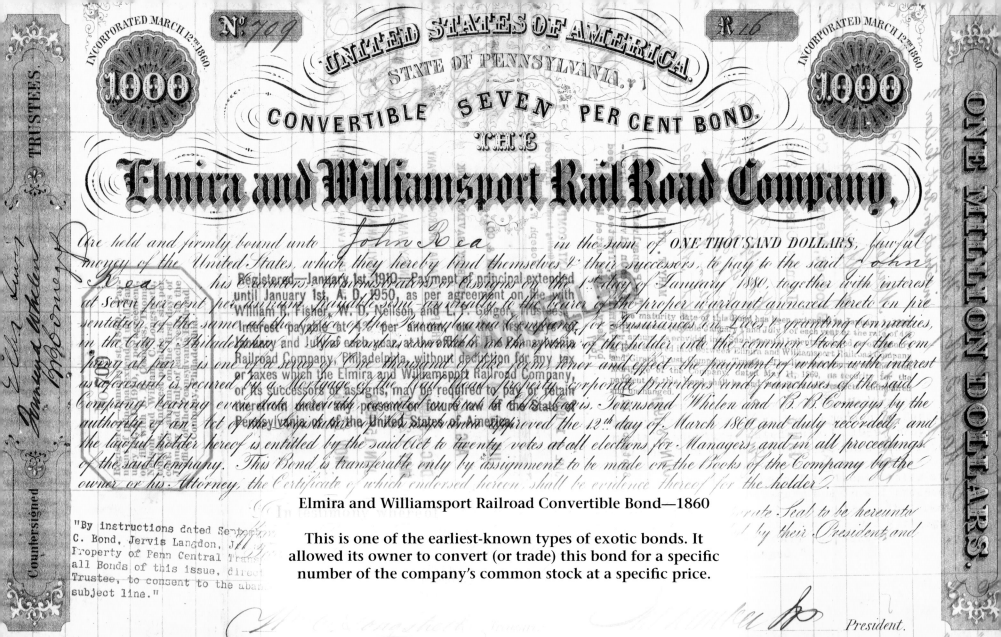

Elmira and Williamsport Railroad Convertible Bond—1860

This is one of the earliest-known types of exotic bonds. It allowed its owner to convert (or trade) this bond for a specific number of the company's common stock at a specific price.

"Industrial, finance, and real estate are the largest issuers of convertible bonds."
The Handbook of Fixed Income Securities, Fabozzi—1983

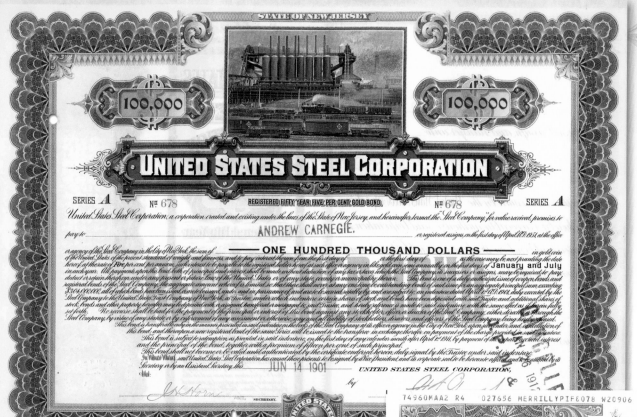

U.S. Steel Bond—1901

The owner of this bond was billionaire Andrew Carnegie. This investment was part of the proceeds from the sale of his steel empire to J.P. Morgan's U.S. Steel. At the time, this was the biggest acquisition in U.S. history, and made Carnegie the second-wealthiest person in world history (worth nearly $300 billion in today's dollars).

RJR Nabisco Bond—1989

The first of the great leveraged buyouts (LBOs) where debt was used to turn publicly traded companies into private enterprises. This bond was used in that $25 billion transaction.

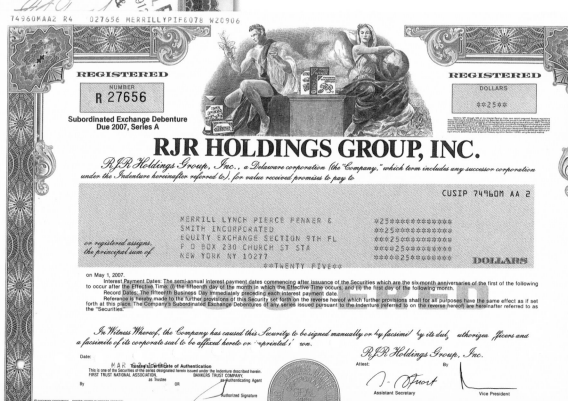

U.S. GOVERNMENT BONDS

*K*NOW all Men by these Presents, That we, *Paine Converse of Killingley & John Babcock of Lebanon both in the State of Connecticut*.

are holden and firmly bound unto the Governor and Company of the ~~English Colony~~ State of Connecticut, in New-England, in the Sum of Three Thousand Pounds, Lawful Money, to be paid to said Governor and Company; To the which Payment well and truly to be made and done, we jointly and severally bind ourselves, our Heirs, &c. by these Presents. Sealed with our Seals, this *8th* Day of *Dec.* A. D. 1776.

*T*HE Condition of the above Obligation is such, That whereas the above bounden *Pain Converse* is appointed Pay-Master to his own Company, now to be raised, to join the Continental Army in *Colo. Mr. Elys Regt.* Now, if the said *Pain* shall faithfully and justly dispose of all the Monies he shall receive out of the public Treasury, for the Purpose of inlisting the Soldiers in, and Paying said Company, and shall account with the Committee of the Pay-Table for the same, when thereto required, the above Obligation to be Void, otherwise to remain in full Force.

pain Converse

Signed, Sealed and Delivered, in Presence of

Wm. Nichols

O. Ellsworth

John Babcock

Colonial government note issued during the American Revolution—1776

Government debt is always at the focal point of discussions about politics and business. The irony is that "we the people" have always owned the bulk of the U.S. government's debt obligations, and our taxes are used to pay the interest on this debt.

Because the government owns a vast amount of assets and can collect taxes from its citizens, it is also the only investment that can legally be called "risk free" of default.

10-Year U.S. Treasury Bond Yields—1800 to 2007

High	15.8%	1981
Low	1.6%	1945
Average	5.1%	
Current	4.0%	

"In scores of ways the U.S. Treasury and Wall Street are brought into close contact."
The Work of Wall Street, Pratt—1916

Gazette of the United States.

PUBLISHED WEDNESDAYS AND SATURDAYS BY *JOHN FENNO*, No. 69, *HIGH-STREET*, BETWEEN *SECOND* AND *THIRD STREETS*, PHILADELPHIA.

[No. 9, of Vol. III.]   SATURDAY, MAY 28, 1791.   [Whole No. 217.]

Gazette of the United States—1791
This newspaper provided the
first price lists of government bonds.

3-Month Treasury Bill Yields—1820 to 2007

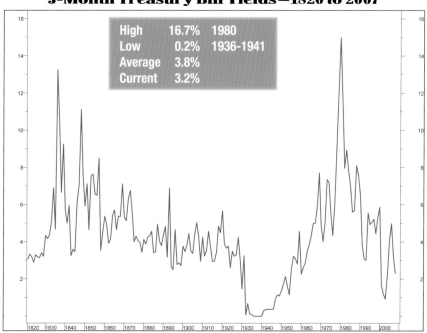

High	16.7%	1980
Low	0.2%	1936-1941
Average	3.8%	
Current	3.2%	

With credit quality assured, the investment focus shifts to maturity. For instance, during times of economic upheaval or high inflation, investors choose to buy Treasury debt with short maturities (usually under 1 year).

As can be seen, Treasury debt yields are hardly static! They have ranged from 17% in late 1980 to .2% throughout the late 1930s.

PRICE CURRENT.—PUBLIC SECURITIES.

FUNDED DEBT.

6 pr. Cents	17ʃ1. 17ʃ2	pr. £.	86	pr. cent.
3 pr. Cents		9ʃ3.	46	do.
Deferred 6 pr. Cents		9ʃ1 9ʃ2	45	do.

UNFUNDED DEBT.

Final Settl. and other Certificates	16ʃ 16ʃ1	80		do.
Indents		9ʃ3	45	do.
N. and S. Carolina debts,	12ʃ6	15ʃ.		

> **"Through budget deficits, there will always be more than enough Treasury bonds to satisfy any and all buyers."**
> *Barron's—February 5, 2007*

MUNICIPAL BONDS

For anyone who doubts the power of taxes on investment decisions, you have to look no further than municipal bonds!

These low-yielding debts have been issued since Colonial times and have been a longtime favorite of wealthy investors. Why? Under Constitutional law, interest earned on any municipal bond cannot be taxed by the U.S. Government. In other words, interest earned on these investments is tax-free to most investors.

In the chart below, you will notice that yields on municipal bonds have ranged from 13% in 1981 to 1.5% in 1945 and have generally had lower yields than Treasury or corporate bonds.

City and County of San Francisco Bond—1863

Municipal Bond Yield—1800 to 2007

High	13.2%	1981
Low	1.5%	1945
Average	4.9%	
Current	5.1%	

"Although tax-exempt munis vary in the degree of credit strength backing them,
and although there have been some famous defaults,
their safety record has generally been excellent,
earning them a place between Treasuries and high-grade corporate bonds."
Barron's Finance & Investment Handbook, Downes—1998

"The divine doctrine of state sovereignty,
which makes a State too dignified to be sued for its debts
ought to make it also too respectable to cheat its creditors."
Henry Clews—1885

TAX FREE VS.   TAXABLE INCOME

This table gives the approximate yields that taxable securities must earn in various income brackets to produce, after tax, yields equal to those on tax-free bonds yielding from 5 to 6.9 percent. The table is computed on the theory that the taxpayer's highest bracket tax rate is applicable to the enti[re] increase or decrease in his taxable income resulting from a sw[itch] to tax-free securities, or vice versa.

© MERRILL LYNCH, PIERCE, FENNER [...]

JOINT RETURN (Taxable income in thousands)	$8 to $12	$12 to $16	$16 to $20	$20 to $24	$24 to $28	$28 to $32	$32 to $36	$36 to $40	$40 to $44	$44 to $52	$52 to $64	$64 to $76	$76 to $88	$88 to $100	$100 to $120	
TAX BRACKET BY PERCENTAGE	22	25	28	32	36	39	42	45	48	50	53	55	58	60	62	
TAX EXEMPT YIELD																
5.00%	6.41	6.67	6.94	7.35	7.81	8.20	8.62	9.09	9.62	10.00	10.64	11.11	11.90	12.50	13.16	13
5.10	6.54	6.80	7.08	7.50	7.97	8.36	8.79	9.27	9.81	10.20	10.85	11.33	12.14	12.75	13.42	14
5.20	6.67	6.93	7.22	7.65	8.13	8.52	8.97	9.45	10.00	10.40	11.06	11.56	12.38	13.00	13.68	14
5.30	6.79	7.07	7.36	7.79	8.28	8.69	9.14	9.64	10.19	10.60	11.28	11.78	12.62	13.25	13.95	14
5.40	6.92	7.20	7.50	7.94	8.44	8.85	9.31	9.82	10.38	10.80	11.49	12.00	12.86	13.50	14.21	15
5.50	7.05	7.33	7.64	8.09	8.59	9.02	9.48	10.00	10.58	11.00	11.70	12.22	13.10	13.75	14.47	15
5.60	7.18	7.47	7.78	8.24	8.75	9.18	9.66	10.18	10.77	11.20	11.91	12.44	13.33	14.00	14.74	15
5.70	7.31	7.60	7.92	8.38	8.91	9.34	9.83	10.36	10.96	11.40	12.13	12.67	13.57	14.25	15.00	15
5.80	7.44	7.73	8.06	8.53	9.06	9.51	10.00	10.55	11.15	11.60	12.34	12.89	13.81	14.50	15.26	16
5.90	7.56	7.87	8.19	8.68	9.22	9.67	10.17	10.73	11.35	11.80	12.55	13.11	14.05	14.75	15.53	16
6.00	7.69	8.00	8.33	8.82	9.38	9.84	10.34	10.91	11.54	12.00	12.77	13.33	14.29	15.00	15.79	16
6.10	7.82	8.13	8.47	8.97	9.53	10.00	10.52	11.09	11.73	12.20	12.98	13.56	14.52	15.25	16.05	16
6.20	7.95	8.27	8.61	9.12	9.69	10.16	10.69	11.27	11.92	12.40	13.19	13.78	14.76	15.50	16.32	17
6.30	8.08	8.40	8.75	9.26	9.84	10.33	10.86	11.45	12.12	12.60	13.40	14.00	15.00	15.75	16.58	17.50	18.53
6.40	8.21	8.53	8.89	9.41	10.00	10.49	11.03	11.64	12.31	12.80	13.62	14.22	15.24	16.00	16.84	17.78	18.82
6.50	8.33	8.67	9.03	9.56	10.16	10.66	11.21	11.82	12.50	13.00	13.83	14.44	15.48	16.25	17.11	18.06	19.12
6.60	8.46	8.80	9.17	9.71	10.31	10.82	11.38	12.00	12.69	13.20	14.04	14.67	15.71	16.50	17.37	18.33	19.41
6.70	8.59	8.93	9.31	9.85	10.47	10.98	11.55	12.18	12.88	13.40	14.26	14.89	15.95	16.75	17.63	18.61	19.71

Muni Bond Ad—1934

Tax Equivalent Yield Table—1974

"For tax reasons, municipal-bond investors often invest in the bonds of the city in which they reside, so they face double jeopardy. In the first place, if city officials are committing fraud, their bonds will turn out not to be so sound…
The second risk is that they will have to pay higher taxes to cover shortfalls in their city's budget."
The Wall Street Journal—November 27, 2006

FOREIGN BONDS

Reichsmark 100.—

Ford Motor Company, Berlin Division—1929

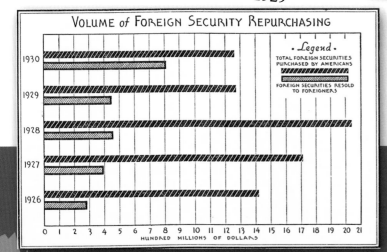

Foreign Investment Chart—1930

Americans have had a long love affair with international investing. Though stocks in foreign companies usually get most of the attention in the media, the bonds of foreign governments and international corporations have proven to be an especially good investment during times of declines in the value of the U.S. dollar.

Foreign Bond Trading Cartoon—1932

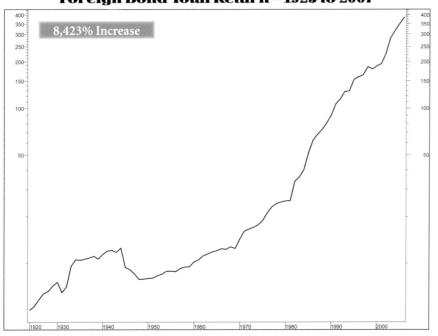

In the chart on this page, you will notice that in the post-World War II era, there has been a continuous bull market in foreign corporate bonds when returns are adjusted in U.S. dollars.

"Since the United States has taken the position of a creditor nation, it is becoming a great marketplace for foreign bonds."
Investment Fundamentals, Babson—1930

BOND INVESTOR TOOLS

The New York Stock Exchange Bond Market.

Liberty bond booth at left, main bond market to right, ticker dispatch station between them.

Figure 15

Though the yields of various types of bonds do seem to move in the same direction, they don't move to the same degree, and bond investors are constantly comparing yields in different bonds looking for the best deals. One of the tools that helps make these comparisons is yield spread charts.

These are built by simply subtracting the yield of one type of bond from another. The higher and lower numbers mark the extreme historical ranges between the two types of bonds and thus serve as reference points for future investments between corporate bonds and preferred stocks or Treasury versus municipal bonds.

Bond Research—1890

A CAREFULLY SELECTED LIST OF
THOROUGHLY SOUND INVESTMENTS,
Combining Safety of Principal, Assured Dividends and Future Enhancement in Price.

SEVEN PER CENT BONDS.	Interest Payable.	Date of Issue.	Date of Maturity.	Amount Outstanding.
Chicago, Burlington & Quincy consol....	J. & J.	1873	July 1, 1903	$28,914,000
Chicago, Milwaukee & St. Paul consol....	J. & J.	1875	July 1, 1905	8,702,000
Chicago, Mil. & St. Paul, Hast. & Dak. Ext. 1st....	J. & J.	1880	Jan. 1, 1910	5,680,000
Chicago, Mil. & St. Paul, Iowa & Dak. Ext. 1st....	J. & J.	1878	July 1, 1908	8,339,000
Chicago & No. Western consol. s. f....	Q.-F.	1865	Feb. 1, 1915	10,380,000
Chicago & No. Western gen. consol. g....	J. & D.	1872	Dec. 1, 1902	10,492,000
Cincinnati, Ham. & Dayton consol. 1st....	A. & O.	1875	Oct. 1, 1905	996,000
Cleveland, Colo., Cin. & Ind. consol....	J. & D.	1874	June 1, 1914	3,991,000
Denver & Rio Grande 1st m. g....	M.& N.	1871	Nov. 1, 1900	1,934,000
Erie Ry. 1st consol. m. g....	M.& S.	1870	Sept. 1, 1920	3,689,500
Erie Ry. N. Y. L. E. & W. funded g....	M.& S.	1878	Sept. 1, 1920	3,698,500
Lake Shore & Mich. So. consol. 1st....	J. & J.	1870	July 1, 1900	9,153,000
Lake Shore & Mich. So. consol. 2d....	J. & D.	1873	Dec. 1, 1903	8,725,000
Michigan Central 1st consol....	M.& N.	1872	May 1, 1902	8,000,000
Nashville, Chat. & St. L. 1st....	J. & J.	1873	July 1, 1913	6,300,000
New York & Harlem consol....	M.& N.	1872	May 1, 1900	12,000,000

REFER TO BOND TABLE (PAGE 319) FOR RANGE OF PRICES DURING PAST TEN YEARS.

We offer BONDS in lots of $1,000 and upward; also, RAILROAD STOCKS in lots of 10 shares and upward, subject to sale or changes of the market.

Orders for the Purchase and Sale of GOVERNMENT, STATE, MUNICIPAL and RAILROAD SECURITIES executed.

Write for "Investor's Manual' and our Lists of the Safest and Most Profitable Investments.

243

General Electric 1965

GENERAL ELECTRIC OVERSEAS CAPITAL CORPORATION
4¼% GUARANTEED BOND DUE 1985
DUE DECEMBER 1, 1985
(CONVERTIBLE FROM MAY 1, 1967 TO NOVEMBER 30, 1975 INTO GENERAL ELECTRIC COMPANY COMMON STOCK)

$1000 · 1000 · 1000 · 1000

Nº 770

General Electric Overseas Capital Corporation, a corporation duly organized and existing under the laws of the State of New York (herein called the Company) for value received, hereby promises to pay to bearer the principal sum of

ONE THOUSAND DOLLARS ($1,000)

A CAREFULLY SELECTED LIST OF
THOROUGHLY SOUND INVESTMENTS,
Combining Safety of Principal, Assured Dividends and Future Enhancement in Price.

FOUR PER CENT BONDS.	Interest Payable.	Date of Issue.	Date of Maturity.	Amount Outstanding.
Atchison, Topeka & Santa Fe, gen. gold....	A. & O.	1895	Oct. 1, 1995	$137,023,000
Chesapeake & Ohio, R. & A. Div. 1st cons. g....	J. & J.	1890	Jan. 1, 1989	6,000,000
C. B. & Q., Denver Div....	F. & A.	1881	Feb. 1, 1922	5,760,500
C. B. & Q., Neb. Div. $20M. p. m....	M.& N.	1887	May 1, 1927	26,110,000
Chicago, Milwaukee & St. Paul, gen. ser. A, gold....	J. & J.	1889	May 1, 1989	23,676,000
Chicago, Rock Island & Pacific gen. m. g....	J. & J.	1898	Jan. 1, 1988	47,971,000
Chicago Ter. Tfr. R. R., gold....	J. & J.	1897	July 1, 1947	13,000,000
Illinois Central, Col. tr. gold....	A. & O.	1888	Apr. 1, 1952	15,000,000
Louisville & Nashville, Unified, gold....	J. & J.	1890	July 1, 1940	14,994,000
Missouri, Kansas & Texas, 1st gold....	J. & D.	1890	June 1, 1990	39,813,000
Missouri Pacific, Pac. of Mo., 1st gold....	F. & A.	1888	Aug. 1, 1938	7,000,000
New York, Chicago & St. Louis, 1st m. gold 4f....	A. & O.	1887	Oct. 1, 1937	19,425,000
New York, Ontario & Western, refd. gold....	M.& S.	1892	June 1, 1992	11,531,000
Rio Grande & Western, 1st gold....	J. & J.	1889	July 1, 1939	15,300,000
St. Paul, Minn. & Man. Mont. Ext. 1st g....	J. & D.	1887	June 1, 1937	7,805,000
West Shore, 1st m. guaranteed N. Y. C....	J. & J.	1885	Jan. 1, 2361	50,000,000

REFER TO BOND TABLE (PAGE 319) FOR RANGE OF PRICES DURING PAST TEN YEARS.

240

"Since the selection of high-grade bonds has been shown to be in good part a process of exclusion, it lends itself reasonably well to the application of definite rules and standards."

Security Analysis, Graham & Dodd—1962

Yield Spread

Corporate Bonds
(High to Low Quality)—1875 to 2007

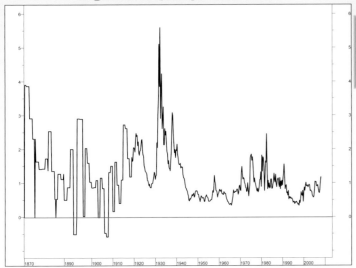

High	5.6%	1932
Low	(.6%)	1907
Average	.8%	
Current	1.2%	

Corporate Bonds (High-Quality)
to Preferred Stocks—1902 to 2007

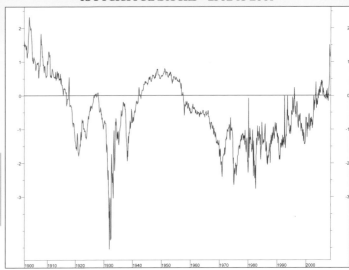

High	2.3%	1903
Low	(4.9%)	1932
Average	(1.2)%	
Current	1.6%	

Corporate Bonds (High-Quality)
to Treasury (10-Year) Bonds—1830 to 2007

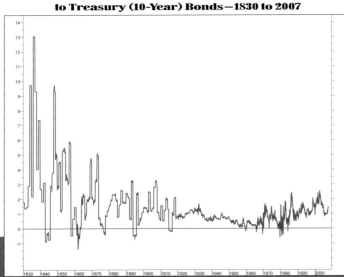

High	13.4%	1836
Low	(1.4%)	1862
Average	0.5%	
Current	2.1%	

Treasury (10-Year) Bonds to
Municipal Bonds—1800 to 2007

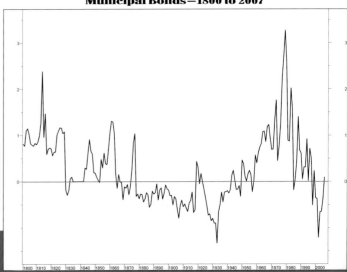

High	3.4%	1979
Low	(1.3%)	1933
Average	1.4%	
Current	.3%	

"Bonds often act as a leading indicator of stocks… A technical analysis of stocks
is incomplete without a corresponding analysis of the bond market."
Intermarket Technical Analysis, Murphy—1991

BOND FACTS and OBSERVATIONS

U.S. CORPORATE BONDS SINCE 1862

Positives

- U.S. corporate bonds have produced a 5,775%% cumulative gain (an 6.7% average annual return). In fact, $1 invested in corporate bonds in December 1863 is worth $8,375 today ($271 after inflation)!

- They have been able to double in value 13 times (every 11 years on average).

- 96% of the total return was from interest income.

- The best annual return was 38.5% in 1982!

- Corporate bonds outperform common stocks 41% of the time and preferred stocks 45% of the time.

Negatives

- U.S. corporate bonds have posted negative years 16% of the time (2% of these corrections were consecutive negative years).

- The average loss in a negative year was -3.5%, and the worst yearly loss was -14% in 1931.

10-Year U.S. Treasury Bond Yields Since 1800

- The record high was 15.8% in 1981.

- The record low was 1.6% in 1945.

- The average is 5.1%.

- They have averaged 1.3% higher than 3-month T-Bills.

Municipal Bond Yields Since 1800

- The record high was 13.2% in 1981.

- The record low was 1.5% in 1945.

- The average is 4.9%.

- Although their average yield is below 10-year Treasuries, "munis" generally outperform on an after-tax basis.

"Recent peak yields were far above the highest prime long-term rates reported in the United States since 1800, in England since 1700, or in Holland since 1600."
A History of Interest Rates, Homer—2005

"Students of the bond market are constantly in danger of falling into the mental habit of thinking that the 'bond market' represents a single unified thing, which behaves in the same way throughout all its parts. A time like the present illustrates the highly composite nature of the bond market, and the variations in the responses of its different sections to the influences which affect it."
The Magazine of Wall Street—September 29, 1923

It is perfectly possible to speculate in bonds, and periodically fortunes are made and lost in the bond markets. It is also perfectly possible to see a portfolio of high-grade bonds decline in value at a time when the majority of common stocks are climbing upward. Nevertheless there is a basic truth to the simile: of the vehicles available to investors, bonds are among the most conservative."
The Anatomy of Wall Street, Rolo—1968

COMMODITIES
GOLDEN OPPORTUNITY OR A LEAD BALLOON?

Gold and Silver (in British Pounds)—1257 to Present

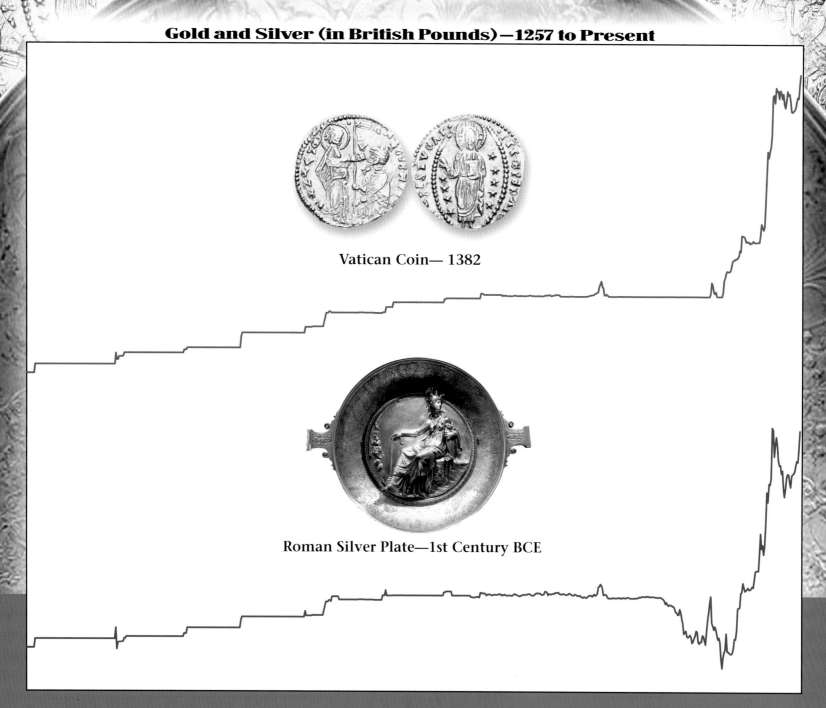

Vatican Coin— 1382

Roman Silver Plate—1st Century BCE

Gold and Silver per Ounce
in U.S. Dollars—1800 to 2007

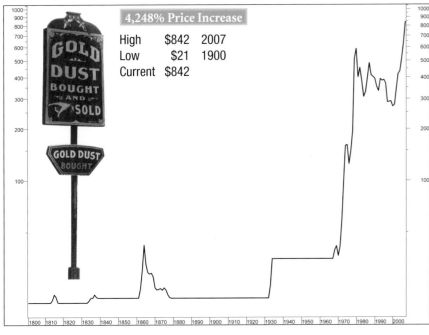

4,248% Price Increase

High	$842	2007
Low	$21	1900
Current	$842	

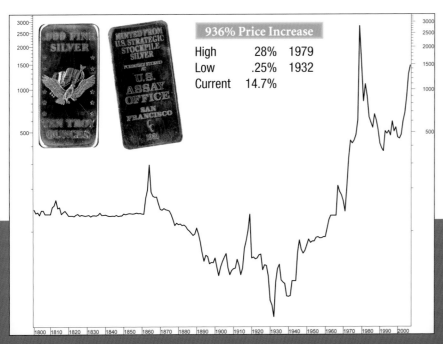

936% Price Increase

High	28%	1979
Low	.25%	1932
Current	14.7%	

1870

"The conventional wisdom of the 1700s equated national wealth, and the power wealth could purchase, with stockpiles of gold and silver. British imperial policy sought to secure for the mother country as much precious metal as possible, even at the expense of Britain's colonies."
The Age of Gold, H. Brands—2002

"The turmoil in the stock market overflowed into the futures markets yesterday, sending livestock, cotton, grain plummeting. Precious metals futures meanwhile soared as investors sought safe havens for their money."
The New York Times—October 20, 1987

COMMODITY INDEXES (Spot Prices)—1800 to 2007

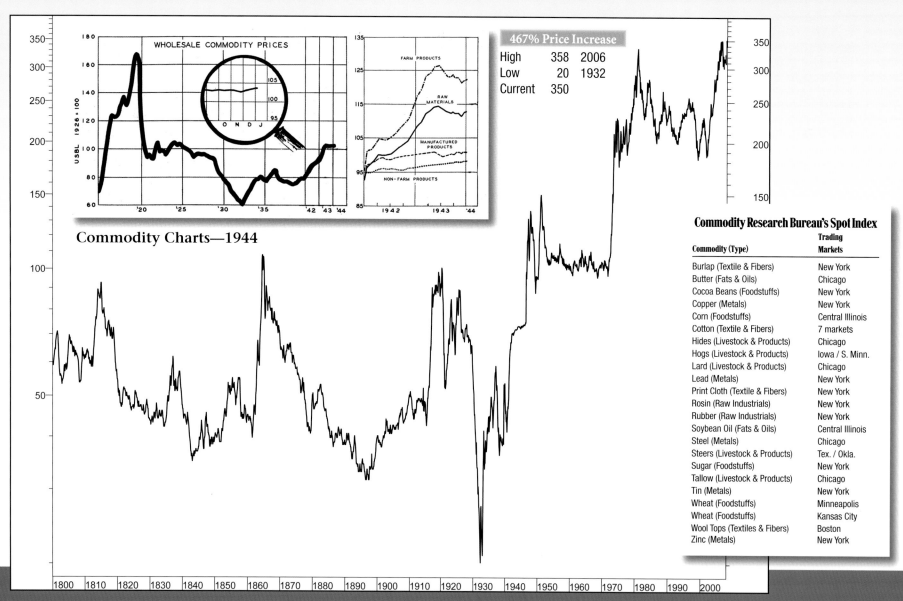

467% Price Increase

High	358	2006
Low	20	1932
Current	350	

Commodity Charts—1944

Commodity Research Bureau's Spot Index

Commodity (Type)	Trading Markets
Burlap (Textile & Fibers)	New York
Butter (Fats & Oils)	Chicago
Cocoa Beans (Foodstuffs)	New York
Copper (Metals)	New York
Corn (Foodstuffs)	Central Illinois
Cotton (Textile & Fibers)	7 markets
Hides (Livestock & Products)	Chicago
Hogs (Livestock & Products)	Iowa / S. Minn.
Lard (Livestock & Products)	Chicago
Lead (Metals)	New York
Print Cloth (Textile & Fibers)	New York
Rosin (Raw Industrials)	New York
Rubber (Raw Industrials)	New York
Soybean Oil (Fats & Oils)	Central Illinois
Steel (Metals)	Chicago
Steers (Livestock & Products)	Tex. / Okla.
Sugar (Foodstuffs)	New York
Tallow (Livestock & Products)	Chicago
Tin (Metals)	New York
Wheat (Foodstuffs)	Minneapolis
Wheat (Foodstuffs)	Kansas City
Wool Tops (Textiles & Fibers)	Boston
Zinc (Metals)	New York

"Speculation is a method now adopted for adjusting differences of opinion as to future values, whether of products or securities. In former years the results of a crop were known only when it came to the market. Now almost everything affecting its future value is known with a fair degree of accuracy before the crop is harvested."

Twenty-Eight Years in Wall Street, H. Clews—1887

CRUDE OIL or "BLACK GOLD"–1860 to 2007

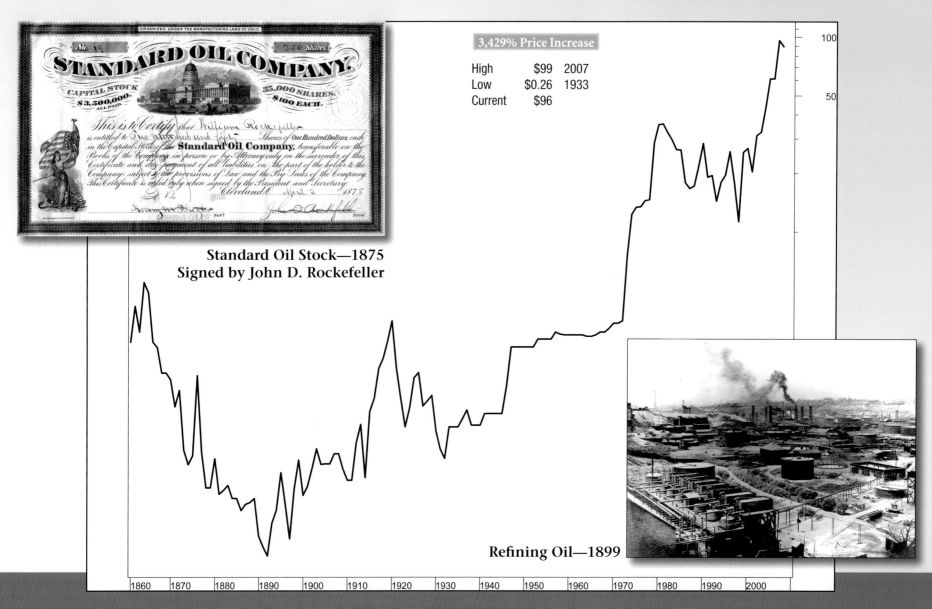

Standard Oil Stock—1875
Signed by John D. Rockefeller

3,429% Price Increase

High	$99	2007
Low	$0.26	1933
Current	$96	

Refining Oil—1899

1860 1870 1880 1890 1900 1910 1920 1930 1940 1950 1960 1970 1980 1990 2000

"As Mr. Greenspan engineered low real interest rates in 2001-04, the prices of commodities, particularly oil and other minerals, started to climb in advance of a general price increase. Since commodity prices are determined by trading on fast-moving auction markets, they respond swiftly."

The Wall Street Journal—September 20, 2004

FOREIGN EXCHANGES

British Foreign Currency Table—1830

Denmark, Norway, etc.
Copenhagen, Sound, Bergen, Drontheim.

Poland and Prussia.
Cracow, Warsaw, &c.
Konningsberg.

FRANCE.
Lisle, Cambray, &c.

Italy.
Leghorn, Florence, &c.

Italy.
(Denari — Quatrini — Soldi — Craca — Quilo — Lir — Piastre of Ex. — Ducat — Pistole)

Portugal.
Lisbon, Oporto, &c.

Italy.
Genoa, Novi, &c.
Corsica, Bastia.

Italy.
Rome, Civita, Veechia, Ancona, &c.

Italy.
VENICE, Berghamo, &c.

Germany.
Hanover, Lunenburg, Zell, &c.

Spain.
Madrid, Cadiz, Seville, &c.

Spain.
Gibraltar, Malaga, Denia, &c.

Italy.
Turin, Chamberi, Cagliari, Sardinia.

Italy.
NAPLES, Gaieta, Capua, &c.

Holland.
Amsterdam, Rotterdam, Middelburg, Flushing, &c.

Germany.
Dresden, Leipsic, &c.
Wismar, Kiel, &c. SAXONY.

Germany.
Vienna, Trieste, &c.
Augsburg, Ulm, Blenheim.

Russia and Muscovy.
Petersburg, Archangel, Moscow, &c.
(Denusca — Copec — Altin — Grivener — Polpolin — Poltin — Rouble — Nervonitz — Imperial — Double)

Livonia.
Riga, Revel, Narva.
(Grosh — Vording — Whiten — Marr — Florin — Rix Dollar — Albertus)

Turkey.
Constantinople, Candia, Cyprus, Smyrna.

INDIA.
Bengal, Calcutta.
Calicut.

INDIA.
Bombay, Dabul, Malabar.

INDIA.
Goa, Visapoor.

Switzerland.
BASIL, Zurich, Zug, &c.

Switzerland.
St. GALL, Appensel, &c.

Switzerland.
BERN, Lucerne, &c.
Neufchatel, &c.

BARBARY.
Algiers, Tunis, Tripoli, &c.

New Coins in FRANCE.
Paris, &c.

China.

Japan.
Jeddo, Meaco.

British West Indies.
Jamaica, Antigua, Barbadoes.
Grenada.
(Halfpenny — Penny — Bit — Shilling — Dollar — Crown)

West Indies.
Domingo, Martinique, Guadaloupe.

MOROCCO.

UNITED STATES.

ENGLAND & SCOTLAND
THE BANK OF ENGLAND.

IRELAND.

Explanation of the Course of Exchange.
Amsterdam gives London ... Flemish for 1l. Sterling
Hamburgh gives ... Flemish for 1l. Sterling
Paris gives ... French for 1l. Sterling
Madrid gives the Piaster for ... British
Leghorn gives the Dollar for ... British
Naples gives the Ducat for ... British
Genoa gives the Piece for ... British
Venice gives 50 Livres for ... British
Lisbon gives the Milree for ... Sterling
Dublin gives 5l. for 1l. British Sterling

British Pound (in U.S. dollars)—1800 to 2007

55% Price Decrease

High	$12.80	1864
Low	$1.10	1985
Current	$2.00	

"The substitution of paper in the room of gold or silver money, replaces a very expensive instrument of commerce."

Wealth Of Nations, A. Smith—1776

COMMODITIES SUMMARY

The noisy, fast-moving trading pits found around the world for buying and selling hundreds of types of commodity contracts evolved from the barter system of ancient times, where merchants would meet at an agreed-upon price and location to transact business for the delivery of goods.

Today's future markets trade everything from carbon emission allowances to butter, with each contract (called "cars") covering a specified price and amount of the commodity to be delivered at a specified date in the near future without the buyer and seller ever meeting each other. Traders can sell the contract before maturity or pay and physically take delivery of the commodity on maturity. Ironically, the vast majority of commodity contracts are "closed out" prior to the maturity date.

Futures provide investors a liquid, high-leveraged way to speculate in commodity bull markets (high demand and low supply) or bear markets (low demand and high supply). But high leverage is a two-edged sword! Because the purchaser of a futures contract is required to commit and maintain a cash deposit equal to exchange-imposed margin requirements as low as 10% (stock investments allow a maximum of 50% initial margin), volatile swings in the value of a futures account can occur in both directions quickly.

Commodity futures can be very profitable in the hands of disciplined traders who are equally skilled at handling bull and bear markets, and are comfortable with the fact that most of their trades will result in a loss. But history has shown that they are not the best choice for investors who like to maintain only "long" positions with "loose" stop loss orders.

Tools—Most of the tools used by practitioners of technical analysis (ranging from moving averages to advanced statistical models) have their roots in commodity trading, where hyper-monitoring of price action is required to prevent financial disaster.

Performance—Because commodities are not designed to be long-term investments, it is difficult to directly compare their long-term performance to growth investments such as stocks and real estate. Although history suggests that stocks and real estate have produced superior cumulative returns over the past 100 years, it can be seen that many commodities are setting all-time price records, and have outperformed U.S. stock and U.S. homes since 2000.

Tables and Ads from early 1900s

Commodity	(Per Contract) Margin Requirements	2007 Price (Spot)	Since 1900 High (Year)	Since 1900 Low (Year)	Cumulative Percentage Returns Since 1900	1950	1975	2000
Gold	$4,050 – $2,500	842	842 (2007)	20.67 (1900)	na	na	421%	211%
Silver	$6,075 – $3,000	14.72	28 (1979)	.25 (1932)	1,874%	1,504%	208%	180%
CRB Spot Index	$8,100 - $5,400	349.6	357.5 (2006)	20.2 (1932)	810%	165%	83%	53%
Crude Oil	$6,075 – $4,500	96	98.8 (2007)	.26 (1933)	21,233%	3,635%	618%	258%
British Pound	$2,700 – $2,000	2.0	6.3 (1914)	1.1 (1985)	(59%)	(29%)	11%	34%
DJIA					18,660%	5,535%	1,456%	23%
Winans International Real Estate Index					10,079%	4,116%	495%	41%

WORLD'S WHEAT CROP.

The following table shows the total crop of wheat in the principal wheat producing countries in the world for sixteen years:

1884	2,290,069
1885	2,104,034
1886	2,198,997
1887	
1888	
1889	
1890	
1891	
1892	
1893	
1894	
1895	
1896	
1897	
1898	
1899	
1900	

Canada Is Harvesting the Greate[st] Wheat Crop in Her History

As approximately three-quarters of this crop of over 450,000,000 bushels will be available for export, the effect will be stimulating to every branch of business in the Dominion.

The opportunities for profitable investment in Canadian Securities were never as attractive.

If you are interested, The Greenshields Review for October carefully reviews conditions. We will gladly mail you a copy.

Write Dept. A for a copy.

...ll... & Company

CORN CROP OF THE WORLD.

The following table shows approximately the corn crop of the comprising the principal corn growing countries:

	1900.	1899.
Argentina	48,000,000	72,000,000
Austria-Hungary	142,000,000	135,000,000
Bulgaria and E. R.	34,000,000	14,000,000
Canada	20,000,000	
Italy	60,000,000	21,600,000
Roumania		86,000,000
Russia	80,000,000	
United States	30,000,000	27,000,000
Egypt		14,000,000
Uruguay	2,105,000	

COLLECTIONS

TURNING HOBBIES INTO WEALTH

Almost everybody collects something at some point during his or her life. Children often collect sports trading cards, common coins (such as Lincoln pennies), and even rocks. The passion of collecting stays with many people throughout their lives as they acquire rare, expensive items through their increased financial capacity. The world's richest families have amassed large collections of artwork, books and manuscripts, and various types of antiques that are shared with the public through museum exhibits and publications (such as the display of antique financial documents used throughout this book).

Yet many investors perceive collectibles as a mere hobby and don't recognize the huge financial gains that are possible. As shown in the following table, several rare, vastly different items have significantly outperformed both stocks and homes since 1960.

Collectibles are broken into two general groups: (1) those graded by respected third parties (similar to the ratings applied to bond investments) such as coins, stamps and vintage wine and (2) unique, non-rated items such as historical memorabilia and works of art.

Gathering long-term, reliable data on this subject is challenging, so the focus is on collectibles that are popular and actively acquired. Morgan Silver Dollars and Beaulieu Vineyard's Georges de Latour Reserve Cabernet Sauvignon are studied as two extensively rated items that are collected in very different ways by investors. In the "wild west" of unrated collectibles, we examine historical memorabilia tied to the Apollo 11 Lunar Landing in 1969. This fast-growing area is a favorite of baby boomers (who followed the space program as kids), and has annual "space" sales at major auction houses.

Collections Performance Overview
Since 1960

S&P 500 Index	2,486%
Winans International Real Estate Index	1,694%
Gold Bullion	2,306%
Morgan Silver Dollar (1883-S)	19,900%
1958 Beaulieu Vineyards	
G. Latour Reserve Cabernet Sauvignon	16,700%
Old Masters Paintings	11,400%
C13 Zeppelin Stamps (1931)	1,976%

"With prices rising faster than ever, savvy collectors are shifting their strategies for nabbing deals."
The Wall Street Journal—July 21, 2007

"The wine auction market has experienced a surge in the past three years… Wine collecting has gone from esoteric to mainstream—from geek to chic."
Wine Spectator—November 30, 2007

"In over ten years the hobby has grown enormously. There are now said to be 100,000 collectors or 'dabblers' in the field, some 200 dealers and 20 to 30 auction houses scattered across the world."
Scripophily, The Art of Finance, Hollender—1994

SILVER COINS

The Morgan Silver Dollar has an interesting history. It was born out of politically scandalous legislation in 1878 to force the U.S. Treasury to buy more silver than it needed at premium prices from mines in Nevada and California. More than 378 million were produced (or minted) by five mints across the country between 1878 and 1921. The silver dollar was headed for extinction when 282 million were melted down in 1918 and 1942 to help pay for both world wars. It is estimated that only 17% of all "Morgans" minted have survived, with certain years and mintages very hard to find.

Today, it is one of the most popular collector coins, and is an ideal coin for preliminary study of numismatics as an investment.

Two common mistakes are made in novice coin collectors' thinking: (1) "Older is more valuable" and (2) "All coins with a high grade are valuable." Though the ANA grading given by respectable grading agencies (based on the condition of a coin) is more important than the coin's age, a coin's rarity is the most important determinant of value.

> "In the complex world of coin investing, third parties (grading services) play a key role."
> *The Wall Street Journal*
> *November 25, 2006*

WALL STREET BULL

Morgan Silver Dollar
Issued 1878–1921

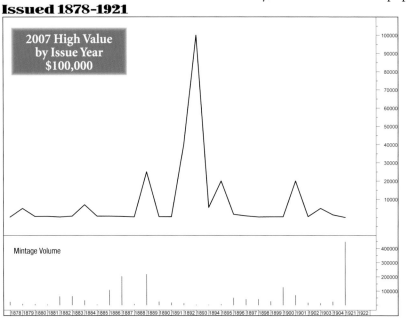

2007 High Value by Issue Year $100,000

Mintage Volume

> "Caution is given that, before spending large sums of money on collectible coins, you should take the time to learn coin grading…
> Slight differences in grade can mean thousands of dollars in value."
> *Crime of 1873, Van Ryzin—2001*

1893-S Morgan Silver Dollar

1950-2007 Return
49,900%

1888-O Morgan Silver Dollar

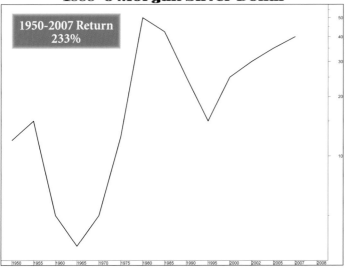

1950-2007 Return
233%

On the previous page, the chart of the 2007 high values of mint state (MS) 60 rated "Morgans" from 1878 to 1921 shows that an 1893 coin is valued at $100,000 while the older 1878 coin's highest value is only $275.

In comparing the best and worst performances of various Morgan dollars with a MS-60 grade, it is seen that they have had wide-ranging returns over the past 57 years. The best was the 1893-S with a 49,900% return (875% annualized). The worst was the 1888-O with a 233% return (4% annualized).

Furthermore, the 1888 coin had five 5-year periods of negative returns while the 1883 had only two.

Though the Morgan Silver Dollar can be a great long-term investment, a collector needs to develop the expertise and dealer network to be successful in the end.

	U.S. Morgan Silver Dollar Best and Worst Performance (MS-60 Grade)			
	1883-S		1888-O	
	Price	% Change	Price	% Change
12/31/1950	200		12.00	
12/31/1955	300	50%	15.00	25%
12/31/1960	500	67%	5.00	-67%
12/31/1965	4,500	800%	3.50	-30%
12/31/1970	5,250	17%	5.00	43%
12/31/1975	20,000	281%	12.50	150%
12/31/1980	25,000	25%	50.00	300%
12/31/1985	17,500	-30%	42.50	-15%
12/31/1990	16,500	-6%	25.00	-41%
12/31/1995	25,000	52%	15.00	-40%
12/31/2000	30,000	20%	25.00	67%
12/31/2002	40,000	33%	30.00	20%
12/31/2005	75,000	88%	35.00	17%
12/31/2007	100,000	33%	40.00	14%

"Coin prices rise when: (1) The economic trend is inflationary. The number of collectors increases, while coin supplies remain stationary or decrease through attrition or melting. (2) Dealers replace their stocks of coins only from collectors or other dealers, who expect a profit over what they originally paid. (3) Speculators buy large quantities. (4) Bullion gold and silver prices rise sharply."

A Guide Book of United States Coins, Yeoman—2001

CABERNET SAUVIGNON WINE

Winemaking has been done in America since Colonial times, and the first vineyards in California have their roots in the 1849 gold rush. Although different types of California wines have come and gone, collectors have long preferred the Cabernet Sauvignon due to its long shelf life and great taste. In fact, wine collecting's key price index, The Wine Spectator Auction Index, lists eight California "Cabs" out of the 32 wines used.

One of the oldest, continuously produced premium Cabernet Sauvignon wines is Beaulieu Vineyard's Georges de Latour Private Reserve. First produced in 1958 and named in honor of the vineyard's founder, it has a worldwide audience and is regularly listed with high rankings. In fact, a 1960s bottle of this hearty wine is still drinkable today.

Napa and Sonoma Wine Company—1874
Owned by Krug and Beringer

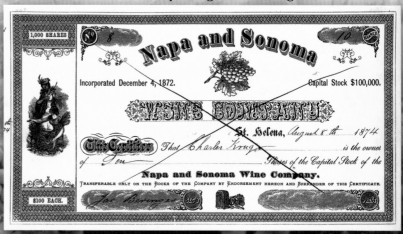

Eisen Vineyard
1872–1926

"Some of the best wines are made in ridiculously small quantities.
We wouldn't say that quantity and quality are necessarily incompatible in winemaking,
but at the very highest echelons of quality, there usually isn't much to go around."
Wine for Dummies, McCarthy—2006

Beaulieu Vineyard Cabernet Sauvignon
Georges de Latour Private Reserve

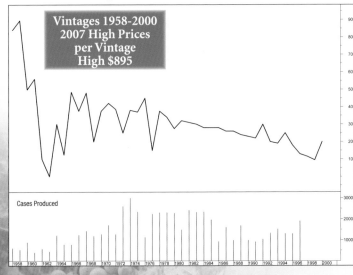

Vintages 1958-2000
2007 High Prices
per Vintage
High $895

Cases Produced

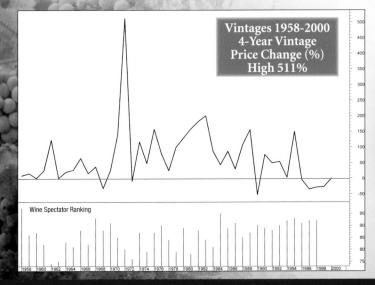

Vintages 1958-2000
4-Year Vintage
Price Change (%)
High 511%

Wine Spectator Ranking

As can be seen in the first chart, this wine's current prices vary significantly between vintages (the year bottled). Last year, the 1959 vintage was most prized by collectors at $895 per bottle, while the 1962 wine was a mere $100 per bottle. Both vintages had been made in limited quantities.

The second chart shows that though published rankings from respected third parties (such as *The Wine Spectator Magazine*) are important in determining the wine's quality, their influence on price appreciation isn't always clear-cut. Over the past four years, the low-ranked (WS 80) 1972 vintage had the largest price increase of 511% while higher-ranked 1969 (WS 88) actually declined -32% during this current wine bull market.

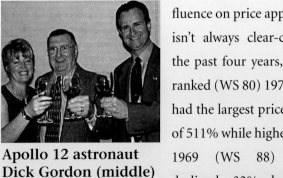

Apollo 12 astronaut Dick Gordon (middle) drinking the 1969 vintage

	$ 2007	$ 2003	% Chg	Cases Produced	Wine Spectator Rank
1958	840	775	8.4%	5,984	97
1959	895	775	15.5%	5,227	86
1960	499	na	0	8,760	87
1961	560	450	24.4%	3,930	82
1962	100	45	122.2%	5,672	74
1963	na	na	0	4,332	75
1964	300	250	20.0%	12,145	83
1965	125	99	26.3%	7,715	81
1966	485	295	64.4%	7,659	88
1967	375	325	15.4%	12,396	82
1968	480	350	37.1%	14,260	93
1969	200	295	-32.2%	11,830	88
1970	375	299	25.4%	12,750	91
1971	420	175	140.0%	17,000	85
1972	385	63	511.1%	12,680	80
1973	250	275	-9.1%	26,000	76
1974	380	175	117.1%	29,900	87
1975	370	250	48.0%	23,390	79
1976	450	175	157.1%	11,290	87
1977	150	84	78.6%	22,400	90
1978	375	300	25.0%	23,000	84
1979	340	170	100.0%	23,000	79
1980	275	120	129.2%	22,700	89
1981	320	124	158.1%	14,900	78
1982	310	110	181.8%	24,100	88
1983	300	100	200.0%	23,200	84
1984	280	150	86.7%	23,350	81
1985	280	195	43.6%	19,600	95
1986	280	150	86.7%	9,230	89
1987	260	200	30.0%	16,000	91
1988	260	125	108.0%	9,750	85
1989	240	94	155.3%	16,800	87
1990	230	480	-52.1%	9,825	90
1991	220	125	76.0%	9,100	89
1992	299	200	49.5%	10,300	88
1993	200	130	53.8%	13,300	90
1994	190	185	2.7%	15,200	92
1995	250	100	150.0%	13,000	93
1996	180	189	-4.8%	13,000	91
1997	130	199	-34.7%	19,000	92
1998	115	161	-28.6%	na	92
1999	95	130	-26.9%	na	na
2000	200	na	0.0%	na	na

Wine Information Table

"During the dot-com boom of the late 1990s, Napa Valley Cabernet Sauvignons–
cult Cabernets in particular–enjoyed heady price increases, higher than those of all other regions…
Then the NASDAQ plummeted, Silicon Valley hit hard times and cult Cabs saw a steep decline."
Wine Spectator—November 30, 2007

NON-RATED COLLECTIBLES

Apollo 11 Memorabilia

The raw capitalism of auctions for non-rated collectibles (artwork and historic artifacts) resembles the excitement on a casino floor when a "one-of-a-kind" item is placed on the block and emotional bidding drives its price into the stratosphere.

When compared to the endless supply of sports and political collectibles, Apollo memorabilia is the perfect picture of limited supply and rising demand. On the supply side, only 27 men traveled to the moon and of those only 12 walked on its surface. On the demand side is a growing number of middle-aged collectors who enthusiastically watched these historical events unfold during their childhood.

Apollo 11 items are the most popular space collectibles. They are regularly sold at auctions and command the best prices. Also because Neil Armstrong rarely signs autographs, it is easier to track the history of each item.

396 🖊 **1969 NEIL ARMSTRONG, MICHAEL COLLINS & BUZZ ALDRIN AUTOGRAPHS .... PH $1000-$1500**
They have signed on a NASA 8"x10" color crew lithograph above or below a set of autopen autographs. Attractive and a great genuine/autopen comparison piece of memorabilia. Armstrong has signed in blue. Attractive and scarce.

Apollo 11 Crew Autographed Portrait

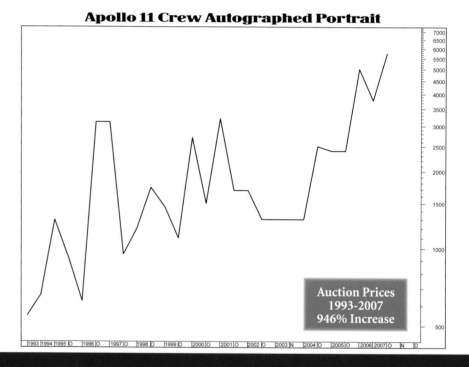

Auction Prices
1993-2007
946% Increase

"Three decades after the last moonwalk finally qualifies as one huge antique...
objects that once wizzed overhead have finally acquired,
for collectors, the mellow patina of Chippendale end tables."
Forbes—November 27, 2000

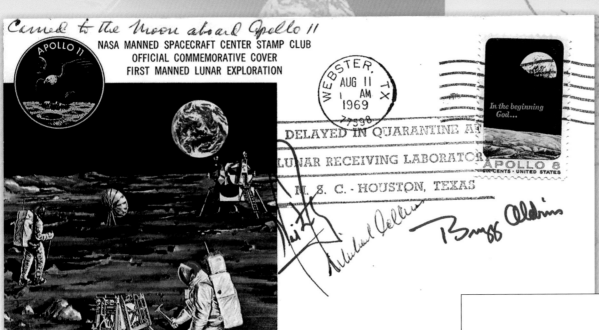

Carried to the Moon aboard Apollo 11

NASA MANNED SPACECRAFT CENTER STAMP CLUB
OFFICIAL COMMEMORATIVE COVER
FIRST MANNED LUNAR EXPLORATION

WEBSTER, TX
AUG 11
1 AM
1969
77598

DELAYED IN QUARANTINE AT
LUNAR RECEIVING LABORATORY
M.S.C. - HOUSTON, TEXAS

In the beginning
God...

APOLLO 8
SIX CENTS · UNITED STATES

Apollo 11 Crew Autographed Items
(Unflown)

Auction Prices
1993-2007
402% Increase

# of Items Sold

The Reynolds Winans Apollo Collection Index (RWACI) tracks the prices of Apollo 11 autographed crew portraits and other crew-signed items. As can be seen, prices of Apollo 11 memorabilia have risen dramatically. A mint condition, Apollo 11 crew-signed portrait (an 8 ½ x 10 photo) sold in 2007 for $5,750. This same photo has appreciated 946% over 14 years (DJIA increased 286% during the same time).

It is also interesting that personal items the astronauts took on their lunar missions have sold for as much as $250,000!

"Armstrong, Collins, and Aldrin are said to have taken 214 postal covers along…
All of the Apollo 11 flown covers were autographed by the three crewmen during post-flight quarantine…
Apollo 11 crew signatures are probably the most commonly encountered forgeries on the market in the United States."
Relics of the Space Race, Still—1995

	Lot	Price
.00	376	$295.00
.00	382	$147.00
.80	385	$354.00
.00	388	$...
.00	392	$233.00
.00	401	$59...
.00	404	$5...
.00	405	$1,...
.00	413	$...
.40	414	$1...
.40	415	$...
.00	425	$...
.50	434	$...
.00	435	$177.00
.00	438	$97...
.50	453	$177.00
.00	456	$424.00
.50	463	$265.50
.50	465	$472.00
.00	466	$472.00
.00	467	$472.00
.50	468	$3,981.25
.00	475	$1,062.00

COLLECTIBLES SUMMARY

Collectibles can be a profitable addition to an investment portfolio. Here are some important things to remember to be a successful collector.

Be an Expert—Experienced collectors are experts in their specific field of interest. They balance the emotional desire to add a unique item to their portfolio with its costs. Many have built their own database of historical prices and have developed an extensive network of other collectors and dealers to keep them posted on desirable items for sale at good prices.

Watch Out for Fades or Collecting Bubbles—Remember Cabbage Patch Dolls or Beenie Babys? They were HOT collectibles that rose in price to ridiculous levels and rapidly collapsed in value as interest waned. Stick with conventional items that your grandparents would have collected.

Numerous Costs—Collecting is expensive, with numerous expenses. Auction costs, storage and security expenses, and insurance premiums are just a few of the costs that serious collectors with extensive portfolios have to contend with. Also tax laws surrounding collectibles can be complicated.

Stick With Rare Items for at Least a 5-Year Holding Period—Focus on expensive, marquee items with an appealing appearance for long-term investment. Scarcity is the key to profitable collecting, so it is better to have a smaller collection of expensive items that will command good prices in soft times.

The Internet Has Changed Collecting—The Internet has had an immense impact on collecting through auction websites, such as eBay, over the past decade. In fact, eBay is one of the few companies created during the Internet boom of the 1990s to survive the dot-com bubble (see chart). Like all change, there are good and bad aspects to it. The good news is that auctions costs have fallen drastically, and ease of access has attracted many new collectors into niche areas such as historical memorabilia. The bad news is that because you can't personally inspect the items before bidding, there is an increased risk of buying fake or forged items.

"If you are a buyer and you're looking for a real steal, you might be hard-pressed to find one on a desirable item at eBay.
Although the sellers benefit from having six million sets of eyes seeing their items, this is often a curse for buyers…
don't expect to find an autographed Babe Ruth baseball card without others seeing it as well."
OnlineAuctions@eBay.com, Prince—1999

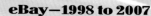

eBay—1998 to 2007

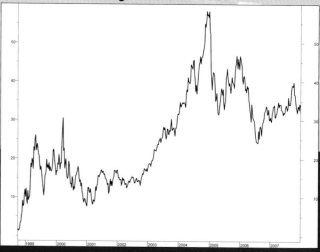

"The Romans, like the Greeks before them, also understood that the greatness of a culture could be conveyed to the world by the artistry of its coins."
Double Eagle, Frankel—2006

1923 Currency

1870 Currency

1933 Cartoon

CASH –
CAN BE KING

High   155   1985
Low   25   1864

Currency— 2001

Colonial Pound, Shilling,
and Pence—1771

"Every dollar bill issued by the Treasury or the Fed since 1863 is as good today as it ever was.
You can even use one today to pay your tax."
"GreenBack" J. Goodwin—2003

The 186-year relationship between the value of the U.S. dollar (versus foreign currencies) and the level and direction of short-term U.S. interest rates (T-Bills and commercial paper) isn't as strong as commonly believed.

The highs and lows of the U.S. dollar and U.S. short-term interest rates don't match up well. The dollar's value (versus the British pound—America's longtime trading partner) had sharply fallen to a low point in 1864 during the U.S. Civil War while interest rates increased modestly.

The U.S. Dollar Index (a basket of major foreign currencies) hit an all-time high in 1985 while short-term interest rates were 47% below their highest levels of 17% in 1980.

While short-term interest rates were near 0% at their all-time low point during the Great Depression of the 1930s, the dollar's value versus the British Pound was near the value it had been at since the late 1800s.

CHART NOTES

• The 90-Day T-Bill chart is calculated arithmetically.

• Commercial Paper and U.S. Dollar Index are shown in a semi-logarithmic format.

90-Day T-Bills

Current Level 3.3%	High	16.7%	1980
	Low	.06%	1932
	Mean	3.8%	

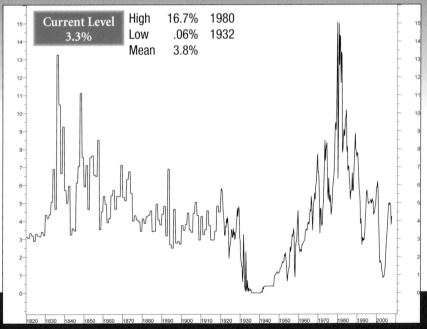

Commercial Paper

	High	30%	1873	Current Level 4.1%
	Low	.5%	1941	
	Mean	4.1%		

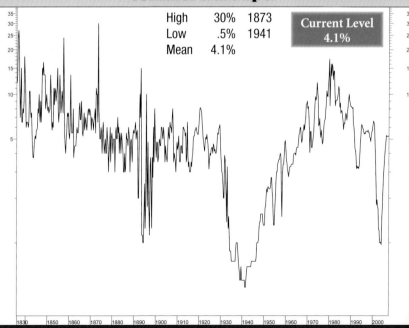

"All cares, hopes, joys, affections, virtues, and associations seemed to be melted down into dollars."

Charles Dickens, author—1844

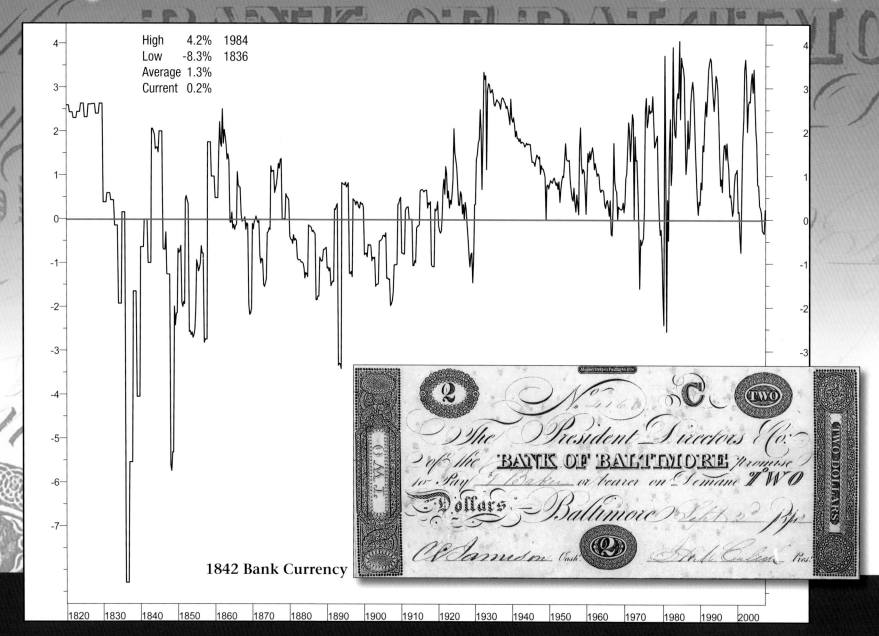

High   4.2%   1984
Low   -8.3%   1836
Average 1.3%
Current 0.2%

1842 Bank Currency

BANK OF BALTIMORE

"Inverted yield curves often come toward the end of Fed rate-increase cycle."
The Wall Street Journal—January 8, 2007

GO TO CASH?

"Go to Cash" is an instinctive move for investors that is just a phone call or "enter" keystroke away during scary, volatile times. It can be the defining judgment that allows investors to keep the easy profits made during an investment bubble that sets an investor up for life. Think of the lucky souls who "went to cash" in August 1929, December 1972, or March 2000.

While consistently getting out "at the top" is pure luck, investors need to remember that stocks and real estate have had declines more than 28% of the time since 1850. It is essential that investors decide whether they plan to ride through the bear markets or pay the taxes and commissions and cash out after making significant gains to come back to fight another day.

Fortunately, money market instruments (mutual funds that mostly hold short-term debt obligations of governments and corporations and one of Wall Street's greatest inventions) are universally used by all investors at some time, and make it easy to "go to cash" regardless of the investor's time frame and not skip a beat in collecting interest.

INFORMATION TABLE

90-Day T-Bill Yield

High	16.70%	1980
Low	.06%	1932

Average Return since

1850	4.2%
1900	3.8%
1950	5.0%
1975	5.9%
2000	3.0%

"The really sophisticated investors liquidate to cash at each bear market rally"

A few key facts to remember

Not all money market accounts are the same

Thinking it's "always" insured by the government, many investors pick the highest-yielding money market account offered by a brokerage house and investigate no further than the fund's name. Caveat emptor—like all other types of investments, there are high-quality and low-rated products. This is not the place to take risk—stick to quality versus yield!

Cash-equivalent investments hedge well against inflation

Because short-term rates have changed quickly, they have adjusted for inflationary pressures well over the past 100 years (average T-Bill yield, 3.8% versus CPI, 3.1%).

Inverted yield curves are common

As can be seen on the previous chart (Treasury Yield Spread), there have been long periods of time when short-term investments pay higher yields than longer-term bonds.

Money market returns have changed rapidly in both directions

Short-term interest rates are heavily influenced by government actions and can rapidly drop in favor of other types of investments. Remember the swings of 1999 and 2002!

The dollar's value is relative

Though it is easy to view "a dollar earned as a dollar saved," in today's global economic environment you can lose wealth on an international scale as your dollar-based investments devalue during adverse currency swings that can last considerable lengths of time. Bottom line: Keep an eye on the direction of the dollar.

SAME ADVICE OVER TIME

"At a certain point he should secure his profits,
temporarily placing the proceeds in some type of security
such as high-grade short-term Government bonds or the like,
waiting for some favorable opportunity
on which to repurchase his investment stocks."
Magazine of Wall Street—May 8, 1928

"A move to a money market fund is usually available at no costs,
gives the investors the option of moving back
into the stock market with as much ease as they left."
New York Times—October 20, 1987

"When bond investors see a recession coming,
they tend to buy (short-term) Treasury securities for two reasons.
First, they are safer than stocks.
Second, they are appealing when inflation is low,
and recessions tend to beat down inflation."
The Wall Street Journal—January 8, 2007

AND THE WINNERS ARE...

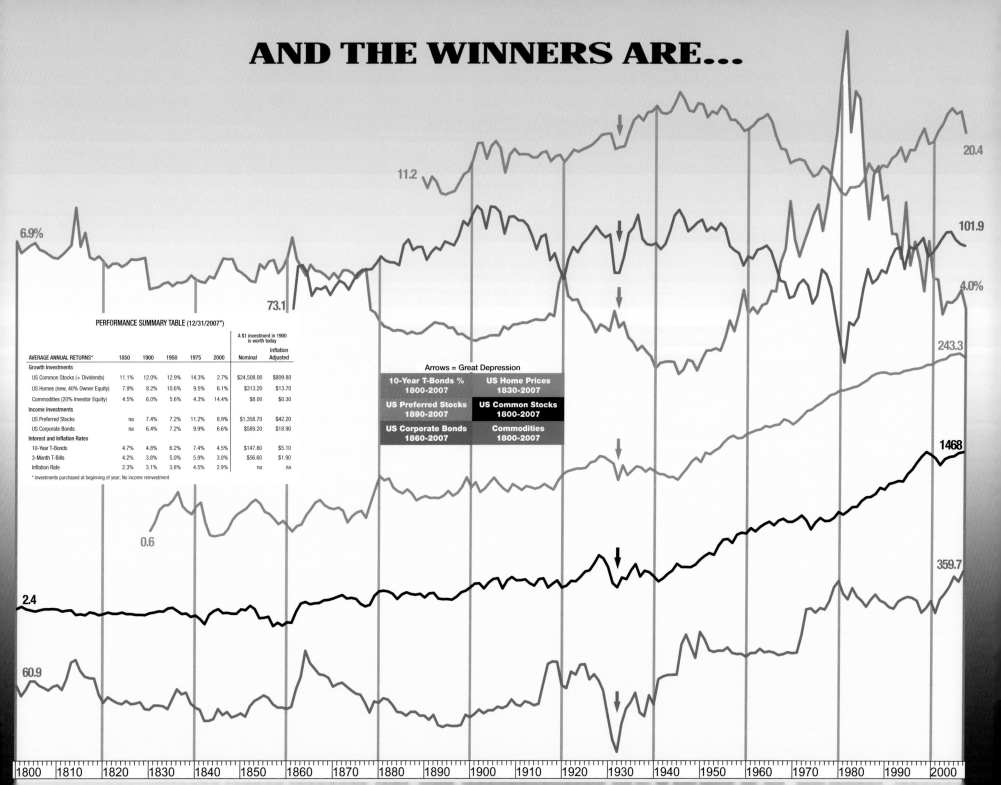

PERFORMANCE SUMMARY TABLE (12/31/2007*)

AVERAGE ANNUAL RETURNS*	1850	1900	1950	1975	2000	A $1 investment in 1900 is worth today Nominal	Inflation Adjusted
Growth Investments							
US Common Stocks (+ Dividends)	11.1%	12.0%	12.9%	14.3%	2.7%	$24,508.00	$809.80
US Homes (new, 40% Owner Equity)	7.9%	8.2%	10.6%	9.5%	6.1%	$313.20	$13.70
Commodities (20% Investor Equity)	4.5%	6.0%	5.6%	4.3%	14.4%	$8.00	$0.30
Income Investments							
US Preferred Stocks	na	7.4%	7.2%	11.2%	8.9%	$1,358.70	$42.20
US Corporate Bonds	na	6.4%	7.2%	9.9%	6.6%	$589.20	$18.90
Interest and Inflation Rates							
10-Year T-Bonds	4.7%	4.8%	6.2%	7.4%	4.5%	$147.80	$5.10
3-Month T-Bills	4.2%	3.8%	5.0%	5.9%	3.0%	$56.60	$1.90
Inflation Rate	2.3%	3.1%	3.8%	4.5%	2.9%	na	na

* investments purchased at beginning of year; No income reinvestment

Arrows = Great Depression

10-Year T-Bonds % 1800-2007	US Home Prices 1830-2007
US Preferred Stocks 1890-2007	US Common Stocks 1800-2007
US Corporate Bonds 1860-2007	Commodities 1800-2007

6.9%

11.2

20.4

101.9

4.0%

73.1

243.3

1468

0.6

359.7

2.4

60.9

1800 1810 1820 1830 1840 1850 1860 1870 1880 1890 1900 1910 1920 1930 1940 1950 1960 1970 1980 1990 2000

BEAR MARKETS
The Expressions Never Change!

1906

1857   1987   1962

MARKET CYCLES
FROM EASY MONEY TO CRASH LANDINGS

In the last section, we reviewed the overall performance of six different types of investments. Though this knowledge is important, when to buy or sell can be as important as what to buy or sell, especially when investment debt is used to try to enhance returns. History has repeatedly shown that investors "blow up" portfolios of sound investments in stocks and real estate by using lethal levels of high leverage during bear markets.

This section will focus on the most significant bull and bear markets for U.S. common stocks and homes since 1850, and how time-tested tools can provide important early clues to possible changes in direction for stocks and real estate.

"It is possible to lose money in a Bull Market—
and likewise to lose money trading short in a Bear Market."
Technical Analysis of Stock Trends, Edwards and Magee—1948

BULL MARKETS—THE BEST OF TIMES

U.S. COMMON STOCKS

Four stock bull markets have exceeded seven years in duration since 1850. Their average annual return was 81% higher than the market's normal performance (20% vs. 11%). Although the Roaring 20s posted the best annual average return of 25%, the 18-year run of the "Decade of Greed" and the era of dot-coms took first place as the longest-running stock bull market in the past 157 years in spite of the 1987 crash.

U.S. Common Stocks
Longest Bull Markets—1850 to 2007

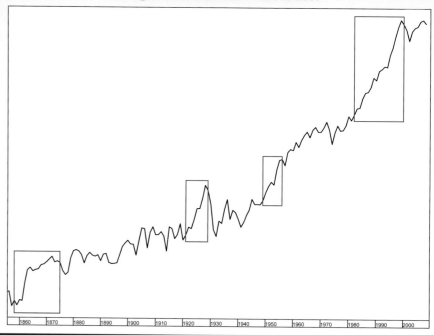

U.S. Common Stocks: Longest Bull Markets

Period	Number of Years	Total Return	Annual Returns				Dividend Yield
			Average	Median	Best	Worst	
1982-1999	18	329%	17%	20%	37%	-3%	3%
1860-1872	13	219%	17%	13%	61%	-2%	6%
1947-1956	10	187%	19%	18%	51%	-1%	6%
1921-28	8	202%	25%	31%	43%	3%	6%
Average	12.3	234%	20%	20%	48%	-1%	5%

Criteria
Time frame to exceed 7 years
No negative year to exceed -3%
Total return to exceed 150%

"A history of the Great Bull Market of 1982-99 is more than a financial story. Ultimately, that breakneck ride would mark an epoch in U.S. cultural history. While share prices spiraled, investing replaced baseball as the national pastime. CNBC's stars began to edge the soaps off the screen. The New Economy spawned a New Society, and, as the baby boomers aged, even the symbols of success changed: SUVs trumped BMW. Trophy mansions replaced trophy wives."

U.S. NEW HOMES

Five real estate bull markets have exceeded five years in duration since 1850. Their average annual return was 120% higher than the market's normal unleveraged performance (11% vs. 5%). The 20-year run of the 1971-1990 market was the longest, but the second-best bull market started one year later, the 15-year run of the 1992-2006 bull market.

U.S. Residential Real Estate
Longest Bull Markets—1850 to 2007

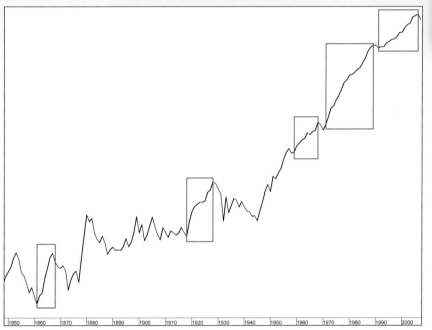

U.S. Homes: Longest Bull Markets

Period	Number of Years	Total Return	Annual Returns			
			Average	Median	Best	Worst
1971-1990	20	192%	10%	10%	20%	0%
1992-2006	15	75%	5%	3%	14%	0%
1919-1928	10	129%	13%	8%	36%	0%
1959-1968	10	70%	7%	6%	19%	-3%
1862-1867	6	122%	20%	22%	37%	6%
Average	12.2	118%	11%	10%	26%	0%

Criteria
 Time frame to exceed 5 years
 No negative year to exceed -3%
 Total return to exceed 70%
 No leverage

"You're seeing people now for whom investing in real estate is their life.
It's a move taken straight from the old day traders of the stock market."

Fortune—June 6, 2005

MARKET TOPS
Is it Time to Sell? How to Tell

There are several tools that stock investors can use to gauge the health of an old bull market similarly to how doctors use various tests during physical exams on their patients. Unfortunately, many investors fruitlessly search for a magic indicator to pick the top of a bull market. Experienced investors use a series of indicators to gain a consensus as to the market's overall strength.

U.S. COMMON STOCKS

Although many tools are used in stock market analysis, the 40-week moving average of broad market index (such as the S&P 500 Index) combined with the NYSE Advance Decline Line are used to evaluate the market tops of 1929 and 2000.

U.S. Common Stocks—1928 to 1930
with 40-week Moving Average

Moving averages are used to determine market direction. If the index is above the moving average, then the index is in an uptrend. If the index is below the moving average, then the index is in a downtrend.

NYSE Advance/Decline Line—1928 to 1930
with 40-week Moving Average

This measures the number of individual stocks where prices are moving up versus down. It uses the 40-week moving average similar to price charts.

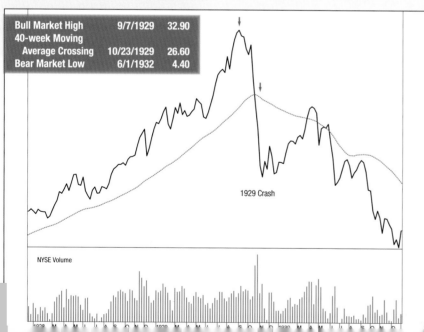

Bull Market High	9/7/1929	32.90
40-week Moving Average Crossing	10/23/1929	26.60
Bear Market Low	6/1/1932	4.40

1929 Crash

NYSE Volume

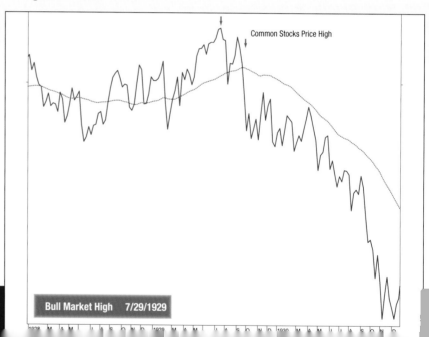

Common Stocks Price High

Bull Market High   7/29/1929

U.S. Common Stocks in 1929 and 1999

As can be seen in both examples, the internal strength of the market had been eroding many months before a new high was made on the index itself. For example, the NYSE Advance Decline Line had started to decline many months before the S&P 500 Index crossed below the 40-week moving average, thus beginning a new bear market in both cases.

U.S. Common Stocks—1999 to 2001
with 40-week Moving Average

Moving averages are used to determine market direction. If the index is above the moving average, then the index is in an uptrend. If the index is below the moving average, then the index is in a downtrend.

NYSE Advance/Decline Line—1999 to 2001
with 40-week Moving Average

This measures the number of individual stocks where prices are moving up versus down. It uses the 40-week moving average similar to price charts.

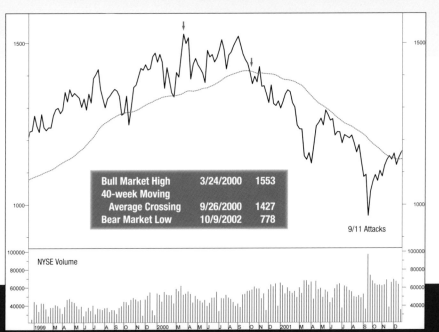

Bull Market High	3/24/2000	1553
40-week Moving Average Crossing	9/26/2000	1427
Bear Market Low	10/9/2002	778

9/11 Attacks

NYSE Volume

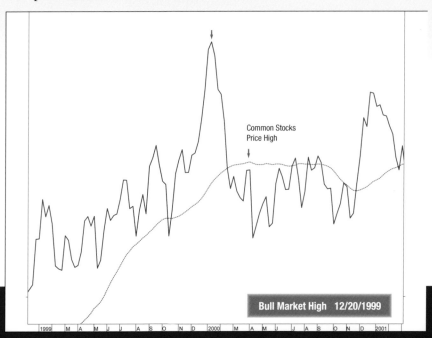

Common Stocks Price High

Bull Market High 12/20/1999

"Despite the pitfalls of public high-tech investing, many experts remain bullish on its prospects for the future."

MARKET TOPS
U.S. Residential Real Estate

Many of the tools used for market analysis of real estate did not exist before the 1960s, so attention is focused on the bull markets of the 1960s and 2000s.

Although there are many tools used in market analysis, the 15-month moving average of the Winans International Real Estate Index™ combined with the number of months a new house was on the market before it was sold are used to evaluate the market tops of 1968 and 2007.

U.S. New Home Prices—1968 to 1970
with 15-month moving average

Moving averages are used to determine market direction. If the index is above the moving average, then the index is in an uptrend. If the index is below the moving average, then the index is in a downtrend.

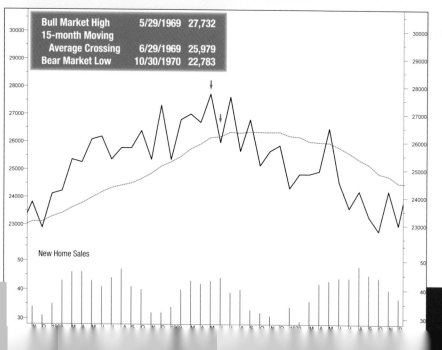

Months That New Homes Were on the Market
1968 to 1970

This measures the number of months that new houses in the United States were for sale before they were sold.

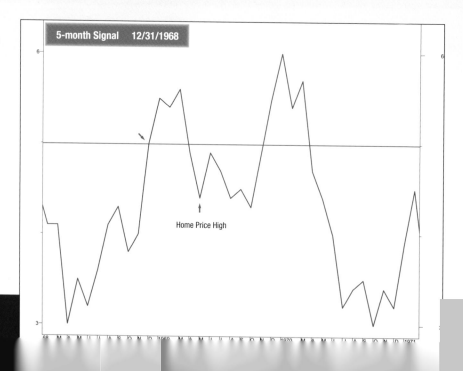

New Homes in 1968 and 2007

As can be seen in both examples, when the WIREI™ crossed below its 15-month moving average, and the months on market climbed above five months, there was strong evidence that the bull markets were coming to an end. It is important to note that the current bear market in residential real estate has recently surpassed the 1969 bear market as the worst percentage drop since the 1940s.

U.S. New Home Prices—2005 to 2007
with 15-month moving average

Moving averages are used to determine market direction. If the index is above the moving average, then the index is in an uptrend. If the index is below the moving average, then the index is in a downtrend.

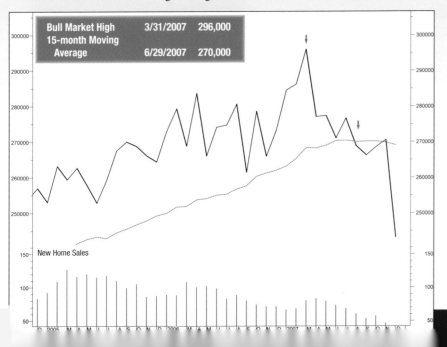

Months That New Homes Were on the Market
2005 to 2007

This measures the number of months that new houses in the United States were for sale before they were sold.

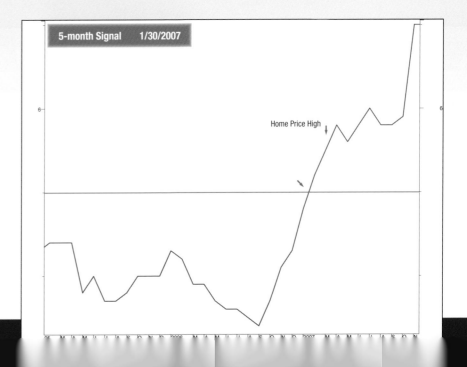

BEAR MARKET–THE WORST OF TIMES

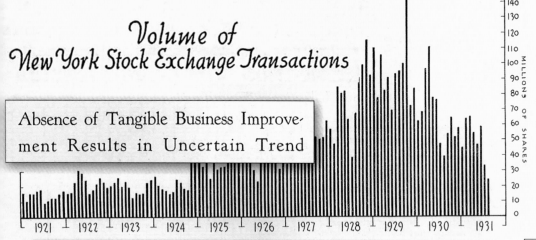

Volume of New York Stock Exchange Transactions

Absence of Tangible Business Improvement Results in Uncertain Trend

MILLIONS OF SHARES

1921 1922 1923 1924 1925 1926 1927 1928 1929 1930 1931

U.S. COMMON STOCKS

Five stock bear markets have exceeded two years in duration since 1850. Their average annual decline was –16% and it took nearly nine years on average to return to the market's previous high. The four-year decline of the Great Depression was the worst decline in 157 years, with a total decline of 83% from its close in 1928.

How Far Can This Market Go?

U.S. Common Stocks: Longest Bear Markets

Period	Number of Years	Total Return	Annual Returns				Dividend Yield
			Average	Median	Best	Worst	
1929-1932	4	-83%	-21%	-17%	-8%	-42%	5%
2000-2002	3	-43%	-14%	-12%	-10%	-22%	1%
1973-1974	2	-37%	-19%	-19%	-13%	-24%	5%
1913-1914	2	-31%	-15%	-15%	-5%	-26%	5%
1853-1854	2	-26%	-13%	-13%	-6%	-20%	8%
Average	2.5	-44%	-16%	-15%	-8%	-27%	5%

Criteria
Time frame to exceed 2 years
No positive year to exceed 2%
Minimum total return -25%

U.S. Common Stocks
Longest Bear Markets—1850 to 2007

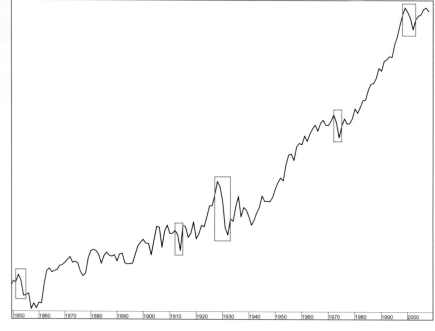

1850 1860 1870 1880 1890 1900 1910 1920 1930 1940 1950 1960 1970 1980 1990 2000

"During the long continued rise in stocks which began in 1924 the slogan 'common stocks for investment' became a popular watchword. People were obsessed with the notion that bear markets were a thing of the past and could never recur."

U. S. NEW HOMES

Five housing bear markets have exceeded three years in duration since 1850. Their average annual decline was –14%, and it took nearly 12 years on average to return to the market's previous high. The six years of decline during World War II was the longest decline in 157 years. But the five-year decline of 1854-1858 was far worse, with a total decline of -77%.

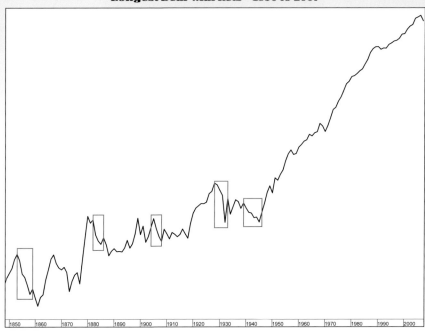

U.S. Residential Real Estate
Longest Bear Markets—1850 to 2007

U.S. Homes: Longest Bear Markets

Period	Number of Years	Total Return	Annual Returns				Recovery Time Years
			Average	Median	Best	Worst	
1940-1945	6	-38%	-6%	-9%	1%	-10%	2
1854-1858	5	-77%	-15%	-15%	-7%	-25%	9
1929-1932	4	-68%	-17%	-11%	-3%	-44%	19
1883-1885	3	-46%	-15%	-12%	-7%	-27%	16
1906-1908	3	-56%	-15%	-15%	-15%	-15%	12
Average	4.2	-55%	-14%	-12%	-6%	-24%	11.6

Criteria
 Time frame to exceed 3 years
 No positive year to exceed 2%
 Minimum total return -40%
 No leverage

"Brace yourself: Home prices could fall an additional 25%, on average, before bottoming out. Such a drop would be unprecedented in modern times."

Business Week—February 11, 2008

MARKET BOTTOMS
Is it Time to Buy? How to Tell

Stock investors can use several tools to determine if a bear market is getting close to ending. Unfortunately, many investors fruitlessly search for a magic indicator to pick the bottom of a bear market. Experienced investors use a series of indicators to gain a consensus as to the market's overall strength or weakness and learn to ignore all the doom and gloom projections coming from media sources.

U.S. COMMON STOCKS

Although many tools are used in market analysis, the 40-week moving average of broad market index (such as the S&P 500 Index) combined with the NYSE advance decline line are used to evaluate the market bottoms of 1932 and 2002.

U.S. Common Stocks
with 40-week Moving Average—1931 to 1933

Moving averages are used to determine market direction. If the index is above the moving average, then the index is in an uptrend. If the index is below the moving average, then the index is in a downtrend.

NYSE Advance/Decline Line—1931 to 1933
with 40-week Moving Average

This measures the number of individual stocks where prices are moving up versus down. It uses the 40-week moving average similar to price charts.

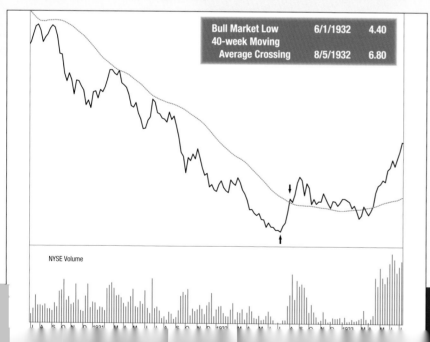

Bull Market Low 6/1/1932 4.40
40-week Moving Average Crossing 8/5/1932 6.80

NYSE Volume

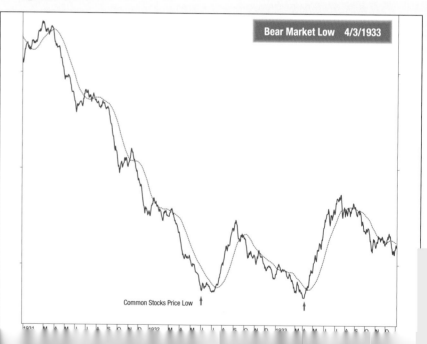

Bear Market Low 4/3/1933

Common Stocks Price Low

U.S. Common Stocks in 1932 and 2003

As can be seen in both examples, waiting for both the indicators to cross above their individual 40-week moving averages gave a strong indication the bear market was coming to an end.

U.S. Common Stocks—2002 to 2004
with 40-week Moving Average

Moving averages are used to determine market direction. If the index is above the moving average, then the index is in an uptrend. If the index is below the moving average, then the index is in a downtrend.

NYSE Advance/Decline Line—2002 to 2004
with 40-week Moving Average

This measures the number of individual stocks where prices are moving up versus down. It uses the 40-week moving average similar to price charts.

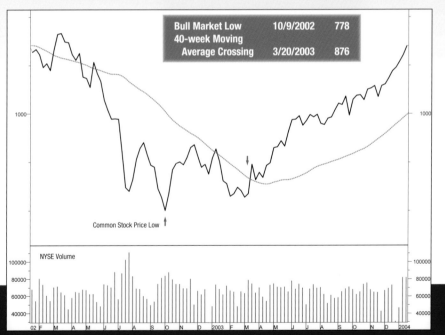

Bull Market Low	10/9/2002	778
40-week Moving		
Average Crossing	3/20/2003	876

Common Stock Price Low

NYSE Volume

Bear Market Low   10/9/2002

Common Stocks
Price Low

"While the 1921-1932 period is the shortest gap between bear market bottoms it was still accompanied by significant structural change in the stock market. There were many more securities to choose from in 1932 compared to 1921."

MARKET BOTTOMS
U.S. Residential Real Estate

Many of the tools used for market analysis of real estate did not exist before the 1960s, therefore attention is focused on the bear markets of the 1970s and 1990s.

Although many tools are used in market analysis, the 15-month moving average of the Winans International Real Estate Index™ combined with the number of months a new house was on the market before it was sold are used to evaluate the market bottoms of 1970 and 1992.

U.S. New Home Prices—1970 to 1972
with 15-month moving average

Moving averages are used to determine market direction. If the index is above the moving average, then the index is in an uptrend. If the index is below the moving average, then the index is in a downtrend.

Months That New Homes Were on the Market
1970 to 1972

This measures the number of months that new houses in the United States were for sale before they were sold.

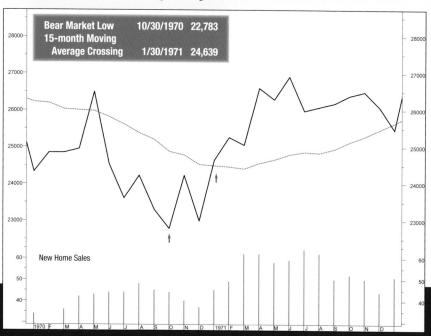

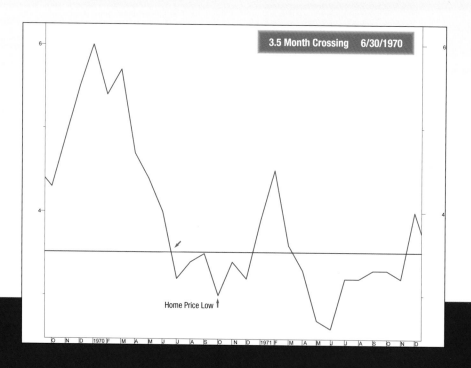

"Home prices have been rising steadily for most of this boom since 1975 with the slight exception of the early 1990s."

New Homes in 1970 and 1992

As can be seen in both examples, when the WIREI crossed above its 15-month moving average, and the months on market reached 3.5 months, there was strong evidence that the bear markets were reaching a close.

U.S. New Home Prices—1991 to 1993
with 15-month moving average

Moving averages are used to determine market direction. If the index is above the moving average, then the index is in an uptrend. If the index is below the moving average, then the index is in a downtrend.

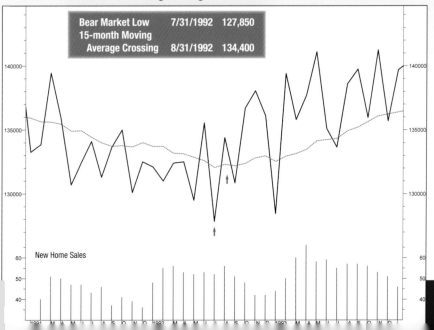

Bear Market Low 7/31/1992 127,850
15-month Moving
Average Crossing 8/31/1992 134,400

New Home Sales

Months That New Homes Were on the Market
1992 to 1994

This measures the number of months that new houses in the United States were for sale before they were sold.

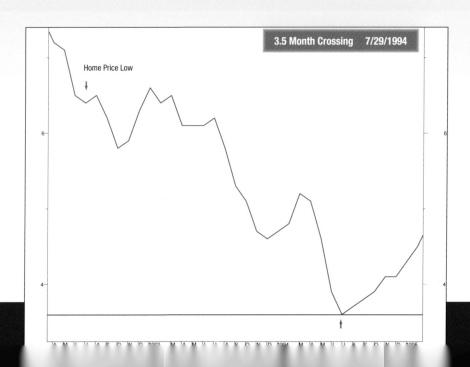

3.5 Month Crossing 7/29/1994

Home Price Low

BUBBLES, FADES, and SCANDALS

Trading Scheme—1902

Email Scam—2007

20 YEARS IN WALL STREET.

NEW YORK TELEGRAPH BUREAU.

*Private Telegraphic Cypher Code Used.
Highest Bank and Mercantile Agency References.
Detailed Report on any Market Subject Furnished
Free of Charge.
CORRESPONDENCE SOLICITED.*

82 WALL STREET,

NEW YORK.

"He who goes into Wall Street to get rich usually gets poor, but he who goes into Wall Street to make a living may become rich."

WE HAVE NO AGENTS.

LEGITIMATE SPECULATION AS A BUSINESS.

As a twentieth century business man you are no doubt interested in the affairs of Wall Street and the New York Stock and Cotton Markets, and possibly, may be interested in legitimate speculation. It is needless for us to say that market operations have been a failure to 90% of the speculating public as a means of making money, and why?—the answer is simply this: They are continually advised to buy—buy—buy.

To be successful in market transactions, you must always be prepared to operate on either side of the market. The great powers in Wall Street never confine their operations to the buying side of the market, they play the Short as well as the Long side. It is a well known fact by well informed people of the street, that these pools or cliques that are formed for the purpose of carrying on a manipulative campaign in some certain commodity, win practically every battle they enter into. These pools are known under various names. The most important is that known as the Standard Oil Pool, commonly called 26 Broadway. Others in importance are the Morgan clique, composed of vast banking interests in this country and Europe. The Savin Pool, operating chiefly in the Atchison shares. The Lower Wall Street Crowd, referring to Havemeyer and the insiders on Sugar. The Western Crowd, headed by John W. Gates and his powerful following, sometimes referred to as the big Store, who operate all through the market, but principally in Western Stocks. The First National Bank Crowd, operating in the Coal Stocks. The Hanover Bank Clique, operating largely in Tennessee Coal and Iron. The Wormser Party and their followers. The Copper Crowd, headed by Thomas W. Lawson of Boston. The Knickerbocker Ice Clique, with E. R. Thomas at its head, and the Keene Crowd, with James R. Keene, said to be the greatest manipulator of stocks who has ever invaded Wall Street. The Up-Town Clique, composed of Jakey Field and his friends, who make their headquarters at the Waldorf Astoria. The Rapid Transit Crowd, which includes Belmont, Ryan and several other multi-millionaires. The Moore Brothers, of Diamond Match fame, who operate heavily through Sidney C. Love. The Harriman Party, operating principally in the Pacifics. The Hill Contingent, referring to Jim Hill and his St. Paul friends.

In the cotton market we have the celebrated Theodore Price, who always operates with a powerful pool—the Edward Weld combination. Mitchell, who operates for different pools. McFadden, known as the "Spot House." The New Orleans Clique, who usually follow one of these leaders, and the big Exchange Clique, made up of a few powerful men of the N. Y. Stock Exchange, who are always interested in the Cotton markets.

Now as a strictly business proposition, if you were to get advance inside information as to the actual workings of these leaders occasionally, would you not feel safe in following them in a small way? The New York Telegraph Bureau is composed of expert telegraph operators, who were brought up within the very shadow of the New York Stock and Cotton Exchanges. Having acquaintances in all the large banking, stock exchange and cotton exchange houses, together with our long experience in market affairs, we are in a position to collect more correct data concerning deals and contemplated deals, than can be obtained through any other channel. Of course we all cannot be a Rockefeller, or a Morgan in the Stock Market, or a Theodore Price in the Cotton Pit, but we contend that if you are operating in the markets and you can learn that Mr. Morgan or Mr. Price is running a deal in some favorite commodity, if it is good enough for them, it should be good enough for you. We wish to impress upon you that in dealing through us, you are not receiving the public gossip or discounted information, such as is sent out from Wall Street by unscrupulous dealers in news. The references attached herewith should convince any one on this point. This Bureau is in a position to give you advance information of the very highest class. Our clientage extends throughout the entire United States and Canada, and the best references we can offer you are our customers who follow our advices from one end of the year to the other. If you are interested in legitimate speculation let us explain to you our plans, it will cost you nothing. Get in communication with us,

---

Ken Winans

From:	"frank jrn wilson" <franklywilson23@hotmail.fr>
To:	<undisclosed-recipients:>
Sent:	Thursday, June 28, 2007 2:00 AM
Subject:	SPAM: Investment Proposal

FROM:FRANK JRN WILSON
C/O: REFUGEE CAMP-ABIDJAN
ABIDJAN COTE D'IVOIRE,
WEST AFRICA,

Dearest One,
I got your contact address on my desperate search for a reliable person/company for partnership investments overseas,I am also believing that you will not expose or betray the trust and confidence I am about to establish with you.

I have decided to contact you with greatest delight and personal respect.Well, I am FRANK JRN WILSON,son to Dr.FRANK WILSON late former Director of finance Sierra-Leone diamond and mining corporation.Few days before the death my father, he confided in me and ordered me to go to his underground safe and move out immediately, with a Deposit Agreement and Cash Receipt he made with a BANK in Abidjan Cote d'Ivoire where he deposited USD$6.2 million dollars cash(SIX MILLION,TWO HUNDRED THOUSAND DOLLARS).This money was made from the sells of Gold and Diamond by my father and he have already decided to use this money for future investment of the family.

Thereafter, I rushed down to Abidjan with these two documents and confirmed the deposit of the fund by my father. Also, I have been granted political stay as a Refugee by the Government of Cote d'Ivoire.Meanwhile, my father have instructed me to look for a trusted foreigner who can assist me to move out this money from Cote d'Ivoire immediately for investment.
Based on this,I solicit for your assistance to transfer this fund into your Account, but I will demand for the following requirement:

(1) Could you provide for me a safe Bank Account where this fund will be transferred to in your country
(2) Could you be able to introduce me to a profitable business venture that would not require much technical expertise in your country where part of this fund will be invested?
(3) Your full name.
(4) Your residential house address.
(5) Your direct telephone and fax number.
(6) Your age
(7) Marital status.
Please, all these requirements are urgently needed as it will enable me to establish a stronger business relationship with you hence I will like you to be the general overseer of the investment there after.I am trusthing you and I will please want you to handle this transaction based on the trust I have established on you.For your assistance in this transaction, I have decided to offer you 25% percent commission of the total amount at the end of this business. The security of this business is very important to me and as such,I would like you to keep this business very confidential.If you are willing to assist me.Please kindly reply me immediately.
Your Faithfull
Frank Jrn Wilson

In the aftermath of bull markets rests the wreckage of stocks representing bubbles, fades, or scandals. Here are just a few of the most notorious examples:

THE BOND OPERATOR.

Fraud Cartoon—1884

Accounting Fraud—2002

WCG17234

WorldCom, Inc.

ORGANIZED UNDER THE LAWS OF THE STATE OF GEORGIA

WorldCom, Inc. – WorldCom Group Common Stock

SEE REVERSE FOR
CERTAIN DEFINITIONS

This Certifies That

CUSIP 98157D 10 6

00017234

0005914908

MINNEAPOLIS MN 55405-1712

is the owner of   **ONE**

SHARES OF ONE CENT (1¢) PAR VALUE EACH OF THE WORLDCOM GROUP COMMON STOCK OF

WorldCom, Inc., a Georgia corporation, fully paid and non-assessable, transferable on the books of the Corporation by the holder hereof in person or by Attorney, upon surrender of this Certificate properly endorsed. This Certificate is not valid until countersigned by the Transfer Agent.

In Witness Whereof, the said Corporation has caused this Certificate to be signed by its duly authorized officers and to be sealed with the Seal of the Corporation.

Dated: AUG 21, 2002

WORLDCOM INC. CORPORATE SEAL A GEORGIA CORPORATION

SECRETARY

PRESIDENT

00017234 000413618

SOUTH SEAS COMPANY TRANSACTION RECEIPT—1720

The dot.com stock of the 1700s! The stock price declined 84% in six months.

South Seas Company Bubble—1711 to 1750

EQUITY FUNDING CORPORATION—1973

Wall Street's Watergate! This insurance company committed a $1 billion fraud, and its stock price went from a high of $80 to $0.50 within nine months. Twenty-two company executives were indicted for fraud and conspiracy.

"When Sir Isaac Newton was asked about the continuance of the rising South Sea Stock? He answered that he could not calculate the madness of people."

"Many investors decided that independent auditors, state examiners and the SEC are not reliable protection against fraud, and they indiscriminately knocked the whole insurance group down ten to twenty-five percent."

PLANET HOLLYWOOD—1996

This company was backed by many of Hollywood's biggest stars. It went public at $32 a share during April 1996 and was trading at only $0.90 by early 1999.

ENRON CORPORATION—2001

The largest bankruptcy in history due to a massive accounting fraud of $111 billion. This blue-chip stock declined from $90 to $0.37 within 15 months. Its top executives received prison sentences between 24 and 45 years.

"Planet Hollywood has stood as a cautionary tale about the perils of celebrity and hype, as the company filed bankruptcy protection not once but twice shortly after the Las Vegas groundbreaking."
The New York Times—September 24, 2007

"Something is rotten with the state of Enron."
The New York Times—September 9, 2001

ACCOUNTING SCAMS
Watch Shareholder Dilution!

During the accounting scandals of 2002, what did companies like Enron, Worldcom, and Tyco have in common (besides stocks that "blew up" due to fraudulent accounting practices)? Excessive shareholder dilution—reckless growth in the number of split-adjusted shares outstanding.

The table below shows shares outstanding between 1991 and 2001. The dilution levels of these three tainted companies were significantly higher than the Dow Jones Industrial Average.

Many companies resort to aggressive accounting methods and high levels of shareholder dilution to hide reckless expansion, ridiculous employee compensation, and illegal business practices.

This statistic can be a good indicator of companies with potential accounting problems. History has shown that if investors want to avoid owning companies that could be using fraudulent accounting practices, then they should avoid companies that have levels of shareholder dilution exceeding 70% over the past 10 years.

Company	Cumulative Outstanding (Millions of Shares)		Dilution (Post splits)
	1991	2001	
Enron	405	752	86%
Worldcom	299	2,965	893%
Tyco International	377	1936	414%
DJIA 30 Stocks Average Cumulative Dilution			17%

"Bubbles lie at the intersection
between finance, economics and psychology."
Famous First Bubbles, Garber—2000

HISTORICAL EVENTS
DOES WALL STREET CARE?

Throughout our lives, we have been shaped by the events we have experienced. Baby boomers have a different take on life than their "Greatest Generation" parents or their "Generation X" kids. This is clearly defined by their investment choices. To this day, many senior citizens still fear (and avoid) the stock market because of painful childhood memories of the 1930s Great Depression. To the other extreme, many of their children enjoy today's conveniences and wide-ranging choices of equity investments offered by the investment community and hold little or no cash for a rainy day.

But are our financial reactions to major events really any different from those of past generations? Can we learn from their investment mistakes and successes during difficult and ecstatic times in the past?

In this section, we review how investors in stocks, homes, and treasury bonds reacted to the major government policies, wars, natural disasters, man-made tragedies, and great national achievements since 1812 in hopes of finding useful investment guidance for future events.

Though it might be difficult to view dark times for all of mankind as investment opportunities, it is important to view these events from many different perspectives and learn from the past actions of uninformed individuals who sold solid investments because of scary headlines rather than learning from the lessons of history.

If there is ever a time to be a logical, disciplined investor, it is during major historical events!

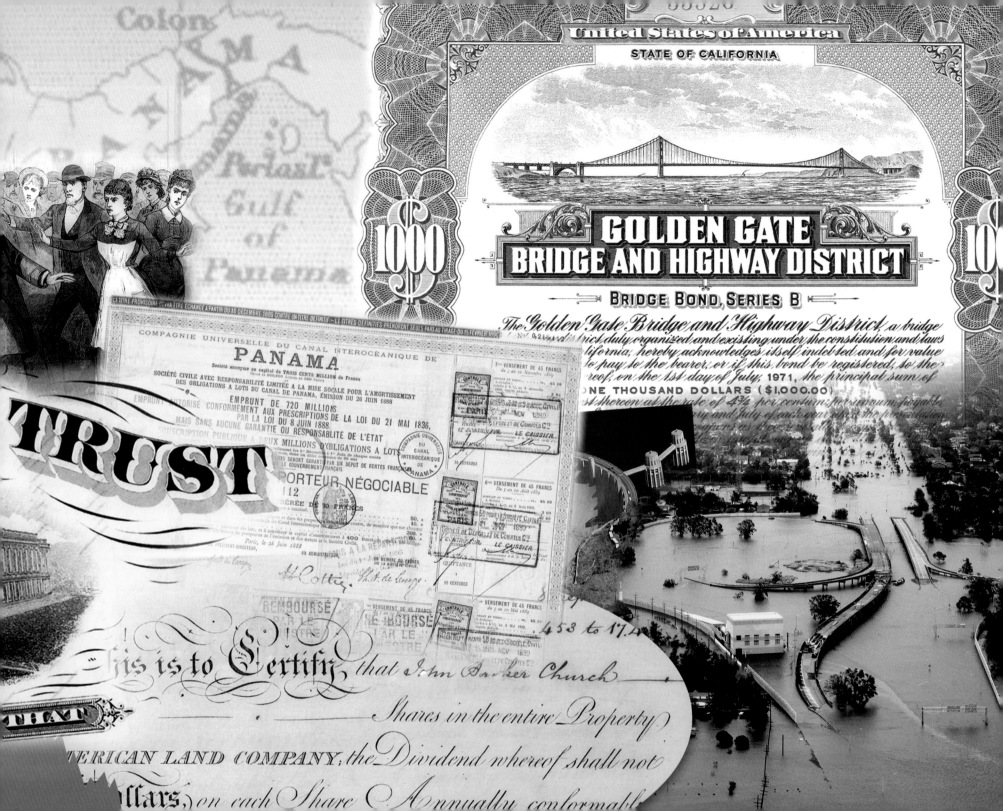

U.S. Capitol building
in Washington, D.C.

Federal Reserve building in Washington, D.C.

IN GOD WE TRUST

THE WHITE HOUSE

TWENTY DOLLARS

UNCLE SAM:

ECONOMIC PARTY ANIMAL
OR PARTY CRASHER?

POLITICS and INVESTING

Since the beginning of our nation's history, many politicians (from opposing parties) have been wealthy, successful investors. In fact, many congressional, senatorial, and presidential campaigns have been financed by the fruits of the candidates' (or their families') investment success.

Do winds of political change really have an effect on investing in America? Ultimately, investors (regardless of their political views) want to see their stocks and real estate holdings appreciate in value within a low-interest-rate environment.

Presidents and Investments		Percentage Change			
		Stocks	T-Bond Yields	Homes	Stocks and Homes
Best Single Terms					
Grant	1877	85%	-38%	265%	350%
Lincoln	1861	109%	-15%	115%	224%
Best Multiple Terms					
Reagan	(1981-1988)	138%	-48%	72%	210%
Coolidge (Harding)	(1921-1928)	150%	-27%	58%	208%
Clinton	(1993-2000)	127%	-13%	46%	173%
Worst Single Terms					
Pierce	1853	-49%	16%	-48%	-97%
Hoover	1929	-53%	5%	-25%	-78%
Worst Multiple Terms					
None					

You might not be surprised to know that Reagan's two terms showed a 138% increase in stocks and 72% increase in new-home prices combined for a total return of 210%, but the best one term was Grant's second term when investments increased an amazing 350%!

Not all bull markets are generated on the Republican side. The best return for a Democrat was Clinton's post-cold-war tenure of 173%, the third best on record!

Clearly the well-followed scandals of the Grant, Reagan, and Clinton administrations didn't matter to Wall Street!

On the flip side, both parties have had bear markets on their watch. The Democrat Pierce and Republican Hoover posted sizeable losses in both stocks and real estate. Finally, voter patience with bear markets is limited and didn't allow a president to serve multiple terms with investment losses.

"The prospect of big losses for business-friendly Republicans in tomorrow's mid-term elections is eliciting more shrugs than fears on Wall Street… The first and most frequently cited rationale for Wall Street's nonchalance at the specter of a Democratic triumph is the old 'gridlock is good' maxim."

The Wall Street Journal —November 5, 2006

North American Land Company Stock Certificate—1795

Founder of this company was Robert Morris,
one of America's earliest millionaires,
who helped finance the American Revolution.
He also signed the Declaration of Independence.

"Since 1833, presidential elections every four years have a profound impact on the economy and the stock market.
Wars, recessions, and bear markets tend to start or occur in the first half of the term;
prosperous times and bull markets, in the latter half."

THE GOP

Republicans and Whigs		Common Stocks			T-Bond Yields			Homes			Stocks and Homes	
Year	Administrations	First Year	Last Year	% Chg	First Year	Last Year	% Chg	First Year	Last Year	% Chg	% Chg	Rank
1841	W. Harrison/Polk	1.6	2.3	48%	4.99	5.47	10%	1,515	487	-68%	-20%	19
1849	Taylor	2.0	2.3	20%	5.41	4.97	-8%	1,011	1,681	66%	86%	9
1861	Lincoln	1.4	2.9	109%	6.58	5.59	-15%	558	1,200	115%	224%	2
1865	Lincoln/Johnson	2.9	3.6	25%	5.59	5.39	-4%	1,200	761	-37%	-12%	18 (tie)
1873	Grant	3.6	2.6	-27%	5.39	5.44	1%	761	895	18%	-9%	17
1877	Grant	2.6	4.9	86%	5.44	3.39	-38%	895	3,270	265%	351%	1
1881	Hayes	4.9	4.2	-14%	3.39	3.23	-5%	3,270	2,083	-36%	-50%	21
1885	Garfield/Arthur	4.2	4.3	2%	3.23	3.14	-3%	2,083	1,790	-14%	-12%	18 (tie)
1893	B. Harrison	3.6	4.3	21%	3.49	3.10	-11%	1,766	2,107	19%	41%	14
1897	McKinley	4.3	5.6	31%	3.10	2.87	-7%	2,107	3,066	46%	76%	10
1901	McKinley/Roosevelt	5.6	8.4	49%	2.87	3.07	7%	3,066	3,596	17%	66%	11
1905	T. Roosevelt	8.4	8.7	3%	3.07	3.45	12%	3,596	2,864	-20%	-17%	19
1909	Taft	8.7	6.9	-21%	3.45	3.58	4%	2,864	2,575	-10%	-31%	20
1921	Harding/Coolidge	7.1	13.7	93%	4.47	3.80	-15%	4,489	5,081	13%	106%	5
1925	Coolidge	13.7	21.4	57%	3.80	3.36	-12%	5,081	7,359	45%	102%	6
1929	Hoover	21.4	10.1	-53%	3.36	3.53	5%	7,359	5,519	-25%	-78%	22
1953	Eisenhower	24.8	40.0	61%	2.59	3.21	24%	9,197	15,474	68%	129%	3
1957	Eisenhower	40.0	71.5	79%	3.21	4.06	27%	15,474	17,381	12%	91%	8
1969	Nixon	92.1	97.5	6%	7.88	6.90	-12%	25,801	36,793	43%	49%	12
1973	Nixon/Ford	97.5	95.1	-3%	6.90	7.78	13%	36,793	55,150	50%	47%	13
1981	Reagan	122.5	209.7	71%	13.98	9.00	-36%	75,600	97,000	28%	99%	7
1985	Reagan	209.7	350.7	67%	9.00	7.93	-12%	97,000	139,750	44%	111%	4
1989	G.H.W. Bush	350.7	468.6	34%	7.93	5.83	-27%	139,750	135,700	-3%	31%	15
2001	G.W. Bush	1161.9	1213.5	4%	5.07	4.24	-16%	204,450	256,950	26%	30%	16
Best Performance		Median	28%			-6%			19%		48%	
Worst Performance		Average	31%			-5%			28%		59%	
		High	109%			27%			265%		351%	
		Low	-53%			-38%			-68%		-78%	

"Just consider Thursday's strong rally in the stock market, which came in the wake of the report, Wednesday night, that President Bush's approval rating had sunk to its lowest level ever… There are lots of things that investors can legitimately worry about these days. But President Bush's low approval rating does not appear to be one of them."

Marketwatch.com—June 15, 2007

Since 1833, the average Republican presidential term has posted a 31% return in stocks, a 28% increase in home prices, and a 5% decline in interest rates. Of the 25 Republican terms, only five had declines in the stock market and only eight had declines in housing prices.

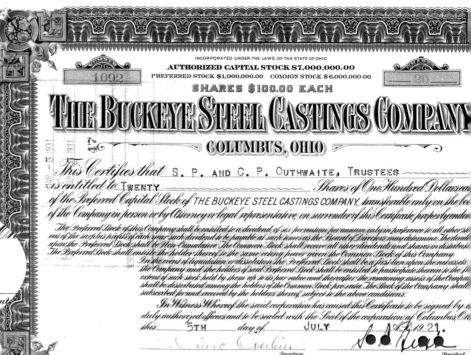

Signed by Samuel Bush
President George W. Bush's great-grandfather

THE DEMS

"The eyes of the U.S. last week turned
anxiously toward Wall Street,
where drama and despair marked
the stock market's worst plunge since 1950.
The sad news on the Big Board did not mean
that the U.S. economy was in bad trouble.
But, it did highlight a dilemma
for the Kennedy Administration."

Time—June 1, 1962

Year	Democrats Administrations	Common Stocks First Year	Common Stocks Last Year	Common Stocks % Chg	T-Bond Yields First Year	T-Bond Yields Last Year	T-Bond Yields % Chg	Homes First Year	Homes Last Year	Homes % Chg	Stocks and Homes % Chg	Rank
1833	Jackson	2.1	1.9	-9%	4.92	4.95	1%	1,373	1,339	-3%	-11%	13
1837	Van Buren	1.9	1.6	-18%	4.95	4.99	1%	1,339	1,515	13%	-5%	12 (tie)
1845	Polk	2.3	2.0	-17%	5.47	5.41	-1%	487	1,011	108%	91%	3
1853	Pierce	2.3	1.2	-49%	4.97	5.77	16%	1,681	870	-48%	-97%	17
1857	Buchanan	1.2	1.4	14%	5.77	6.58	14%	870	558	-36%	-22%	15
1889	Cleveland	4.3	3.6	-17%	3.14	3.49	11%	1,790	1,766	-1%	-18%	14
1913	Wilson	6.9	6.5	-6%	3.58	3.84	7%	2,575	2,597	1%	-5%	12 (tie)
1917	Wilson	6.5	7.1	9%	3.84	4.47	16%	2,597	4,489	73%	82%	4
1933	F. Roosevelt	10.1	10.6	5%	3.53	2.68	-24%	5,519	5,144	-7%	-2%	11
1937	F. Roosevelt	10.6	8.7	-18%	2.68	2.07	-23%	5,144	4,096	-20%	-38%	16
1941	F. Roosevelt	8.7	17.4	100%	2.07	1.67	-19%	4,096	3,337	-19%	81%	5
1945	F. Roosevelt/Truman	17.4	16.8	-4%	1.67	1.80	8%	3,337	7,185	115%	112%	2
1949	Truman	16.8	24.8	48%	1.80	2.59	44%	7,185	9,197	28%	76%	6
1961	Kennedy/Johnson	71.5	92.4	29%	4.06	4.65	15%	17,381	20,839	20%	49%	8
1965	Johnson	92.4	92.1	-0%	4.65	7.88	70%	20,839	25,801	24%	23%	10
1977	Carter	95.1	122.5	29%	7.78	13.98	80%	55,150	75,600	37%	66%	7
1993	Clinton	468.6	970.8	107%	5.83	5.75	-1%	135,700	160,850	19%	126%	1
1997	Clinton	970.8	1161.9	20%	5.75	5.07	-12%	160,850	204,450	27%	47%	9

Best Performance											
Worst Performance		Median	2%			8%			16%	35%	
		Average	12%			11%			18%	31%	
		High	107%			80%			115%	126%	
		Low	-49%			-24%			-48%	-97%	

Shares	100 Shares

C 13899

TEMPORARY CERTIFICATE
Exchangeable for Definitive Engraved Certificate When Ready for Delivery

100 Shares

UNITED STATES LINES COMPANY
INCORPORATED UNDER THE LAWS OF THE STATE OF NEW JERSEY.

COMMON STOCK

This Certificate is transferable in the City of New York or in Hoboken, N.J.

JOHN J. FORD AND ROSE F. KENNEDY
TRUSTEES UNDER INDENTURE OF TRUST MADE
BY JOSEPH P. KENNEDY DATED JAN 27 1926

THIS CERTIFIES that the owner of ———— ONE HUNDRED ———— full-paid and non-assessable shares of the **COMMON STOCK** of the Par Value of $1.00 each of

UNITED STATES LINES COMPANY

transferable on the books of the Corporation by the holder hereof in person or by duly authorized attorney upon surrender of this certificate properly endorsed.

A statement of the powers, preferences and relative, participating, optional or other special rights of the Preferred Stock and of the Common Stock which the Corporation is authorized to issue and of the qualifications, limitations or restrictions of such rights is printed upon the reverse hereof and this Certificate and the shares represented hereby are issued and shall be held subject to all the provisions of the Certificate of Organization of the Corporation and of the amendments thereto (copies of which are on file with the Transfer Agent) to all of which the holder, by acceptance thereof assents.

This certificate is not valid unless countersigned by the Transfer Agent and registered by the Registrar.
WITNESS the seal of the Corporation and the facsimile signatures of its duly authorized officers.

Dated FEB 21 1944

Treasurer

President

COUNTERSIGNED:
BANKERS TRUST COMPANY (New York) Transfer Agent,

Since 1833, the average Democratic presidential term has posted a 12% return in stocks, an 18% increase in home prices, and an 11% increase in interest rates. Of 18 Democratic terms, eight had declines in the stock market, and seven had declines in housing prices.

**Stock certificate issued to a
Kennedy Family Trust—1944**

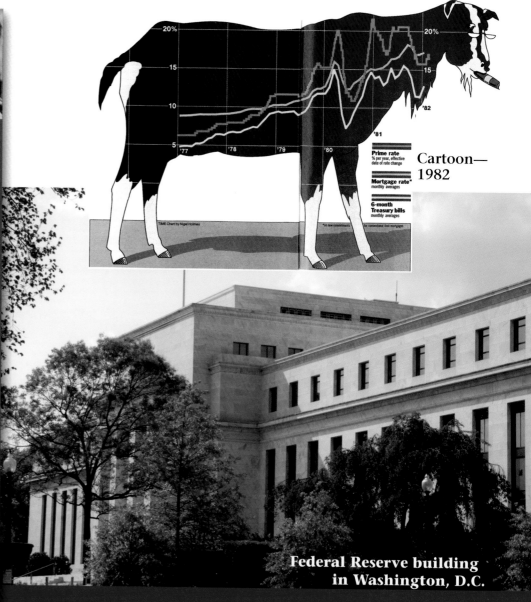

Cartoon—1982

Federal Reserve building in Washington, D.C.

"It is not the responsibility of the Federal Reserve—
nor would it be appropriate—to protect lenders and investors
from the consequences of their financial decisions."

Ben Bernanke, Chairman of the Federal Reserve—September 4, 2007

Who should investors pay the most attention to: the president, Congress, or the Federal Reserve? Historically, the president has been praised and blamed for the economy. For instance, Hoover is the popular choice to blame for the Great Depression, while House Speaker Longworth or Federal Reserve Chairman Young are not even mentioned for their role in the disaster.

Up until Chairman Volcker, the public didn't pay much attention to the Federal Reserve, and yet an argument can easily be made that the actions of this body have the most direct effect on the investment world.

Today, Capitol Hill, the White House, Wall Street, and the media have a love/hate relationship with the "Fed," and there have been times all of them have wanted to "tar and feather" the Fed chairman.

Has America economically performed better with the Federal Reserve at the helm in trying to control inflation and enhance economic growth?

In looking at charts of inflation and economic growth since 1800, it can be seen that economic growth is more stable under the Fed's watch. Deflation is less prevalent, yet inflation still seems to be a persistent problem since the Federal Reserve was established in 1913.

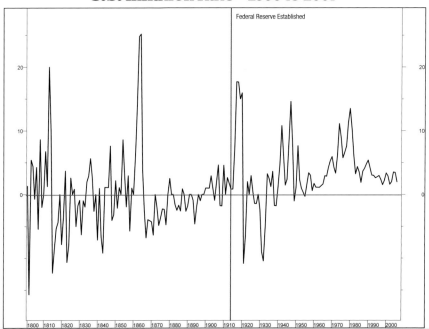

U.S. Gross Domestic Product % Change—1800 to 2007

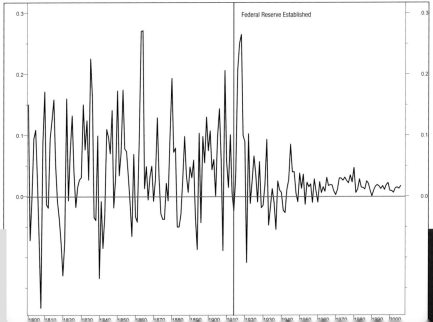

"None of the post-war expansions died of old age.
They were all murdered by the Fed."

"There's an awful lot of power there held by unelected people. I'm not sure it's good for a President to be held responsible for monetary policy when he has no control over it."

Donald Regan, Treasury Secretary—1984

Federal Reserve Chairman			Tenure	Inflation Rate (CPI)			Fed Funds Rate			Common Stocks		Annualized	T-Bond Yields		Annualized	New Home Prices		Annualized	Stocks% and Homes%	
Administration	Start	End	(Years)	High	Low	Average	High	Low	Average	Start	End	% Chg	1st Year	Last Year	% Chg	1st Year	Last Year	% Chg	- Inflation%	Rank
Hamlin	10/10/1914	10/10/1916	2.0	7.4%	0.8%	4.1%	5.0%	3.0%	4.0%	4.7	8.9	44%	3.6%	3.6%	-0%	2,443	2,879	9%	49%	1
Harding	10/10/1916	10/09/1922	6.0	17.7%	-10.8%	3.4%	7.0%	3.0%	5.0%	8.9	8.9	0%	3.6%	4.3%	3%	2,879	4,711	11%	7%	8
Crissinger	05/01/1923	09/15/1927	4.4	2.9%	-6.5%	-1.8%	4.5%	3.0%	3.8%	8.5	17.4	24%	4.4%	3.3%	-6%	4,711	6,393	8%	34%	2
Young	10/04/1927	08/31/1930	2.9	0.1%	-1.4%	-0.7%	6.0%	2.0%	4.0%	17.4	21.4	8%	3.3%	3.3%	-0%	6,393	6,554	1%	9%	7 (tie)
Meyer	09/16/1930	05/10/1933	2.6	-2.4%	-4.9%	-3.7%	4.5%	1.5%	3.0%	21.4	8.8	-22%	3.2%	3.3%	1%	6,554	5,519	-6%	-25%	11
Black	05/19/1933	08/15/1934	1.2	3.2%	-4.9%	-0.8%	3.5%	1.5%	2.5%	8.8	9.0	2%	3.3%	3.1%	-6%	5,519	3,941	-23%	-20%	10
Eccles	11/15/1934	02/03/1948	13.2	14.6%	-1.7%	6.4%	2.0%	0.5%	1.3%	9.2	14.6	4%	3.1%	2.2%	-2%	3,941	6,252	4%	2%	9
McCabe	04/15/1948	04/02/1951	3.0	7.9%	-1.0%	3.4%	1.8%	1.0%	1.4%	15.4	21.3	13%	2.1%	2.3%	3%	6,252	8,548	12%	22%	4 (tie)
Martin	04/02/1951	02/01/1970	18.8	7.6%	-0.3%	3.7%	9.0%	0.6%	4.8%	21.3	85.8	16%	2.3%	7.8%	12%	8,548	24,773	10%	22%	4 (tie)
Burns	02/01/1970	01/31/1978	8.0	11.1%	3.3%	7.2%	14.0%	3.3%	8.6%	85.8	89.2	1%	7.8%	7.9%	0%	24,773	55,400	15%	9%	7 (tie)
Miller	03/08/1978	08/06/1979	1.4	11.3%	6.6%	9.0%	10.9%	5.0%	7.9%	87.8	104.3	13%	8.0%	8.9%	8%	56,550	69,000	16%	20%	5
Volcker	08/06/1979	08/11/1987	8.0	13.5%	1.9%	7.7%	24.0%	5.4%	14.7%	104.3	333.3	27%	8.9%	8.7%	-0%	69,000	117,650	9%	29%	3
Greenspan	08/11/1987	01/31/2006	18.5	5.4%	1.5%	3.5%	9.9%	0.9%	5.4%	333.3	1280.2	15%	8.7%	4.5%	-3%	117,650	272,950	7%	19%	6
Bernanke	02/01/2006	?																		
Top Performance		Median	4.4			3.5%			4.0%			13.0%			-0.1%			8.8%	19.1%	
Worst Performance		Average	6.9			3.2%			5.1%			11.2%			0.8%			5.6%	13.7%	
		High	18.8			9.0%			14.7%			43.8%			12.3%			15.6%	48.5%	
		Low	1.2			-3.7%			1.3%			-22.2%			-6.1%			-23.0%	-24.5%	

"The verdict upon the Federal Reserve System is thus necessarily mixed. Foreign observers regard it with favor, as witness the extensive copying of the System in various countries. Many home critics have blamed it for acts, which constitute its principal claim for merit. It has suffered very greatly from the lack of an informed and effective public opinion which understood the meaning of the different policies that were being applied."

THE FED

Chairman Paul Volcker, seated at rear, presiding at a meeting in Washington of the Governors of the Federal Reserve Board—1980.

There have been 14 chairmen of the Federal Reserve, with tenures ranging from 1.2 to 18.8 years. Stocks and homes posted their best inflation-adjusted gains during the tenures of Hamlin, Crissinger, and Volcker. The long tenures of Martin and Greenspan were marked with strong investment performance even though inflation was nearly twice as high during Miller's terms. The only Fed chairman to have declines in both stocks and housing during his term was Meyer during the 1930s.

Short-term interest rates were more stable in the early days of the Federal Reserve. From 1914-1951, Fed Funds Rate average range was 2.4% (highest inflation averaged per term 6.7%). Since April 1951, the Fed Funds Rate average range increased to 10.5% (highest inflation averaged per term 9.8%). For example, the Greenspan years were inflation benign, yet short-term interest rates ranged from 9.9% to 0.9%.

"The President (Reagan) and the Federal Reserve chairman (Volcker)
shared in the warming glow of public opinion.
Ronald Reagan took personal credit for halting high inflation,
though the task was actually done by the Federal Reserve."
Secrets of the Temple, W. Greider—1987

TAXATION

Department of the Treasury
Internal Revenue Service

The old saying "It's not what you make, but what you get to keep" really holds true with investing and taxes. Taxes strongly influence which investments are used, when profits and losses are realized, and which types of accounts are used (taxable versus tax-deferred). Over time, taxes ebb and flow, and the government has developed a complicated maze of investment-related taxes such as income tax (with dividends taxed twice due to taxes paid by the corporate entity), capital gains, estate taxes, penalties for early and late IRA withdrawals, just to name a few.

Much has been written about taxes on investment, and though these articles and books have been written at different times and situations, they all deal with the need for an individual's investment strategy to strike a balance between realizing maximum profits and minimizing the impact of taxes. Simply put, selling an investment "at the top" is always an investor's goal, and yet in the world of taxes, it might not be the most profitable solution.

"The complexity of some opportunities now being offered in the investment markets and elsewhere make the task of predicting tax results even more daunting."
Investment Taxation, Hibschweiler—2004

Cartoon—1932

Stock Transaction Tax Stamps—1903

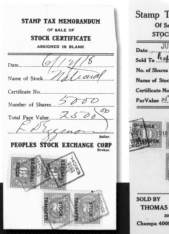

"The art of taxation consists in so plucking the goose as to obtain the largest possible amount of feathers with the smallest amount of hissing."

Personal Income Tax Rate
with Capital Gains Tax Rate—1913 to 2007

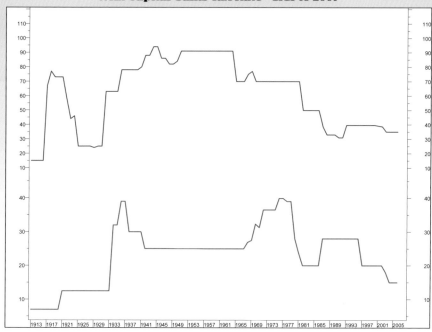

U.S. Common Stocks
with Capital Gains Tax Rate (%)—1913 to 2007

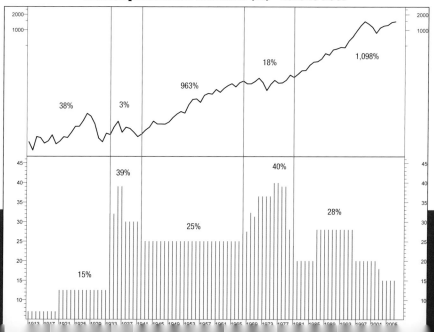

	Investment Taxes					
Year	Corporate Tax	%Chg	Individual Tax	% Chg	Capital Gains Tax	% Chg
Median	35.0	0%	70.0	0%	25.0	0%
Average	33.8	6%	60.9	4%	23.1	2%
High	52.8	200%	94.0	347%	39.9	156%
Low	1.0	-17%	15.0	-46%	7.0	-29%

As can be seen in the charts and tables on this page, income taxes were permanently imposed on U.S. citizens in 1913 and have been increased and reduced on 21 separate occasions. Top income tax rates have ranged from 15% in 1916 to 94% in 1944. Capital gains tax has ranged from 7% in 1913 to 39.9% in 1975. Big jumps in tax rates (such as 1917, 1932, and 1934) were not well received on Wall Street. (See the complete table on page 236.)

There is also a strong inverse relationship between the level of the capital gains tax rate and the stock market. As can be seen in the preceding chart, during the two periods ranging from 8 to 10 years in which this tax exceeded 30%, the stock market performed miserably.

It is also important to note that though the level of tax rates has been in a general decline since the late 1940s, investment tax law has become very complicated and can easily make a good investment into a tax nightmare.

"**Treasury estimates the biggest boost to economic growth comes from the cuts in capital gains and dividend taxes.**"
The Wall Street Journal—January 27, 2006

Rockefeller and Roosevelt—Investors at odds!

Standard Oil shown as a monopoly—1903 Cartoon

"Roosevelt distrusted wealthy businessmen and dissolved
forty monopolistic corporations as a 'trust buster'
(including Standard Oil Trusts).
He was clear, however, to show he did not disagree
with trusts and capitalism in principle
but was only against corrupt, illegal practices."
Wikipedia.com—2007

"Legislation came under the Constitution of Zeno of 483 AD.
This provided for confiscation of property and banishment
for any trade combinations or joint action of monopolies."
Wikipedia.com—2007

Humpty Dumpty Back Together—Again

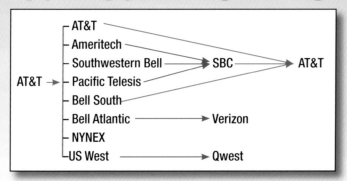

There is such a thing as too much success! Throughout history, governments have always felt compelled to attack monopolistic threats and change the investment landscape.

In the past 100 years, there were two well-publicized government-imposed corporate breakups, Standard Oil (1911) and AT&T (1984), and the near breakup of Microsoft (2001). But political agendas do change, and the election of George W. Bush in 2000 spared Microsoft a breakup. Changes in government policy have also allowed many pieces of the former Standard Oil and AT&T to come back together again.

AT&T

1974 - U.S. Department of Justice initiates an antitrust lawsuit to break up AT&T.
1982 - AT&T agreed to divest of its local phone operations.
1984 - AT&T local phone operations split into 7 "Baby Bells."
2006 - 5 of the 7 "Baby Bells" merged back into AT&T.

Microsoft

1998   U.S. Department of Justice filed civil actions against Microsoft, and alleged that it abused monopoly power.
1999   An open letter to President Clinton from 240 economists printed in the New York Times stated, "Consumers did not ask for these antitrust actions—rival business firms did."
2000   U.S. District Court ruled that Microsoft had violated the Sherman Act and must be broken into two separate units.
2001   D.C. Circuit Court of Appeals overturned the lower court's ruling, and the DOJ reached an agreement with Microsoft, in which the company must share its proprietary application with its competitors.

WHO REALLY CAUSED THE GREAT DEPRESSION?

Cartoon—1930

One of the public's mistaken beliefs about Wall Street is that the 1929 stock market crash caused the Great Depression.

Though the stock market reacted to the deteriorating economic conditions of the 1930s, the U.S. government's disastrous policies of large increases in interest rates, imposing high barriers to foreign trade, increasing income taxes 152%, and a massive increase of the government regulation of business were the real culprits in the economic meltdown and the slow recovery. In fact, it took more than 22 years for both stocks and real estate to get back to their highs of 1929.

"One of the great defects of our kind of monetary system is that its performance depends so much on the quality of the people who are put in charge. We have seen that in the history of our own Federal Reserve System. Surely a computer would have produced far better results during the 1930s and during both world wars."
Milton Friedman—2006

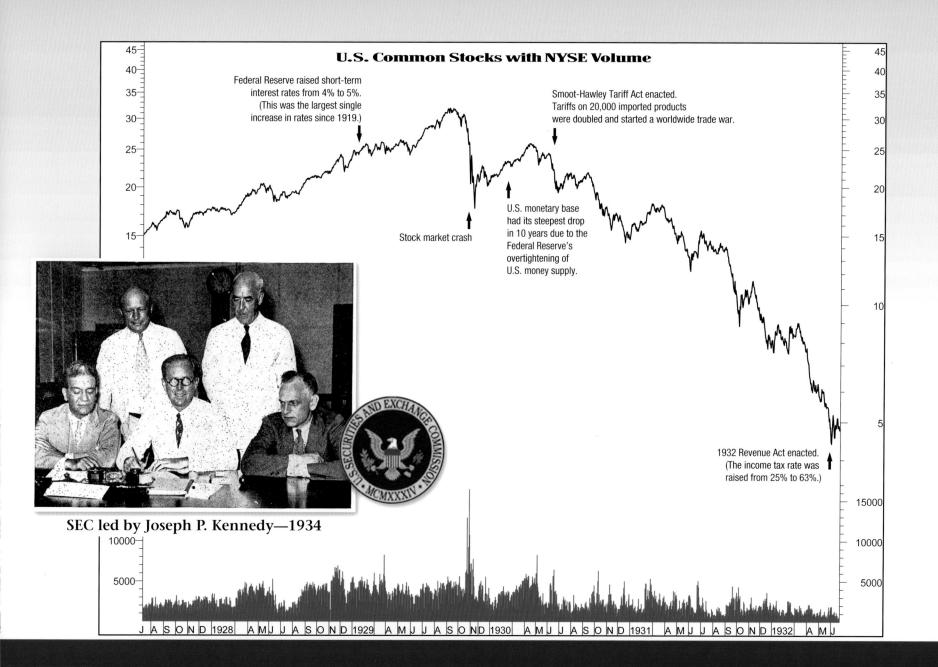

U.S. Common Stocks with NYSE Volume

Federal Reserve raised short-term interest rates from 4% to 5%. (This was the largest single increase in rates since 1919.)

Smoot-Hawley Tariff Act enacted. Tariffs on 20,000 imported products were doubled and started a worldwide trade war.

Stock market crash

U.S. monetary base had its steepest drop in 10 years due to the Federal Reserve's overtightening of U.S. money supply.

1932 Revenue Act enacted. (The income tax rate was raised from 25% to 63%.)

SEC led by Joseph P. Kennedy—1934

J A S O N D 1928 A M J J A S O N D 1929 A M J J A S O N D 1930 A M J J A S O N D 1931 A M J J A S O N D 1932 A M J

"Stock market reform long denied has a way of going to excess, often producing results more distasteful than the abuses aimed at. It appears to be so with proposed Federal regulation of security exchanges."
The Magazine of Wall Street—March 31, 1934

UNCLE SAM SUMMARY

"We come now to the prospects of business
recovering soon enough and fast enough
both to curb extraordinary government outlays
and to provide abundant taxes and public loans.
If it does we shall avoid dangerous inflation of either
the currency or credit through government instrumentality."
The Magazine of Wall Street—February 17, 1934

The table at the right lists taxes (set by the president and Congress), Fed funds rate (set by the Federal Reserve), and stocks and real estate prices. Several key facts materialize when reviewing the investment carnage after 1915, the 1930s, the early 1970s, and the early 2000s:

1. The Federal Reserve significantly increased interest rates prior to and during each of these periods.

2. Investment-related taxes were significantly increased in three of these four periods.

3. The combination of increases in both taxes and interest rates were present during severe, multiyear bear markets in both stocks and real estate.

When it comes to government economic miscues, there is plenty of blame to go around. Who should investors pay the most attention to: the president, Congress, or the Federal Reserve?

Answer: All of them!

Government Actions and Investments

Beginning of Year	President	House Speaker	Individual Income Tax	% Chg	Capital Gains Tax	% Chg	Fed Chairman	Fed Funds Rate	% Chg
			Investment Taxes				**Short-Term Interest Rates**		
1916	Wilson (D)	Clark (D)	15	0%	7	0%	Harding	3.00	0%
1917	Wilson (D)	Clark (D)	67	347%	7	0%	Harding	3.00	0%
1918	Harding (R)	Clark (D)	77	15%	7	0%	Harding	4.00	33%
1929	Hoover (R)	Longworth (R)	24	-4%	12.5	0%	Young	4.50	-10%
1930	Hoover (R)	Longworth (R)	25	4%	12.5	0%	Young	2.00	-56%
1931	Hoover (R)	Longworth (R)	25	0%	12.5	0%	Meyer	3.50	75%
1932	Hoover (R)	Garner (D)	63	152%	12.5	0%	Meyer	2.50	-29%
1933	F. Roosevelt (D)	Garner (D)	63	0%	12.5	0%	Meyer	2.00	-20%
1934	F. Roosevelt (D)	Rainey (D)	63	0%	32	156%	Eccles	1.50	-25%
1935	F. Roosevelt (D)	Byrns (D)	63	0%	32	0%	Eccles	1.50	0%
1936	F. Roosevelt (D)	Byrns (D)	78	24%	39	22%	Eccles	1.50	0%
1937	F. Roosevelt (D)	Bankhead (D)	78	0%	39	0%	Eccles	1.00	-33%
1938	F. Roosevelt (D)	Bankhead (D)	78	0%	30	-23%	Eccles	1.00	0%
1939	F. Roosevelt (D)	Bankhead (D)	78	0%	30	0%	Eccles	1.00	0%
1940	F. Roosevelt (D)	Bankhead (D)	78	0%	30	0%	Eccles	1.00	0%
1941	F. Roosevelt (D)	Rayburn (D)	80	3%	30	0%	Eccles	1.00	0%
1942	F. Roosevelt (D)	Rayburn (D)	88	10%	25	-17%	Eccles	0.50	-50%
1943	F. Roosevelt (D)	Rayburn (D)	88	0%	25	0%	Eccles	0.50	0%
1969	Nixon (R)	McCormack (D)	77	3%	27.5	2%	Martin	8.97	49%
1970	Nixon (R)	McCormack (D)	70	-9%	32.3	17%	Martin	4.90	-45%
1971	Nixon (R)	Albery (D)	70	0%	31.3	-3%	Burns	4.14	-16%
1972	Nixon (R)	Albery (D)	70	0%	36.5	17%	Burns	5.33	29%
1973	Nixon (R)	Albery (D)	70	0%	36.5	0%	Burns	9.95	87%
1974	Ford (R)	Albery (D)	70	0%	36.5	0%	Burns	8.86	-11%
2000	Clinton (D)	Hastert (R)	39.6	0%	20	0%	Greenspan	6.25	9%
2001	GW Bush (R)	Hastert (R)	39.1	-1%	20	0%	Greenspan	1.63	-74%
2002	GW Bush (R)	Hastert (R)	38.6	-1%	20	0%	Greenspan	1.19	-27%
Median			70.0	0%	25.0	0%		3.7	0%
Average			60.6	4%	23.0	2%		4.3	6%
High			94.0	347%	39.9	156%		20.0	141%
Low			15.0	-46%	7.0	-29%		0.5	-74%

Large Tax Rate Decreases
Large Tax Rate Increases

See complete table
on page 234 and 235.

"History has taught us that not only
do regulations not rein in excessive risk taking,
but they often do more harm than good."
The Wall Street Journal —July 22, 2007

WAR

FROM INDIANS TO IRAQ, HOW WARS INFLUENCE INVESTING

VICTORY DAY ON WALL STREET

NOVEMBER 11, 1918

Since 1812, the United States has been involved in 10 major military conflicts. Though war has always been a dark spot on humanity, it has been financially good for American investors. Stocks and real estate generally appreciated in the range of 40%-50% on average during these large military conflicts as huge increases in government spending drove the wartime economy. (In fact, the only conflict in which American shareholders didn't prosper was the War of 1812.) Amazingly, this appreciation occurred during times when U.S. interest rates fluctuated wildly as large amounts of government war debt hit the market.

Even though the conflicts are very different in why, how, and where they have been fought, wartime investments display common, predictable characteristics. In comparing the charts of stock and home prices during The War of 1812, Mexican-American War, Civil War, Indian Wars of the late 1800s, Spanish-American War, World War 1, World War 2, and the "Cold War" battlefields of Korea and

Vietnam, investments usually declined in value during the initial phases of the war, reversed direction while the outcome was uncertain, and were significantly higher at the end of the conflict—win, lose, or draw.

Our wartime adversaries often used their financial markets to finance their military needs, and their financial assets typically moved in the opposite direction of U.S. investments as the winds of war shifted direction. Ironically, U.S. corporations often revived these foreign investment markets after the conflict through peacetime rebuilding efforts and increased worldwide trade at about the same time many of America's business titans were accused of war profiteering.

As you review the following charts, you will notice that the 200-day moving average (shown as a red dotted line) has proven to be a useful indicator in determining the stock market's trend during these turbulent times.

The current war is following its predecessors; it seems that history once again repeats itself!

"Hey, Dad, what war was this?"

The Wall Street Journal—1979

WAR of 1812

Land certificate for 120 acres of public land
for military service in 1812

Stock certificate for the private armed ship *Yorktown*

YORKTOWN SCRIP.

Estimated cost of Ship, Armament and Outfits,

Fifty-Six Thousand Dollars.

Divided into 320 Shares, each Share valued at 175 Dollars.

This Scrip Certifies that
is registered on the Books of the Agents for the
PRIVATE ARMED SHIP YORKTOWN, on her second cruize,
as holding   Share   in the said ship and in the
nett proceeds of all prizes, prize goods, &c. which shall come into the hands
of said agents on account of said cruize.

Signed in behalf of the agents,

Clerk.

"The War of 1812 gave the first genuine impulse to stock speculation. There were endless
fluctuations and the lazy-going capitalists of the time managed to gain or lose handsome fortunes."

War of 1812—U.S. Common Stocks with 200-Day Moving Average

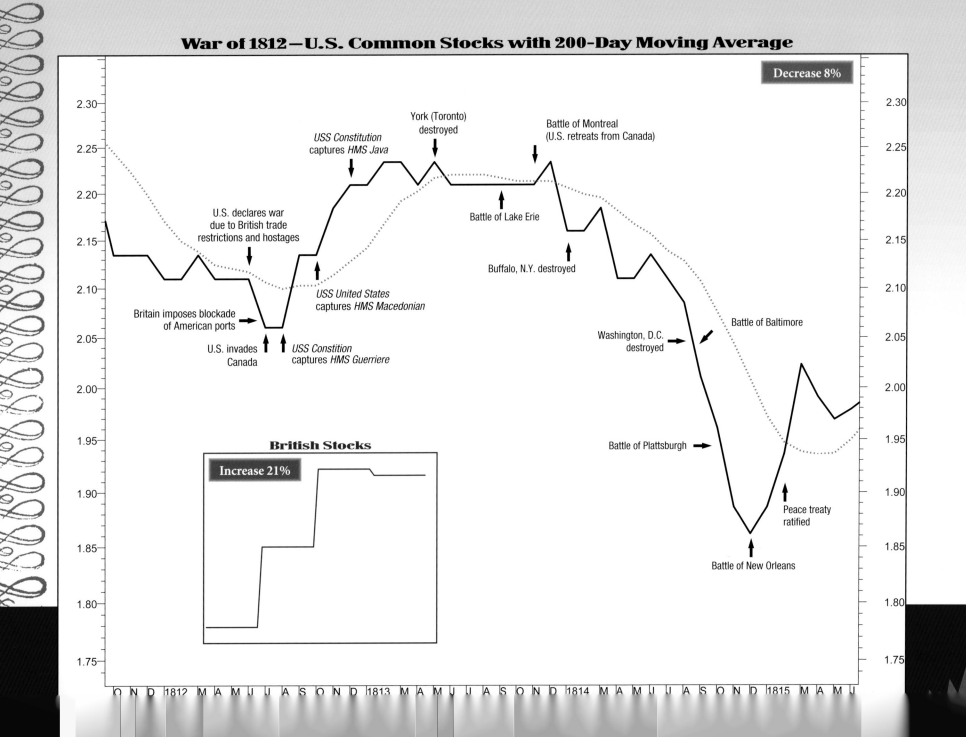

Decrease 8%

York (Toronto) destroyed

USS Constitution captures HMS Java

Battle of Montreal (U.S. retreats from Canada)

U.S. declares war due to British trade restrictions and hostages

Battle of Lake Erie

Buffalo, N.Y. destroyed

Britain imposes blockade of American ports

USS United States captures HMS Macedonian

U.S. invades Canada

USS Constition captures HMS Guerriere

Washington, D.C. destroyed

Battle of Baltimore

Battle of Plattsburgh

Peace treaty ratified

Battle of New Orleans

British Stocks

Increase 21%

O N D 1812 M A M J J A S O N D 1813 M A M J J A S O N D 1814 M A M J J A S O N D 1815 M A M J

PRICE OF STOCKS.

New-York Bank :::::::::: 125 Mutual
Manhattan Bank :.::: 116 1-2 Globe :::
Merchants Bank ::: 117 1-2 Washing
Mechanics Bank :::: 116 1-2 City Lo
Union Bank ::::::::::::::: 103 Ditto Se
Bank of America :::::::: 105 Phœnix
City Bank ::::::::::: 110 1-2 Ocean :::::::: 85 :::::::

U.S. Stocks   down 8%
U.S. Interest Rates   up 15%

CHART NOTES

Early victories were greeted by a strong rally in U.S. stocks. As American forces retreated out of Canada and British forces destroyed American towns and cities, U.S. financial assets suffered huge losses while British stocks and bonds posted equally impressive gains.

PRICE OF STOCKS.

New-York Bank ::::::::: 125	Mutual :::::::::::::::::: 110
Manhattan Bank :.::: 116 1-2	Globe ::::::::::::: 102 1-2
Merchants Bank :::: 117 1-2	Washington ::::::::::: 116
Mechanics Bank :::: 116 1-2	City Loan ::::::::: 100 1-2
Union Bank ::::::::::::: 103	Ditto Seven per ct. 104 105
Bank of America ::::::::: 105	Phœnix ::::::::::::::::::::: }
City Bank ::::::::::::. 110 1-2	Ocean ::::::: 85 :::::::: } nomin.
New-York Manuf. Con'y 100	New-York Fireman :::: }
Six per cents. div. off ::::: 99	—
Louisiana ::::::::::::::: 91	EXCHANGE.
Three per cents. :::::::::: 55	Saturday, March 4, 1815.
Old and Deferred, ::::::::: 95	Bills on London, 60 da. 95 96
N. York Insurance :::: 90 100	:::: :::: Amsterdam ::: }
Treasury Notes :::::::: 4 1-4	::::::: :::: Hamburg ::::: } nom.
United ::::::::::::::: 90 100	::::::: :::: France ::::::::: }
Eagle, div. off ::::::::::: 115	

The first complete price list of stocks ever published in a newspaper—March 10, 1815

U.S. T-Bond Yields

Yield 7%

British Bonds %

Yield 5%

MEXICAN–AMERICAN WAR–1846 to 1848

New York November 30. 1848

Hon Millard Fillmore
    Comptroller State of New York
                    Sir
            You will please assign of the
Bonds of the New York and Erie Rail Road Company, sold
to Messrs Davis Brooks & Co under contract dated Nov 3 1848
filed in your office, one hundred bonds to them, and
deliver the Bonds when so assigned to Nathaniel Marsh
secretary of said Company, taking his receipt therefor.

                    Respectfully Yours
                            F. W. Edmonds ag.
                            N.Y. & E RR Co.

New York & Erie Railroad letter to New York
state comptroller Millard Fillmore
(soon to be 13th U.S. president)
regarding bond investments—November 30, 1848

Hon Millard Fillmore
Comptroller State of New York

"México's cession of Alta California and Nuevo México and its recognition of U.S. sovereignty over all of Texas
north of the Rio Grande formalized the addition of 3.1 million km² (1.2 million mi²) of territory to the United States.
In return the United States agreed to pay $15 million and assumed the claims of its citizens against México."

Mexican-American War—U.S. Common Stocks with 200-Day Moving Average

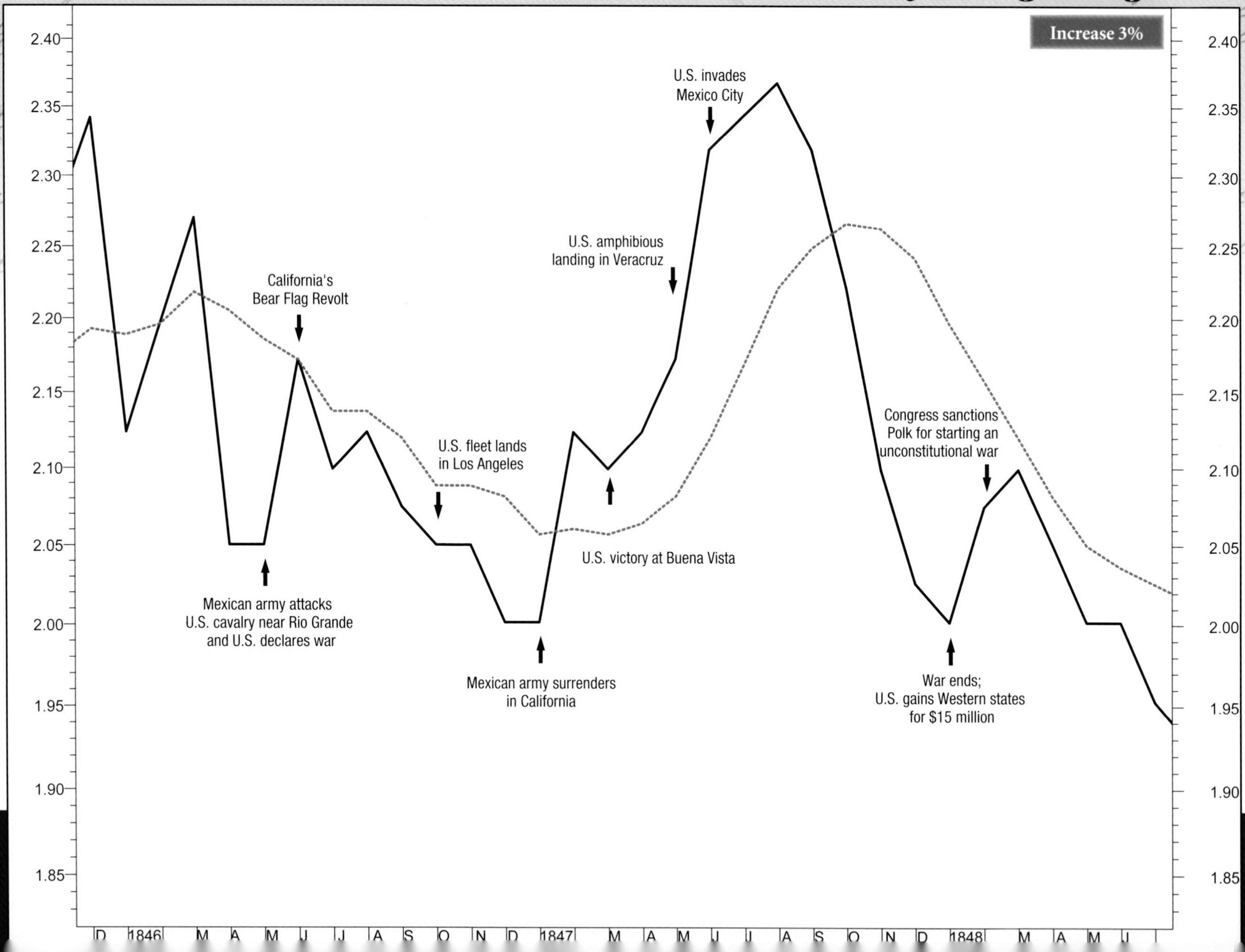
Increase 3%
2.40
2.35
2.30
2.25
2.20
2.15
2.10
2.05
2.00
1.95
1.90
1.85
California's Bear Flag Revolt
Mexican army attacks U.S. cavalry near Rio Grande and U.S. declares war
U.S. fleet lands in Los Angeles
Mexican army surrenders in California
U.S. amphibious landing in Veracruz
U.S. victory at Buena Vista
U.S. invades Mexico City
Congress sanctions Polk for starting an unconstitutional war
War ends; U.S. gains Western states for $15 million
D 1846 M A M J J A S O N D 1847 M A M J J A S O N D 1848 M A M J

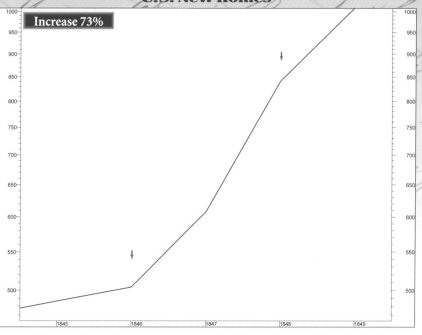

U.S. New Homes

Increase 73%

1845 1846 1847 1848 1849

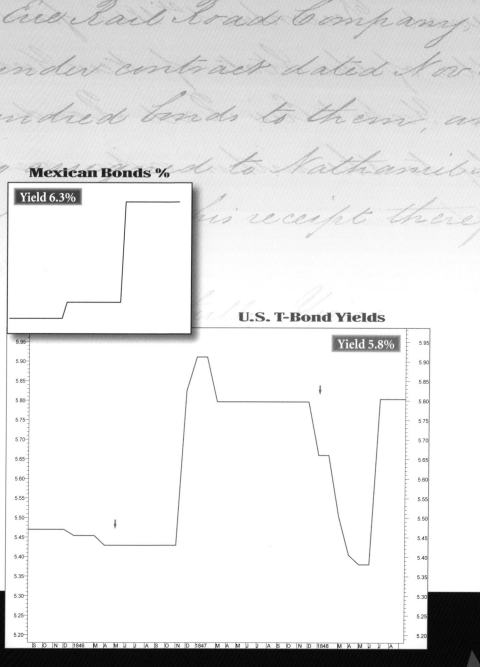

Mexican Bonds %

Yield 6.3%

U.S. T-Bond Yields

Yield 5.8%

S O N D 1846 M A M J J A S O N D 1847 M A M J J A S O N D 1848 M A M J J A

U.S. Stocks	up 3%
U.S. Home Prices	up 73%
U.S. Interest Rates	up 7%

CHART NOTES

Wall Street initially greeted this unpopular war with a whimper. The war rally started after victories in California, and hit a climax with the invasion of Mexico City. Although equity gains were meager, real estate values gained 73% in light of America obtaining valuable new territories. Interest rates in Mexico rose dramatically as the U.S. invaded Mexico City.

Civil War—U.S. Common Stocks with 200-Day Moving Average

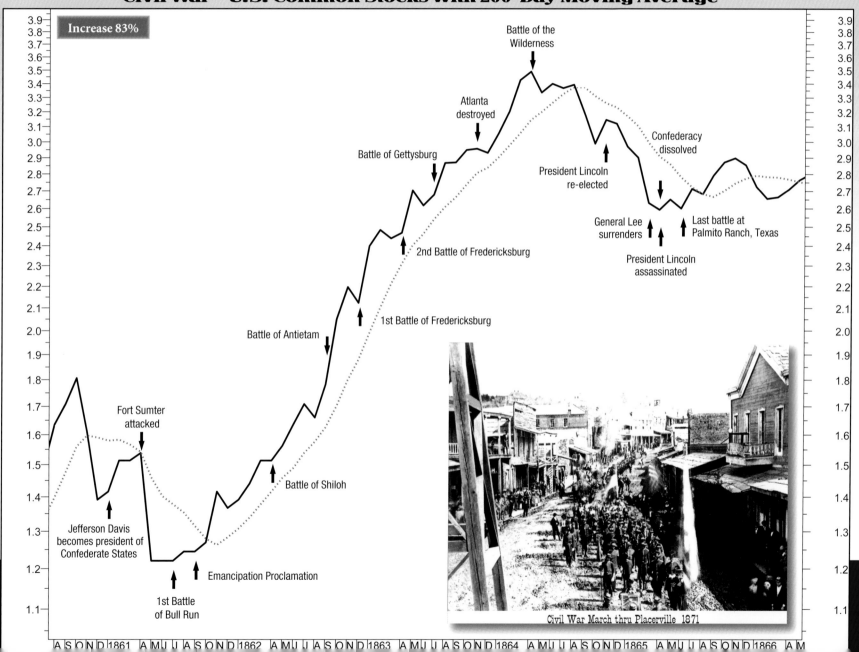

Increase 83%

Battle of the Wilderness

Atlanta destroyed

Battle of Gettysburg

Confederacy dissolved

President Lincoln re-elected

General Lee surrenders

Last battle at Palmito Ranch, Texas

President Lincoln assassinated

2nd Battle of Fredericksburg

1st Battle of Fredericksburg

Battle of Antietam

Battle of Shiloh

Fort Sumter attacked

Jefferson Davis becomes president of Confederate States

1st Battle of Bull Run

Emancipation Proclamation

Civil War March thru Placerville 1871

U.S. Stocks	**up 83%,**
U.S. Home Prices	**up 115%**
U.S. Interest Rates	**down 16%**

CHART NOTES

After the initial decline from the Battle of Fort Sumter, the market hit bottom before the 1st Battle of Bull Run. The stock market's high was made just after the little-known Battle of Wilderness. The returns in stocks and real estate were the highest posted of any wartime period in American history while bonds were relatively stable in light of high inflation and a devalued currency. One of the worst investments of the U.S. Civil War was debts issued by the government of the Confederate States of America. After appreciating through most of 1864, Confederate Cotton Bonds (7%, due 1868) stopped trading in London at 8 cents on $1 shortly after the Confederacy dissolved in early 1865.

The Winans Steam Gun, created by Ross Winans, was captured by General Butler's command near the Relay House, Maryland

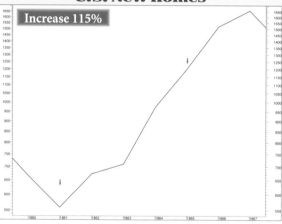

U.S. New Homes

Increase 115%

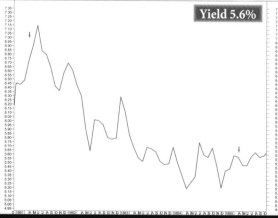

U.S. T-Bond Yields

Yield 5.6%

"It should be that early in the [civil] war,
Union successes were used as arguments in favor of a rise in stocks,
but as the war went on,
Union defeats were used as arguments in favor of a rise."

Ten Years in Wall Street—1870

Confederate 7% Cotton Bond Due 1868—Traded in London

Decrease 91%

INDIAN WARS—1866 to 1890

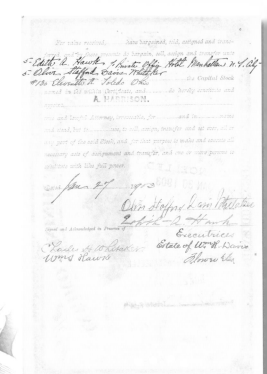

E MINING CO.

D MINING DISTRICT, LAWRENCE COUNTY, DAKOTA TERRITORY.

Homestake Mining stock certificate—1883

Indian Wars—U.S. Common Stocks
with 200-Day Moving Average and NYSE Volume

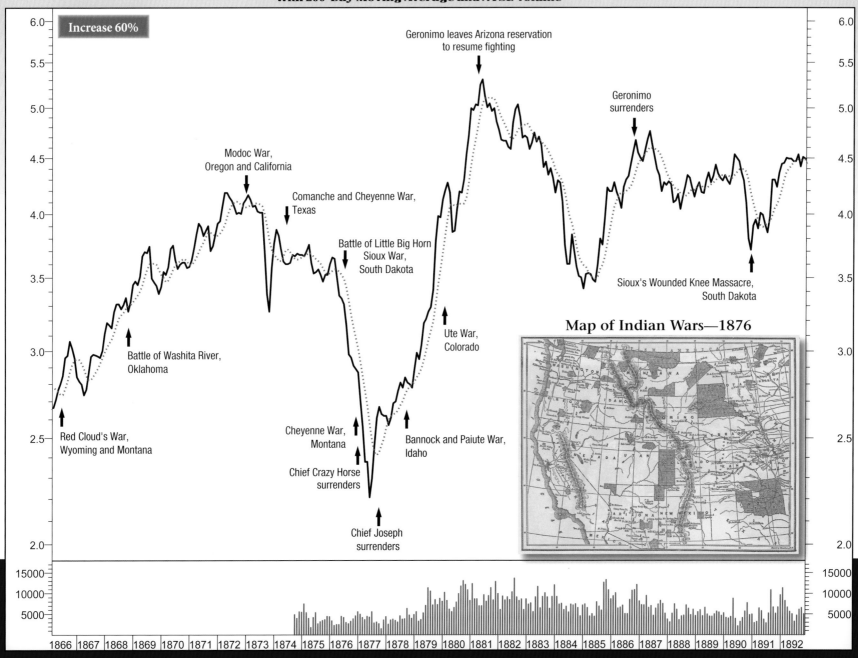

Increase 60%

Geronimo leaves Arizona reservation to resume fighting

Geronimo surrenders

Modoc War, Oregon and California

Comanche and Cheyenne War, Texas

Battle of Little Big Horn Sioux War, South Dakota

Sioux's Wounded Knee Massacre, South Dakota

Ute War, Colorado

Map of Indian Wars—1876

Battle of Washita River, Oklahoma

Red Cloud's War, Wyoming and Montana

Cheyenne War, Montana

Bannock and Paiute War, Idaho

Chief Crazy Horse surrenders

Chief Joseph surrenders

U.S. Stocks	up 60%
U.S. Home Prices	up 58%
U.S. Interest Rates	down 30%

CHART NOTES

The Indian wars of the late 1800s were a series of guerilla-style conflicts by various tribes caused by the great population migration into the Western territories and a series of gold and silver rushes on Indian ancestral lands. The most pronounced decline was tied to the shock of Custer's Last Stand at the Little Big Horn, and the panic of future large-scale Indian attacks on Western settlers. Stock and real estate investments staged impressive gains as Indian leaders such as Joseph and Crazy Horse surrendered.

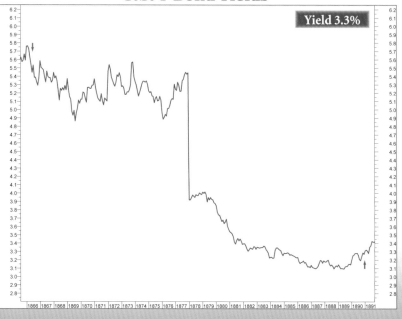

U.S. T-Bond Yields

Yield 3.3%

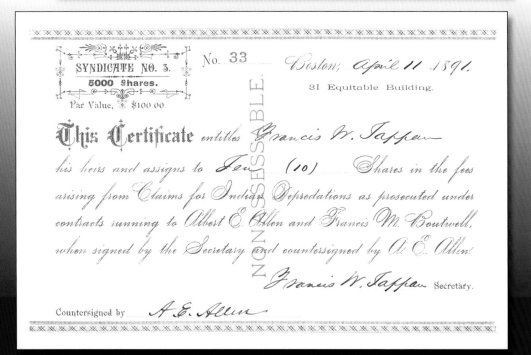

**Claims for Indian depredations—1891
To reimburse victims of crimes**

U.S. New Homes

Increase 58%

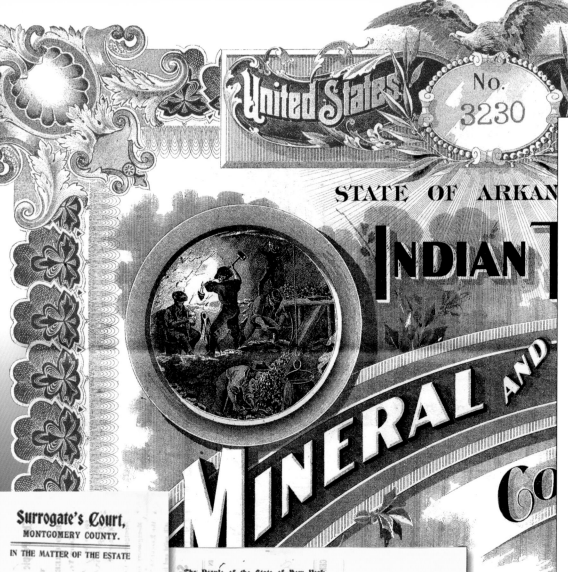

Surrogate's Court,
MONTGOMERY COUNTY.

IN THE MATTER OF THE ESTATE

— OF —

William H. Davis

DECEASED.

CERTIFICATE OF APPOINTMENT
OF EXECUTOR.

The People of the State of New York,

To All whom these Presents shall Come or may Concern.

SEND GREETING:

Know Ye, That at a Surrogate's Court held in the City of Amsterdam and County of Montgomery, on the 17th day of January in the year one thousand nine hundred and three Letters Testamentary of the Last Will and Testament of William H. Davis late of the town of Palatine Montgomery County, N. Y., deceased, were granted and issued by the Surrogate of the County of Montgomery, to Olive Stafford and Whittaker & Edith A. Hawk the Executors named in the Last Will and Testament of said deceased, and that the same are still valid and in full force.

IN TESTIMONY WHEREOF, we have caused the seal of said Surrogate's Court of the County of Montgomery to be hereunto affixed.

WITNESS: W. Barlow Dunlap, Surrogate of our said County of Montgomery, at the City of Amsterdam, the 17th day of January in the year of our Lord one thousand nine hundred and three

CLERK OF THE SURROGATE'S COURT.

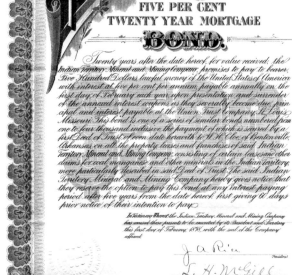

Indian Territory M&M Company—1898

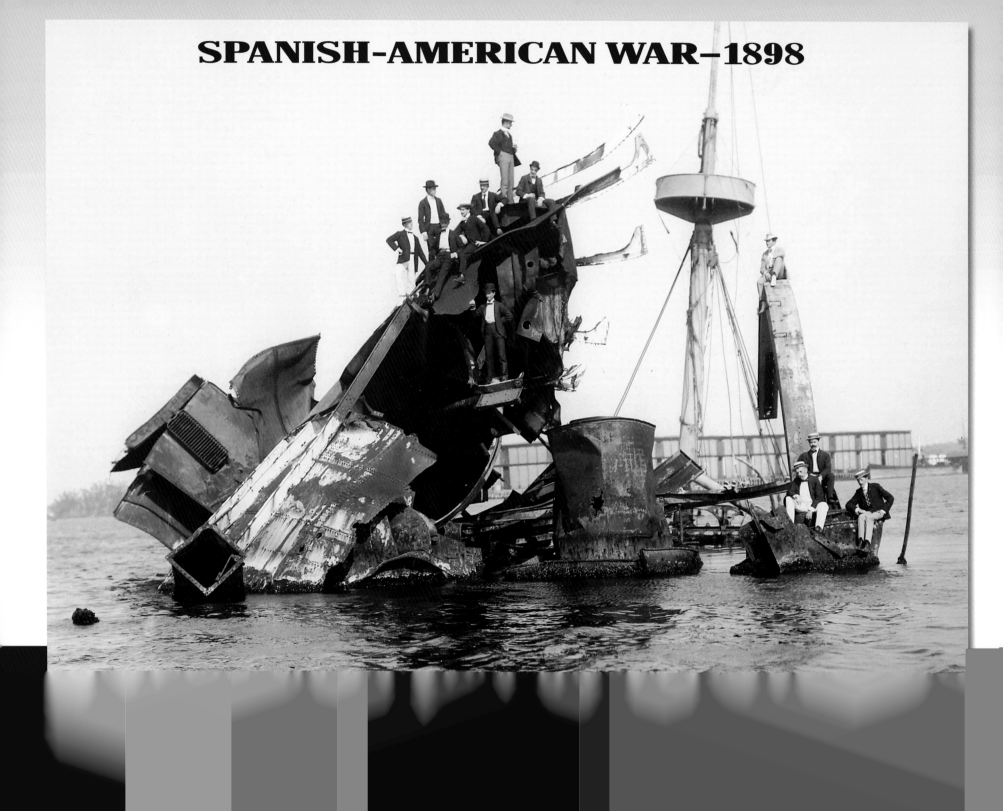

SPANISH-AMERICAN WAR–1898

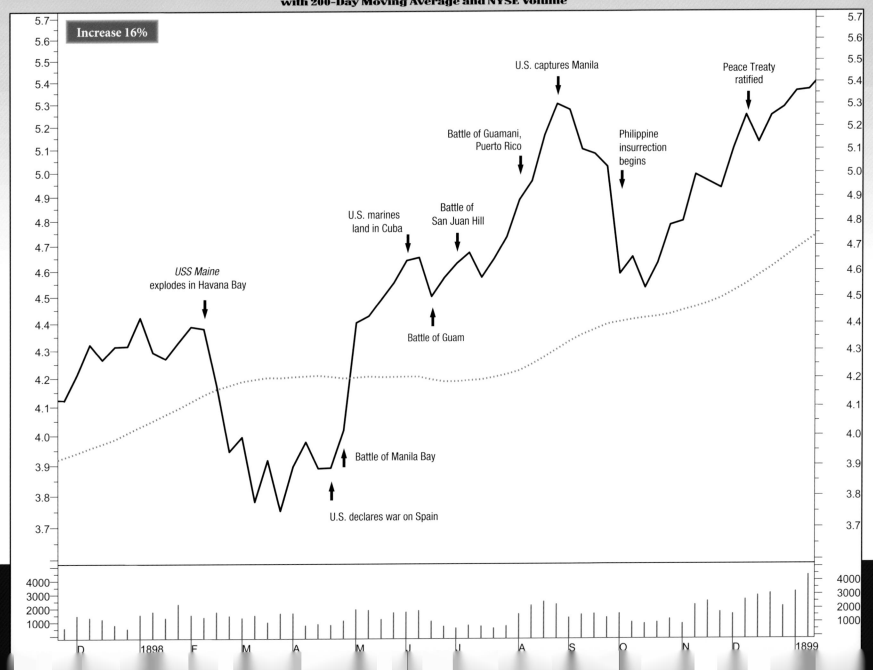

Spanish-American War—U.S. Common Stocks
with 200-Day Moving Average and NYSE Volume

Increase 16%

USS Maine explodes in Havana Bay

U.S. declares war on Spain

Battle of Manila Bay

U.S. marines land in Cuba

Battle of Guam

Battle of San Juan Hill

Battle of Guamani, Puerto Rico

U.S. captures Manila

Philippine insurrection begins

Peace Treaty ratified

U.S. Stocks	**up 16.0%**
U.S. Home Prices	**up 10.0%**
U.S. Interest Rates	**down 0.6%**

CHART NOTES

As can be seen in the *Leslie's Magazine* sketch on the following page, there was an initial panic on Wall Street after the battleship *USS Maine* exploded in Havana Harbor. Investments quickly rebounded after war was declared and Admiral Dewey's victory in the Battle of Manila Bay. Interest rates in Spain declined throughout this short war.

Spanish Interest Rates

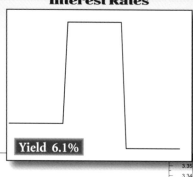

Yield 6.1%

U.S. New Homes

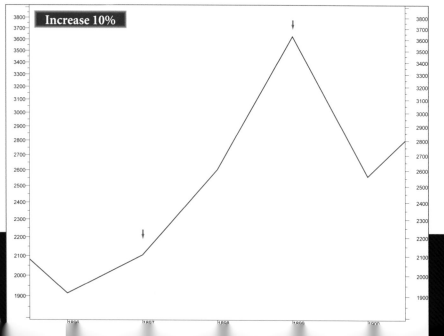

Increase 10%

U.S. T-Bond Yields

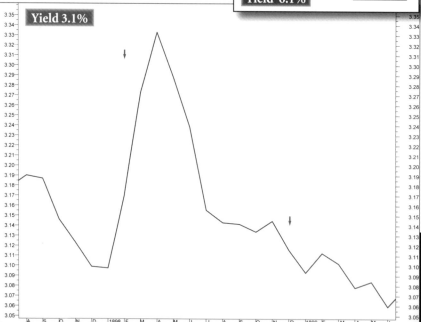

Yield 3.1%

PACIFIC

UNLISTED SECURITIES

WAR RUMORS IN WALL STREET.

San Francisco Dry Docks—1916

"Cordell Hull, American Secretary of State under Franklin Roosevelt, believed that trade barriers were the root cause of World War I."
Wikipedia.com, 2007

World War I—U.S. Common Stocks
with 200-Day Moving Average and NYSE Volume

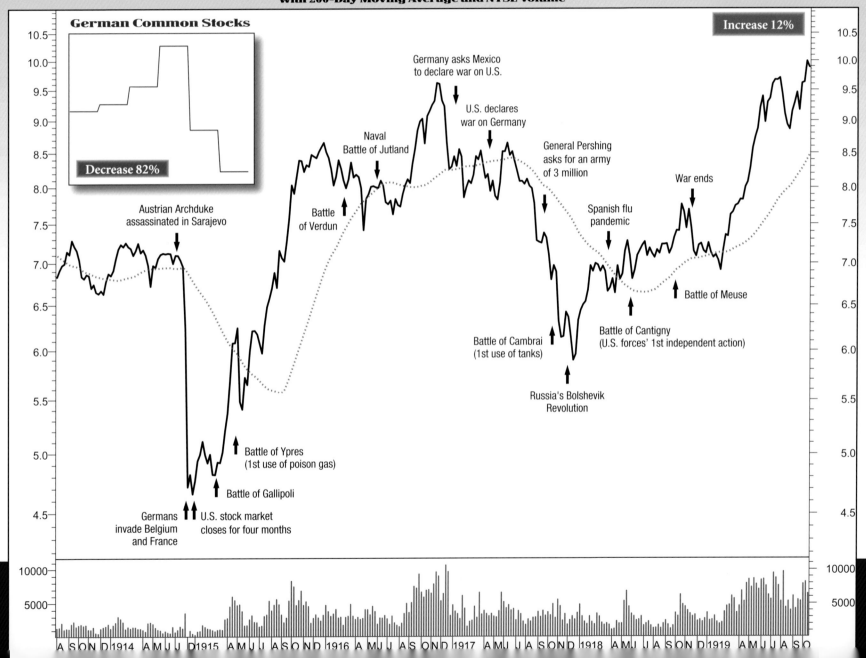

German Common Stocks

Decrease 82%

Increase 12%

Austrian Archduke assassinated in Sarajevo

Germans invade Belgium and France

U.S. stock market closes for four months

Battle of Gallipoli

Battle of Ypres (1st use of poison gas)

Battle of Verdun

Naval Battle of Jutland

Germany asks Mexico to declare war on U.S.

U.S. declares war on Germany

General Pershing asks for an army of 3 million

Battle of Cambrai (1st use of tanks)

Russia's Bolshevik Revolution

Battle of Cantigny (U.S. forces' 1st independent action)

Spanish flu pandemic

War ends

Battle of Meuse

A S O N D 1914 A M J J D 1915 A M J J A S O N D 1916 A M J J A S O N D 1917 A M J J A S O N D 1918 A M J J A S O N D 1919 A M J J A S O

U.S. New Homes

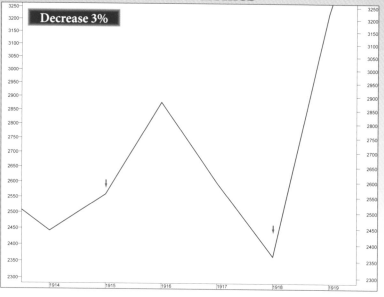

Decrease 3%

	U.S. Stocks	up 12%
	U.S. Home Prices	down 3%
	U.S. Interest Rates	up 3%

CHART NOTES

The beginning of World War I led to the longest disruption in world financial markets of the past 100 years. The NYSE closed for four months after Germany invaded France. When trading resumed, the market quickly rallied until the U.S. entered the war, and General Pershing requested a 3,000,000-man U.S. army for Europe's bloody trenches. Ironically, the beginning of Soviet Communism was met with a significant rally. Real estate was in the midst of a severe bear market through most of the war. German financial markets suffered enormous losses due to their defeat and the financial penalties imposed by the Allies for starting the war.

U.S. T-Bond Yields

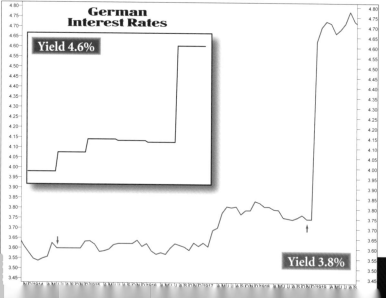

German Interest Rates

Yield 4.6%

Yield 3.8%

French defense bond—1915

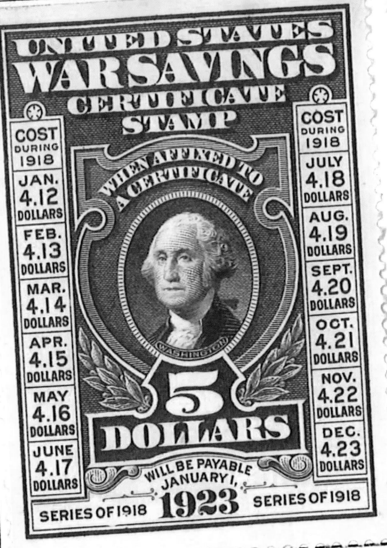

COST DURING 1918

JAN. 4.12 DOLLARS
FEB. 4.13 DOLLARS
MAR. 4.14 DOLLARS
APR. 4.15 DOLLARS
MAY 4.16 DOLLARS
JUNE 4.17 DOLLARS

COST DURING 1918

JULY 4.18 DOLLARS
AUG. 4.19 DOLLARS
SEPT. 4.20 DOLLARS
OCT. 4.21 DOLLARS
NOV. 4.22 DOLLARS
DEC. 4.23 DOLLARS

UNITED STATES WAR SAVINGS CERTIFICATE STAMP

WHEN AFFIXED TO A CERTIFICATE

WASHINGTON

5 DOLLARS

WILL BE PAYABLE JANUARY 1, 1923

SERIES OF 1918

THE TORCH OF LIBERTY

3 — AFFIX ONLY $5.00 WAR-SAVINGS CERTIFICATE STAMP — SERIES OF 1918

4 — AFFIX ONLY $5.00 WAR-SAVINGS CERTIFICATE STAMP — SERIES OF 1918

7 — AFFIX ONLY $5.00 WAR-SAVINGS CERTIFICATE STAMP — SERIES OF 1918

8 — AFFIX ONLY $5.00 WAR-SAVINGS CERTIFICATE STAMP — SERIES OF 1918

13 — AFFIX ONLY $5.00 WAR-SAVINGS CERTIFICATE STAMP — SERIES OF 1918

14 — AFFIX ONLY $5.00 WAR-SAVINGS CERTIFICATE STAMP — SERIES OF 1918

U.S. Government war bond with stamps—1918

Disney War Bond, State of Wisconsin—1944

"Since April 1942 stocks listed on the New York Stock Exchange have risen in value from $31 billion to $73 billion, with almost half the rise taking place in 1945."

World War II—U.S. Common Stocks with
200-Day Moving Average and NYSE Volume

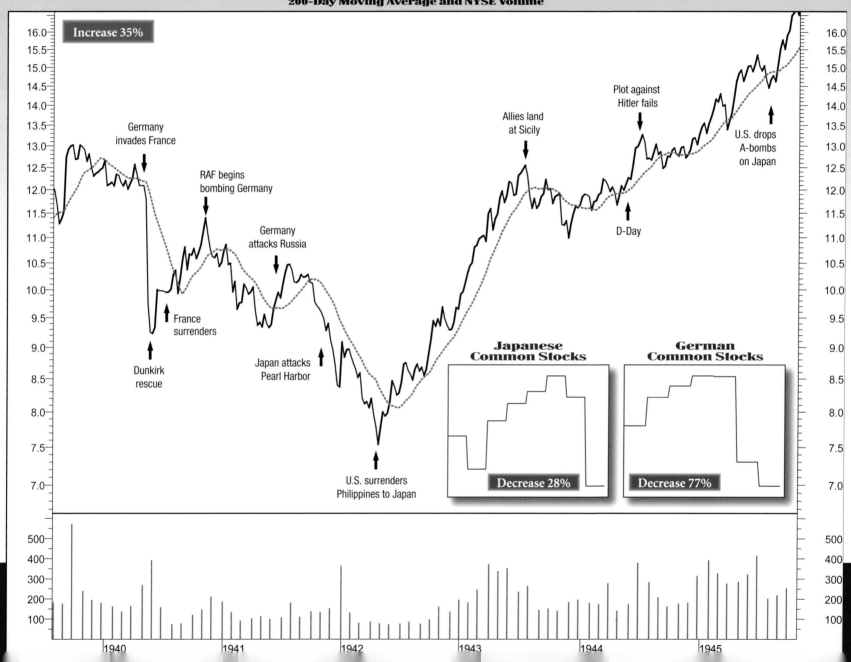

Increase 35%

Germany invades France

Dunkirk rescue

France surrenders

RAF begins bombing Germany

Germany attacks Russia

Japan attacks Pearl Harbor

U.S. surrenders Philippines to Japan

Allies land at Sicily

Plot against Hitler fails

D-Day

U.S. drops A-bombs on Japan

Japanese Common Stocks

Decrease 28%

German Common Stocks

Decrease 77%

U.S. New Homes

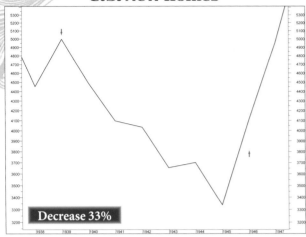

Decrease 33%

Japanese Bonds %

Yield 4.6%

Japanese war bond 1943

German Bonds %

Yield 5.5%

Nazi war bond 1937

U.S. Stocks	up 35%
U.S. Home Prices	down 33%
U.S. Interest Rates	down 39%

CHART NOTES

The stock market started this war in a prolonged downtrend as Allied losses mounted. A powerful rally in stocks started right after America's worst military defeat in history (surrender of the Philippine Islands to Japan) and continued through the end of the war. U.S. Treasury Bonds posted their best wartime performance. German and Japanese equities and bonds followed an inverse course to U.S financial investments, while U.S. real estate suffered its worst wartime performance due to a shortage of mortgages as investors poured savings into the "war bonds" of the most expensive war in American history.

U.S. T-Bond Yields

Yield 1.7%

"Price control, financing, rationing, controls of consumption, investment and international trade have all undergone significant changes in the past twelve months."

"In the past two years, the falling off in demand for stocks has resulted from the fear of higher taxes, the effects of war priorities, and the general uncertainty concerning the future."
The Economics of America at War—1943

U.S. savings bond, Series E—1944

"Scandinavia is one of our chief sources of supply for wood pulp, and when Germany invaded Norway it looked as if our imports of pulp would be cut off for the duration of the war, and, therefore, that pulp stocks might be a good buy. They enjoyed an agreeable rise and about a month later Germany attacked the Netherlands. In view of Germany's all-out method of Blitzkrieg war, it was reasonable to expect that Germany would either defeat France or be defeated herself within a fairly short time period. What should one do, therefore, about the pulp stocks? It did not take much thought to produce the following conclusions:
a) If Germany were defeated, the supplies of pulp from Norway would start coming in again which would be bad for pulp stocks,
b) If France were defeated, the threat of our being involved in the war would have such a serious effect on our economic system that all stocks would be affected."
Making Money in Stock Trading—1943

"Although our maximum military effort still lies ahead, we have already gone over the top in industrial production for war to such an extent that large, although selective, cut-backs in war output are both familiar and increasing."
The Magazine of Wall Street—February 5, 1944

"Actually Germany cannot take much comfort out of the widely publicized difference among the Big Three (i.e. contract scandals)... On the contrary the Allies are united as ever on the paramount objective—which is to defeat the Nazis, although they may see certain related factors with different eyes. No Breaks for the Axis."
The Magazine of Wall Street—February 5, 1944

"The problem in defense spending is to figure how far you should go without destroying from within what you are trying to defend from without."
President Eisenhower—1955

"You say we want war, but you have now got yourselves into a position I would call idiotic, but we don't want to profit by it. If you withdraw your troops from Germany, France, and Britain—I'm speaking of American troops—we will not stay one day in Poland, Hungary, and Romania. But we, Mister Capitalists, we are beginning to understand your methods… It doesn't depend on you whether or not we exist. If you don't like us, don't accept our invitations, and don't invite us to come to see you. Whether you like it or not, history is on our side. We will bury you!"
Nikita Khrushchev, Premier of USSR—November 26, 1956

"In 1958 the U.S. just missed the moon (i.e. response to Russia's lunar satellite). But Wall Street's Bull made it—and over, with ease."
Business in 1958, Time—December 29, 1958

"The Cold War was fought at a tremendous cost globally over the course of more than four decades. It cost the U.S. up to $8 trillion in military expenditures, and the lives of nearly 100,000 Americans in Korea and Vietnam. The military spending, combined with the legacy of the economic structural problems of the 1970s, transformed the U.S. from the world's leading creditor in 1981 to the world's leading debtor. It cost the Soviets an even higher share of their gross national product. By the late years of the Cold War, Moscow had built up a military that consumed as much as twenty-five percent of the Soviet Union's gross national product at the expense of investment in civilian sectors."
Wikipedia.com—2007

KOREAN WAR—1950 to 1953

UNDER THE LAWS OF THE STATE OF DELAWARE

SPERRY CORPORATION

THIS CERTIFICATE IS TRANSFERABLE IN THE CITY OF NEW YORK,OR IN JERSEY CITY, N.J.

---SIGLER & CO---   is the owner of

ONE HUNDRED

Y CORPORA

Sperry Corporation,
a major defense
company

"The wrong war, at the wrong place,
at the wrong time, and with the wrong enemy."
General Omar Bradley, one of six 5-star generals—1951

Korean War—U.S. Common Stocks
with 200-Day Moving Average and NYSE Volume

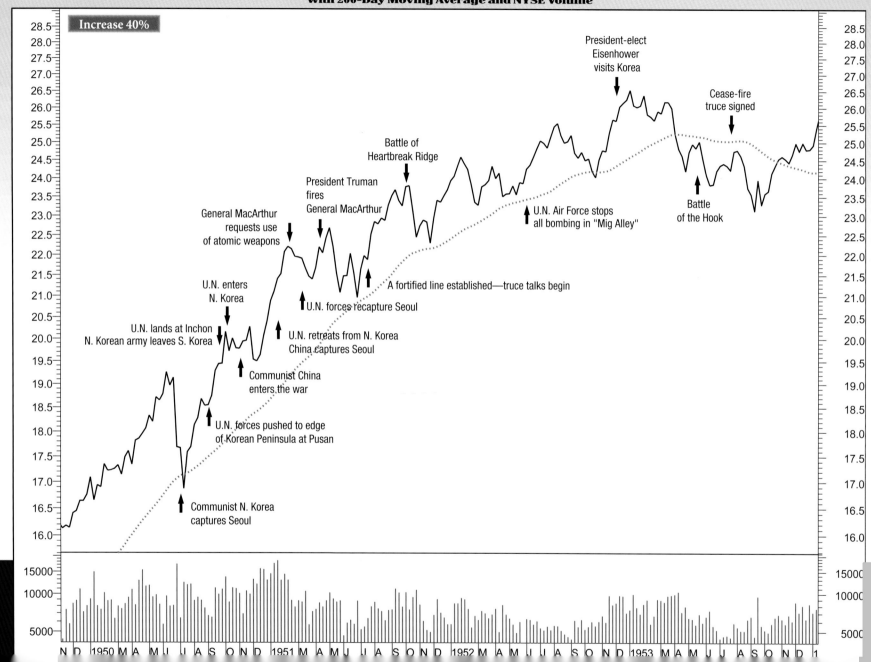

Increase 40%

President-elect Eisenhower visits Korea

Cease-fire truce signed

Battle of Heartbreak Ridge

President Truman fires General MacArthur

General MacArthur requests use of atomic weapons

U.N. Air Force stops all bombing in "Mig Alley"

Battle of the Hook

U.N. enters N. Korea

A fortified line established—truce talks begin

U.N. forces recapture Seoul

U.N. lands at Inchon N. Korean army leaves S. Korea

U.N. retreats from N. Korea China captures Seoul

Communist China enters the war

U.N. forces pushed to edge of Korean Peninsula at Pusan

Communist N. Korea captures Seoul

N D 1950 M A M J J A S O N D 1951 M A M J J A S O N D 1952 M A M J J A S O N D 1953 M A M J J A S O N D 1

"The twin policies of the Truman 'Doctrine and the Marshall Plan' led to billions in economic and military aid. Confronted with the Chinese Revolution and the end of the US atomic monopoly in 1949, the Truman administration quickly moved to escalate and expand the containment policy. Truman administration officials proposed to reinforce pro-Western alliance systems and quadruple spending on defense. And in Congress, Republicans were not disagreeing with the Truman administration by calling for and funding a build up of South Korea's forces."

Wikipedia.com—2007

"Korea's economy had been integrated with the Empire of Japan, and with that relationship now broken, so too was its economy. Japanese forces in Korea surrendered to the Americans in 1945, marking the end of three and a half decades of Japanese rule in Korea. The Russians made matters worse by sealing their zone of occupation from the southern zone, halting coal deliveries to southern Korea, halting also railway traffic, mail deliveries, and the transfer of electrical power southward across the 38th parallel."

MacroHistory.com—2007

U.S. Stocks	up 40%
U.S. Home Prices	up 49%
U.S. Interest Rates	up 51%

CHART NOTES

The first confrontation of the Cold War was met with the shock of Communist North Korea's invasion. But U.S. investments staged a long, linear bull market as U.N. forces pushed Communist troops out of South Korea through to the end of hostilities. At the end of the war, South Korean government bond interest rates exceeded 25%.

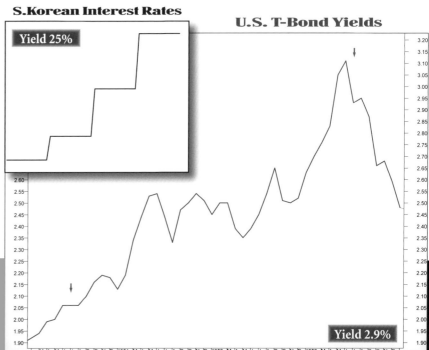

VIETNAM WAR—1964 to 1973

THE WAR IN VIETNA

Common
(No Par

THIS OFFERING INVOLVES

At the present time there is no established
Company. The Company does not have a record
shares being offered hereby was determined by th

THIS MATTER HAS NOT BEEN AP
SECURITIES EXCHANGE COMMISSION,
STATES, THE AMERICAN PEOPLE, OR A
EXCEPT THE PENTAGON, NOR HAS AN
RACY OR ADEQUACY OF INFORMATION
MATTER. ANY REPRESENTATION TO
OFFENSE.

Per Share ....

Total $12

(1) Does not include additional costs and effects, includ
properties, divisiveness of the populace, destruction of the co

This offering involves:

(a) Special Risks concerning the Co

(b) Annual call for additional fund

THE ADMINISTRATION   THE JOINT CH

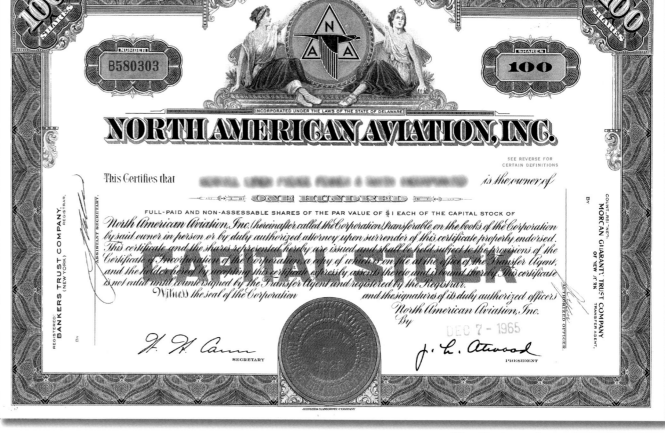

North American Aviation,
major supplier of military aircraft and spacecraft
(dated on 24th anniversary of Pearl Harbor attack)

This prospectus was written by Burton R. Tauber. It is being
Workman Publishing Company, Inc., Monocle Periodicals, Inc., Pen

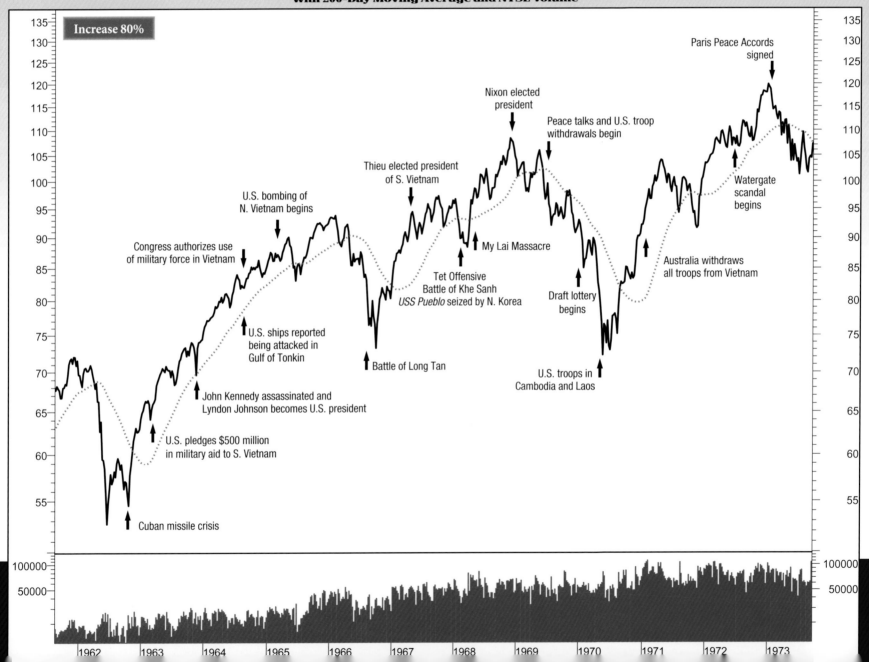

Vietnam War—U.S. Common Stocks
with 200-Day Moving Average and NYSE Volume

Increase 80%

Paris Peace Accords signed

Nixon elected president

Peace talks and U.S. troop withdrawals begin

Thieu elected president of S. Vietnam

U.S. bombing of N. Vietnam begins

Congress authorizes use of military force in Vietnam

My Lai Massacre

Watergate scandal begins

Tet Offensive
Battle of Khe Sanh
USS Pueblo seized by N. Korea

U.S. ships reported being attacked in Gulf of Tonkin

Draft lottery begins

Australia withdraws all troops from Vietnam

Battle of Long Tan

John Kennedy assassinated and Lyndon Johnson becomes U.S. president

U.S. troops in Cambodia and Laos

U.S. pledges $500 million in military aid to S. Vietnam

Cuban missile crisis

1962 1963 1964 1965 1966 1967 1968 1969 1970 1971 1972 1973

Carrier-based pocket bomber packs a nuclear punch

*Defensive systems—ability of such aircraft as the Douglas A4D-2 Skyhawk to range far afield from their floating bases increases our defense-in-depth by thousands of miles.

Aerospace advertising—1962

American priorities

$25 BILLION FOR THIS—

$150 BILLION (PLUS) FOR THIS—

VIETNAM

The Minneapolis Tribune—December 13, 1972

"The Vietnam War cost the United States more than 58,000 lives and claimed hundreds of thousands of Vietnamese. It cost more than $500 billion in today's dollars."

U.S. News & World Report
November 12, 2006

**Draft protest
at the Pentagon—1970**

"By means of their influence on the operation of the Pentagon, military-industry firms seem to get away with large profits."
Seymour Melman, Pentagon Capitalism—1970

> "Even with large gold reserves the dollar
> can be shaken by a drop in confidence.
> Devaluation of the dollar and a concomitant increase
> in the price of gold would lead to a run on gold."
> *Walt Rostow, President Johnson's National Security Advisor*
> *January 13, 1968*

U.S. Stocks	up 80%
U.S. Home Prices	up 86%
U.S. Interest Rates	up 55%

CHART NOTES

After the Cuban Missile Crisis, the stock market started a long bull run with only a couple of "hiccups" such as the initial bombing of North Vietnam that was feared would bring Communist China into the conflict, and the beginning of the peace treaty process followed by initial U.S. troop withdrawals. Next to the Civil War, equities and real estate posted their best wartime performance in spite of the highest interest rates since the War of 1812. At the time of the signing of the peace treaty, South Vietnam's government bond yields exceeded 33%.

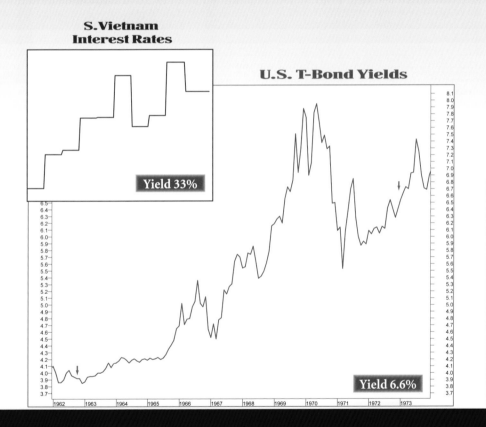

S.Vietnam Interest Rates — Yield 33%

U.S. T-Bond Yields — Yield 6.6%

U.S. New Homes with New Home Sales — Increase 86%

> "Vietnam made clear 'even the mighty United States' lacks
> the means to fight anywhere, anytime and prevail and a call
> for de-escalation and fiscal restraint are needed now"

AL-QAEDA WAR–2001 to ...

NUMBER
GF 13787

HAVE YOU SEEN ME?

I'm about to get my ass nuked off the face of the planet!
Osama Bin Laden
1-HEI-SSO-DEAD

Taped to the outside of
the New York Stock Exchange

"Military procurement is heavily challenged by the
Pentagon's purchase of 'needless gizmos' from defense contractors"

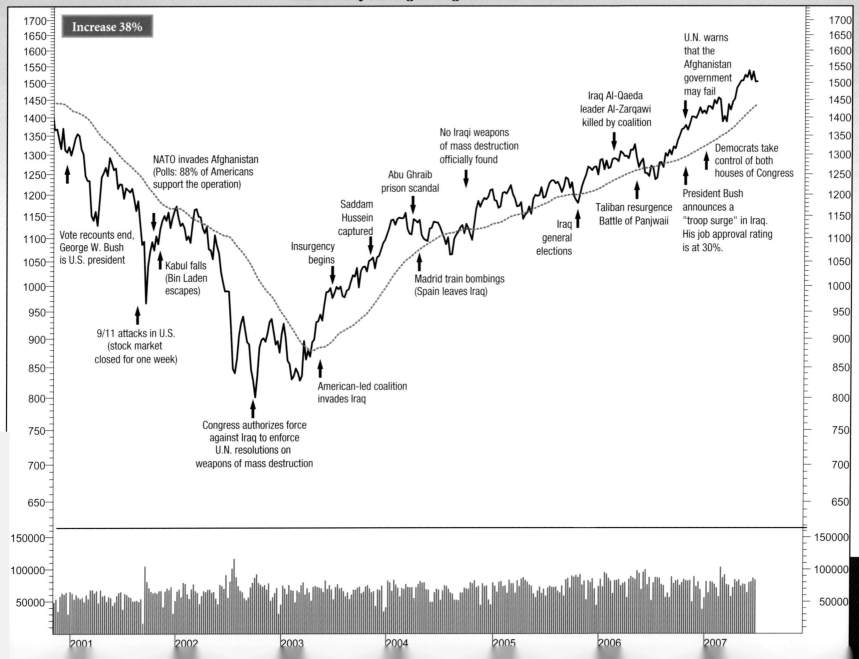

Al-Qaeda War—U.S. Common Stocks
with 200-Day Moving Average and NYSE Volume

"Wall Streeters now fall mainly into two camps:
Those who think the war in Iraq was itself a horrible mistake
and those who think it could have been a good choice
but was bungled in the execution.
It is not the $800 billion the Iraq War is
projected to cost that drives us nuts.
A $13 trillion economy can make adjustments.
But it is the troop draw down,
and the failure to finish the job in Afghanistan."
TomPaine.com—June 26, 2006

Investor's Business Daily—June 2, 2006

Investor's Business Daily—December 22, 2006

"It is a budget fight that highlights the deep stresses
on a military force tussling for more money and manpower
while it struggles to protect expensive combat systems in a time when
war worn equipment remains in need of critical repairs and
posts across the country are struggling to pay their electric bills."
U.S. News & World Report—October 30, 2006

"One after another, the men and women who have stepped
forward to report corruption in the massive effort
to rebuild Iraq have been vilified, fired and demoted."
Santa Barbara News-Press—August 25, 2007

U.S. Stocks	up 38%
U.S. Home Prices	up 46%
U.S. Interest Rates	up 9%

CHART NOTES

After the 9/11 attacks, the U.S. stock and bond markets were closed for five days. After an initial panic, the stock market "bounced" following the prompt invasion of Afghanistan by NATO forces. The stock market hit a low point on the day of Congress' controversial decision to authorize U.S. military force against Iraq as the second front of this war. To date, both stocks and real estate have posted gains similar to the Korean War with the lowest level of interest rates since the late 1950s. Yields on Iraqi Central Bank Rates are at 9%.

Certificate of Martyrdom

Iraqi government bond

Iraqi Interest Rates

Yield 9%

U.S. New Homes with New Home Sales

Increase 46%

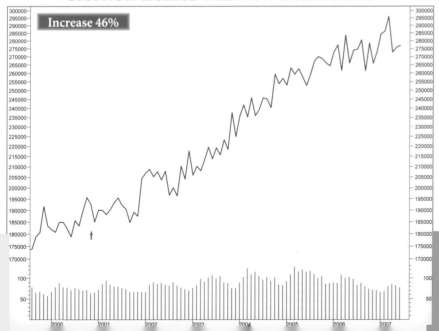

U.S. T-Bond Yields

Yield 4.7%

PAYING FOR A WAR

DEPOSIT FORM.

No 739
14. for $10000

INSTRUCTIONS.—This Deposit Form must contain particulars of the Bonds for one Certificate only; and the Form, when filled up and signed, must be lodged, together with the Bonds, with the NATIONAL SAFE DEPOSIT COMPANY, LIMITED, 1, Queen Victoria Street. E.C. If more than one Certificate be required, a separate Deposit Form must be filled up for each Certificate.

Confederate States of America.

THE RIGHT HON. LORD PENZANCE,
THE HON. THOMAS C. BRUCE, M.P., }
JOHN ELDON GORST, ESQ., Q.C., M.P., } Bondholders'
JOHN B. MARTIN, ESQ., } Trustees.
ROBERT STEWART, ESQ.,

We, (or I) the undersigned, holders of the Bonds of the Confederate States of America, particularized at foot, hereby deposit them with the National Safe Deposit Company, Limited, on the terms and conditions endorsed hereon, to which we (or I) hereby assent, to be exchanged for a Scrip Certificate of the Bondholders' Trustees.

Signature _for G J Tffe_

Address _19 Old Broad St_

Date when left _5 Nov '83_

Number.	%	Amount.	Number.	%	Amount.	Number.	%	Amount.	Number.	%	Amount.
20265	8	500									
20267	"	"									
20279	"	"									
13554	"	"									
13557	"	"									
13558	"	"									
13560	"	"									
13576	"	"									
15744	8	1000									
15745	"	"									
15742	"	"									
15746	"	"									
16184	"	"									
16186	"	"									

$10000

SIXTY-FIFTH CALL.

REDEMPTION OF 5-20 BONDS OF 1865—CONSOLS OF 1865.

1878.
Department No. 84.
Secretary's Office.

Treasury Department,

August 5, 1878.

By virtue of the authority given by the Act of Congress approved July 14, 1870, entitled "An act to authorize the refunding of the national debt," I hereby give notice that the principal and accrued interest of the bonds herein-below designated, known as "Five-twenty Bonds," of the Act of March 3, 1865, Consols of 1865, will be paid at the Treasury of the United States, in the City of Washington, on and after the FIFTH DAY OF NOVEMBER, 1878, and that the interest on said Bonds will cease on that day:

COUPON BONDS, DATED JULY 1, 1865, NAMELY:

$50—No. 69501 to No. 70000, both inclusive. $500—No. 84001 to No. 86000, both inclusive.
$100—No. 120001 to No. 123000, both inclusive. $1,000—No. 157001 to No. 163500, both inclusive.

Total Coupon............$2,500,000

REGISTERED BONDS,

"REDEEMABLE AT THE PLEASURE OF THE UNITED STATES AFTER THE 1ST DAY OF JULY, 1870," AS FOLLOWS:

$100—No. 18451 to No. 18550, both inclusive. $5,000—No. 10251 to No. 10400, both inclusive.
$500—No. 10701 to No. 10750, both inclusive. $10,000—No. 19801 to No. 20500, both inclusive.
$1,000—No. 35851 to No. 36100, both inclusive.

Total Registered..........$2,500,000
Aggregate...............$5,000,000

The amount **outstanding**, included in the numbers above, is five million dollars.

All United States Bonds, forwarded for redemption, should be addressed to the "Loan Division, Secretary's Office," and all Registered Bonds should be assigned to "the Secretary of the Treasury for redemption."

Where parties desire checks in payment for Registered Bonds, drawn to order of any one but the payee, they should assign them to the Secretary of the Treasury for redemption account of the owner or owners, giving name or names thereof.

John B Hawley

Acting Secretary.

1878 Civil War bond redemption notice.
U.S. Treasury started to pay off war debts
10 years after the Civil War.

Confederate States of America deposit form—1883
This was used by foreign investors to collect
principal payments from the defunct Confederacy.

Gas ration book with stamps—1944

Wartime Investments Summary

Conflicts	Period of Time (years)	Percentage Change		
		Stocks	Real Estate	T-Bond Yields
Average (w/o Cold War)	6.4	37%	52%	5%
Median (w/o Cold War)	4	36%	49%	5%
% of Time at a Loss		10%	22%	40%
War of 1812	3	(8%)	na	15%
Mexican-American War	2	3%	73%	7%
Civil War	4	83%	115%	(16%)
Indian Wars	24	60%	58%	(30%)
Spanish-American War	1	16%	10%	(.6%)
World War I	4	12%	(3%)	3%
World War II	6	35%	(33%)	(39%)
Cold War	45	2,054%	3,131%	330%
Korean War	3	40%	49%	51%
Vietnam War	11	80%	86%	55%
Al-Qaeda War	5+	38%	46%	9%

WAR = PROFITS

The following phrase best sums up how to be a wartime investor;

"This is as good a place as any to emphasize the necessity of not letting your mind be paralyzed by the events… Never forget to think and take action!"

Making Money in Stock Trading—1943

WELCOMING THE TROOPS HOME!

Victory Parade—1991

VJ Day, New York City—1945

"War is the trade of Kings."
John Dryden, Poet—1680

"What a country calls its vital economic interests are not the things
which enable its citizens to live, but the things which enable it to make war.
Petrol is more likely than wheat to be a use of international conflict."
Simone Weil, Philosopher—1937

"Wars are made to make debt."
Ezra Pound, Poet—1963

DISASTERS

FROM KENNEDY'S DEATH TO KATRINA:
BUY OR SELL?

163

NATURAL DISASTERS

San Francisco Fire—1906

San Francisco Fire Protection Bond—1920

Hurricanes, tsunamis, tornadoes, volcanic eruptions, earthquakes, fires, pandemics, and environmental catastrophes—there is no place and no one in the world that hasn't been affected by at least one of these natural disasters. Acts of Mother Nature have shaped civilizations past or present. In fact, pandemics have been called a key factor in the decline of the Roman Empire.

How have investors reacted to sudden events and prolonged tragedies?

In this section, 11 major natural disasters in U.S. history (which led to the destruction of four major cities and the deaths of hundreds of thousands of people) are examined in light of their short- and long-term effects on various types of investments to see if they really matter to Wall Street.

Hurricane Katrina—2005

"When a vast destruction of life and property takes place in a few hours, through an earthquake, the big commercial nations seem to realize that humanitarianism and economic interest alike demand both temporary measures of emergency relief, and more fundamental measures for the reconstruction of the economic life of the affected area at the earliest date possible."

The Magazine of Wall Street—September 29, 1923

SAN FRANCISCO EARTHQUAKE – 1906

An ancestor of the author took these photographs.

U.S. Common Stocks with NYSE Volume

1-Year Change
(14.2%)

Coins melted in
San Francisco fire

U.S. New Home Prices

U.S. T-Bond Yields

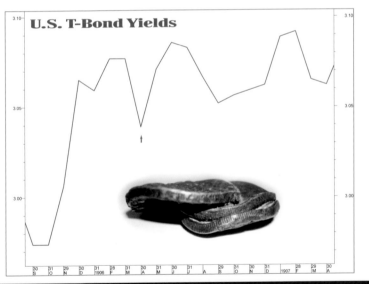

"Right in the path of the largest, hottest blaze, a few dozen men at the San Francisco Mint stood fast.
Led by a political appointee with no experience in crisis management, they fought back against an inferno that
melted the glass in the mint's windows and burned the clothes off their backs. Although their story is largely forgotten,
by safeguarding gold and silver worth $300 million in 1906, they may have saved the U.S. economy from collapse."

FIRES

New York Fire—1835

U.S. Common Stocks

1-Year Change
(13.5%)

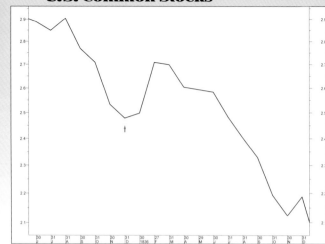

Chicago Fire—1871

1-Year Change
(13.3%)

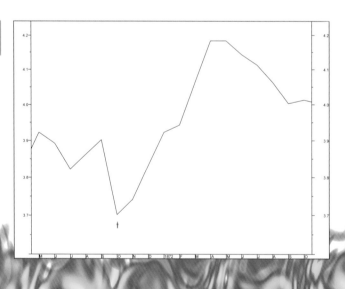

"Within a year of these disasters, the financial district (Wall Street) was restored,
its lightning-like reconstruction driven by an appetite
for commercial speculation that nothing seemed able to dampen."
Every Man a Speculator, Fraser—2005

U.S. T-Bond Yields

U.S. New Homes

"When the Chicago fire occurred it immediately created a panic.
When a calamity occurs at any part of the country the shock is first felt in Wall Street."
Twenty-Eight Years in Wall Street, Clews—1887

HURRICANE ANDREW–1992

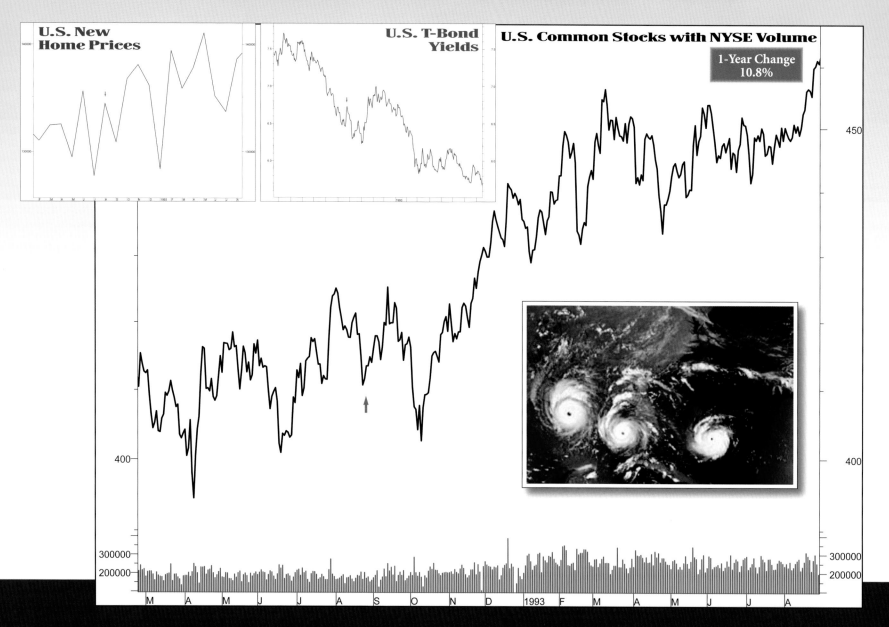

U.S. New Home Prices

U.S. T-Bond Yields

U.S. Common Stocks with NYSE Volume

1-Year Change
10.8%

450

400

300000
200000

300000
200000

M A M J J A S O N D 1993 F M A M J J A

"Unlike most hurricanes, the vast majority of the damage in Florida was caused by winds.
The agricultural loss in Florida was $1.04 billion alone."

Wikipedia.com—2007

TSUNAMI and KATRINA–2005

U.S. Common Stocks with NYSE Volume

1-Year Change
5.8%

Sumatra-Andaman
earthquake and tsunamis

Hurricane Katrina
and flooding
of New Orleans

U.S. New Home Prices

U.S. T-Bond Yields

"In the aftermath of Hurricane Katrina,
Congress passed the Katrina Emergency Tax Relief Act of 2005,
which was signed by the President into law on September 23, 2005."
Your Income Tax, Lasser—2006

169

MOUNT ST. HELENS – 1980

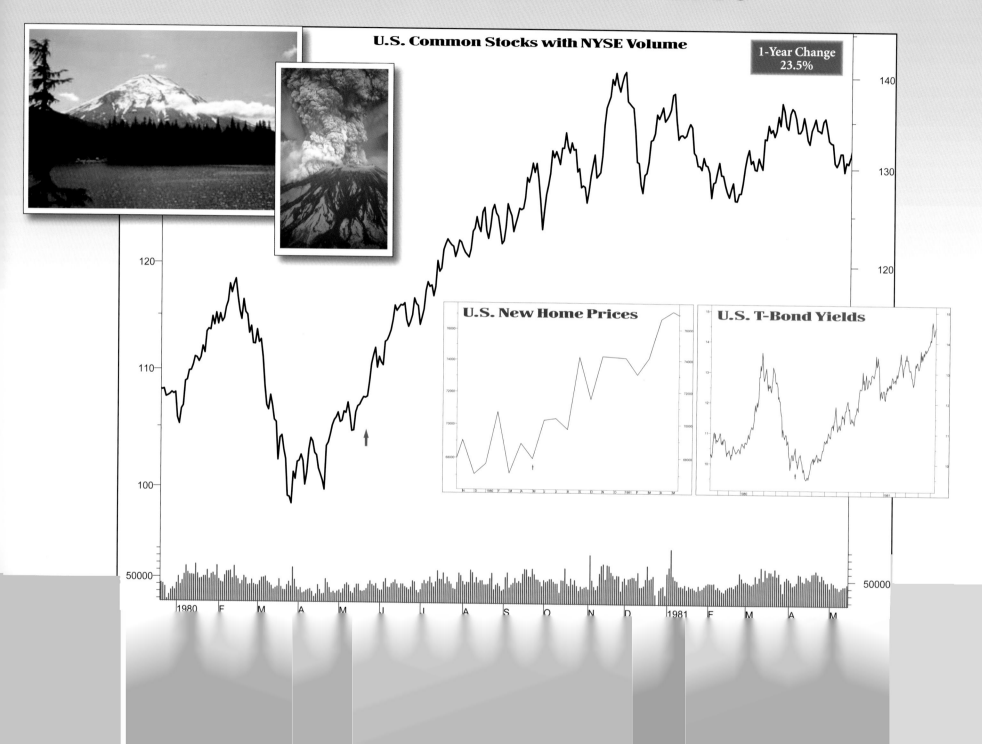

U.S. Common Stocks with NYSE Volume

1-Year Change
23.5%

U.S. New Home Prices

U.S. T-Bond Yields

TORNADO STORMS – 1974

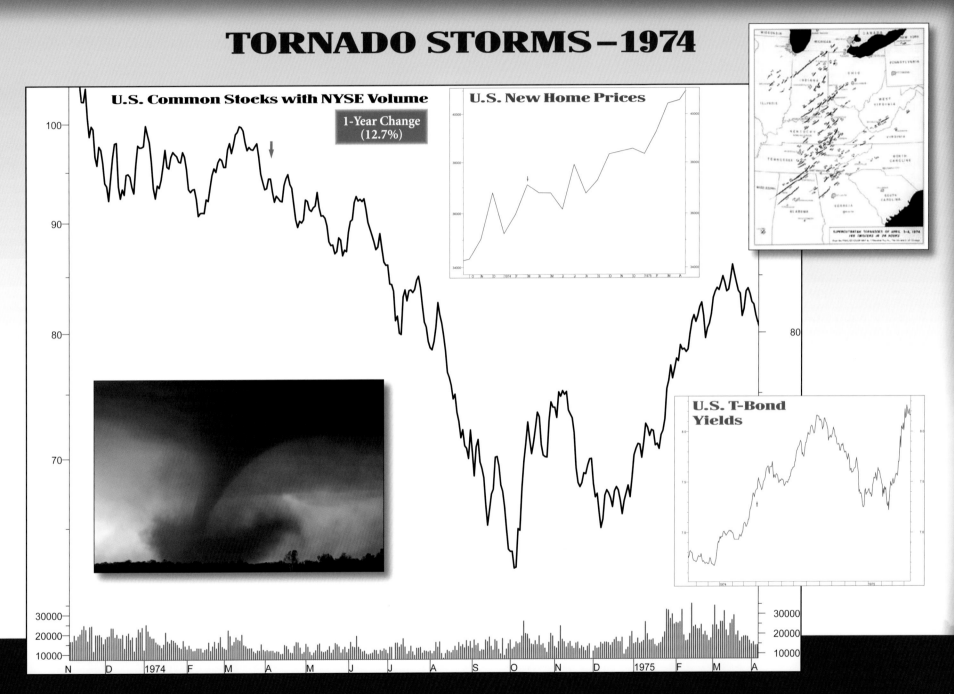

U.S. Common Stocks with NYSE Volume

1-Year Change (12.7%)

U.S. New Home Prices

U.S. T-Bond Yields

"Although [the] number of fatalities [has] decreased,
the number of people affected by tornados and costs incurred continues to increase."

PANDEMICS

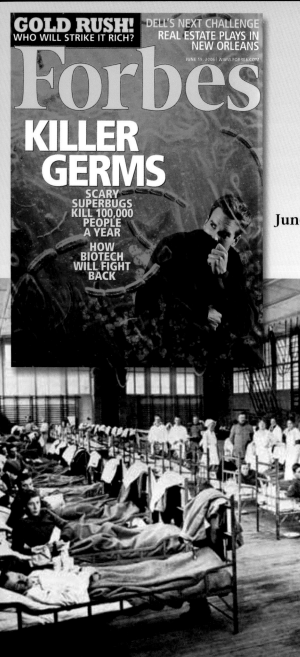

June—2006

Treatment ward
during the
Spanish flu
pandemic

Spanish Flu—1918

Total Change
39%

U.S. Common Stocks with NYSE Volume

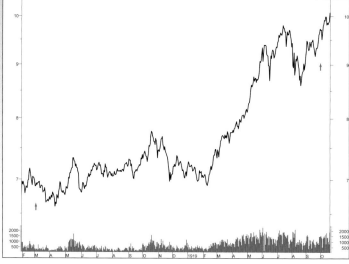

Asian Flu—1957

Total Change
0.7%

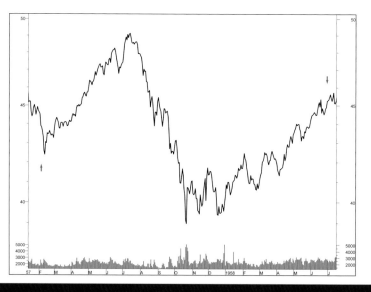

"More and more bugs are becoming untreatable.
But, Big Pharma, rather than riding to the rescue,
has largely abandoned antibiotic research,
a low-ticket business, for more lucrative pursuits."

Forbes—June 2006

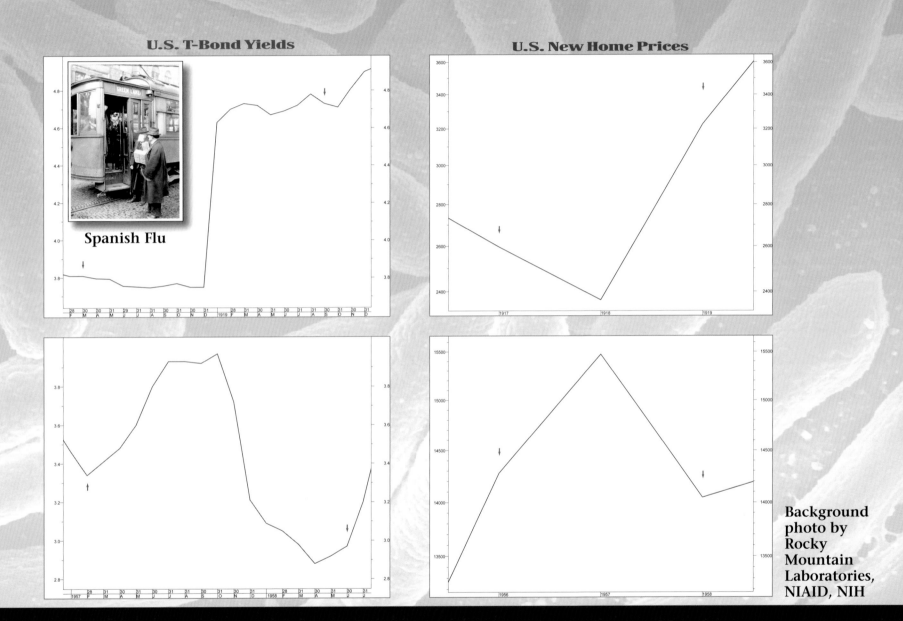

U.S. T-Bond Yields

U.S. New Home Prices

Spanish Flu

Background photo by Rocky Mountain Laboratories, NIAID, NIH

"With people streaming in from all over the world to join the California gold rush, at a time when public health and sanitary conditions were frequently substandard, it now seems amazing that only one major plague ravaged the Golden State during those tumultuous days."

California Disasters, Secrest—1957

ENVIRONMENTAL CATASTROPHE–1933

U.S. Common Stocks with NYSE Volume

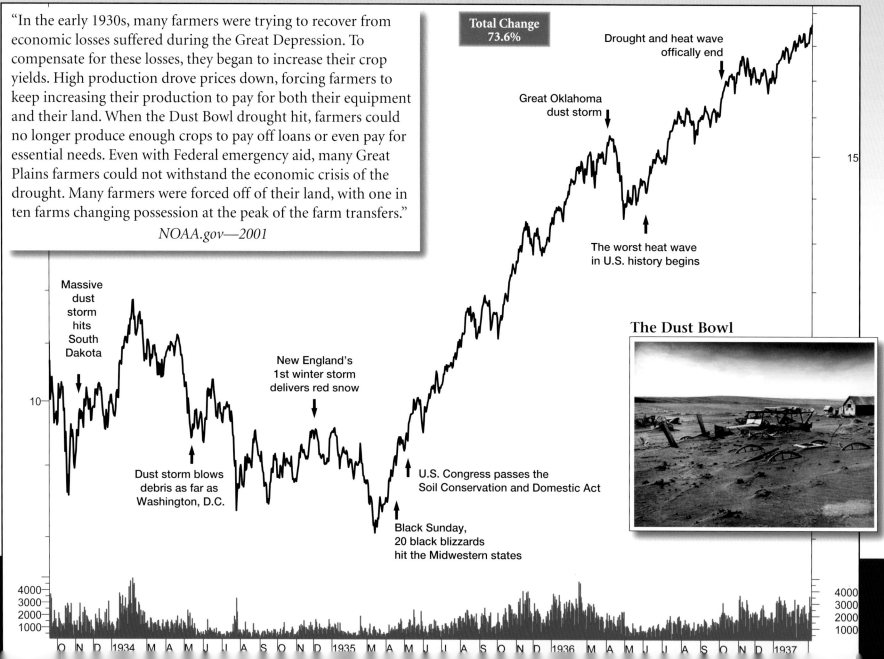

"In the early 1930s, many farmers were trying to recover from economic losses suffered during the Great Depression. To compensate for these losses, they began to increase their crop yields. High production drove prices down, forcing farmers to keep increasing their production to pay for both their equipment and their land. When the Dust Bowl drought hit, farmers could no longer produce enough crops to pay off loans or even pay for essential needs. Even with Federal emergency aid, many Great Plains farmers could not withstand the economic crisis of the drought. Many farmers were forced off of their land, with one in ten farms changing possession at the peak of the farm transfers."

NOAA.gov—2001

Total Change 73.6%

Drought and heat wave offically end

Great Oklahoma dust storm

The worst heat wave in U.S. history begins

Massive dust storm hits South Dakota

New England's 1st winter storm delivers red snow

Dust storm blows debris as far as Washington, D.C.

U.S. Congress passes the Soil Conservation and Domestic Act

Black Sunday, 20 black blizzards hit the Midwestern states

The Dust Bowl

15

10

4000
3000
2000
1000

4000
3000
2000
1000

O N D 1934 M A M J J A S O N D 1935 M A M J J A S O N D 1936 M A M J J A S O N D 1937

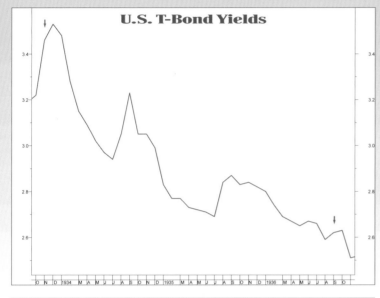

U.S. T-Bond Yields

U.S. New Home Prices

As the table on the next page shows, there have been various market reactions to these destructive disasters. The common pattern is a knee-jerk correction not exceeding (3.4%) in the stock market over a week, followed by annual advances in both equities and real estate. In fact, stocks and home prices combined have advanced 3.7% within one year (investment gains exceeded 6.8% for 63% of the time) of these acts of Mother Nature. Bond yields posted moderate increases.

The great fires in the financial centers of New York (1835), Chicago (1871), and San Francisco (1906) caused large one-year corrections in stocks, while Hurricanes Andrew and Katrina had little effect on stock and real estate values nationwide short- or long-term, while interest rate changes ranged from 14% to (14%) over a year.

Deadly pandemics and the environmental nightmare of the three-year Dust Bowl didn't faze investors, with investment prices advancing 44% on average throughout these events, with single-digit increases in interest rates.

"The direct and indirect economic effects of this disaster
will be enormous and will affect the entire nation.
The loss of wealth will be huge, measured physically,
but measured in money and trade the consequences are problematical."
The Magazine of Wall Street—August 18, 1934

NATURAL DISASTERS SUMMARY

SINGLE EVENTS	Date	Description (What is it? What did it do?)	Common Stocks Price	1 Week After	% Chg	6 Months After	% Chg	1 Year After	% Chg	T-Bond (10 yr) Yield Yields	6 Months After	% Chg	1 Year After	% Chg	Homes Prices	1 Year After	% Chg	Combined % Chg
Great New York Fire (1, 2)	December 16-17 1835	Destroyed 700 buildings (including NYSE) in lower Manhattan, $20 million in damages.	2.5	na	na	2.6	1.9%	2.2	-13.5%	4.83	4.96	2.7%	4.96	2.7%	1,673	2,189	30.8%	17.3%
Great Chicago Fire (1, 2)	October 8-10 1871	The largest U.S. natural disaster of the 19th century, $222 million in damage (four square miles of downtown Chicago destroyed—important commodities exchanges).	3.9	na	na	4.2	7.2%	3.4	-13.3%	5.06	5.39	6.5%	5.14	1.6%	1,274	1,142	-10.4%	-23.7%
Great San Francisco Earthquake and Fire (2)	April 18-20 1906	500 city blocks destroyed; $400 million in damage; 3,000 people killed (15% of population), West Coast's major financial institutions destroyed.	8.5	8.2	-3.4%	8.3	-2.2%	7.3	-14.2%	3.08	3.05	-1.0%	3.07	-0.3%	3,596	2,913	-19.0%	-33.2%
The Super Tornado Outbreak	April 3-4 1974	148 tornadoes struck 13 Midwestern states; $3.5 billion damage over 2,600 miles. Other Factor: Watergate scandal	93.3	92.0	-1.4%	62.3	-33.3%	81.5	-12.7%	7.43	8.04	8.2%	8.15	9.7%	37,112	40,600	9.4%	-3.3%
Mount St. Helens Eruption	May 18 1980	Most destructive volcanic event in U.S. history, $3 billion in damages (185 miles of major Northwest highways destroyed). Other Factor: record interest rates	107.3	110.6	3.0%	139.7	30.1%	132.5	23.5%	10.37	12.95	24.9%	13.80	33.1%	68,850	77,200	12.1%	35.6%
Hurricane Andrew	August 24 1992	Second-most destructive hurricane in U.S. history, $27 billion in damages outside Miami.	414.9	414.0	-0.2%	440.9	6.3%	459.8	10.8%	6.53	6.01	-8.0%	5.60	-14.2%	127,850	138,600	8.4%	19.2%
Sumatra-Andaman Earthquake and Tsunamis	December 26 2004	Second-largest earthquake in recorded history; 285,000 people killed in six countries with strong U.S. financial interest. Other Factors: Hurricane Katrina; Al-Qaeda war	1210.2	1202.1	-0.7%	1190.7	-1.6%	1257.0	3.9%	4.23	3.90	-7.8%	4.34	2.6%	256,950	264,400	2.9%	6.8%
Hurricane Katrina New Orleans Floods	August 23-30 2005	Costliest disaster in U.S. history exceeded $82 billion throughout four states, 80% of New Orleans destroyed; 1,836 people killed	1221.8	1220.3	-0.1%	1287.8	5.4%	1293.0	5.8%	4.22	4.56	8.1%	4.81	14.0%	267,550	280,600	4.9%	10.7%
		Average		-0.5%			1.7%		-1.2%			4.2%		6.1%			4.9%	3.7%
		Median		-0.2%			3.6%		-4.4%			4.6%		2.6%			6.6%	8.7%
		High		3.0%			30.1%		23.5%			24.9%		33.1%			30.8%	35.6%
		Low		-3.4%			-33.3%		-14.2%			-8.0%		-14.2%			-19.0%	-33.2%

EXTENDED EVENTS	Date	Description (What is it? What did it do?)	Common Stocks Beginning	End	% Chg	T-Bond Beginning	End	% Chg	Homes Beginning	End	% Chg	Combined
Spanish Flu Pandemic (2)	March 1918 to September 1919	17 million people died worldwide; 500,000 in U.S. (of 100 million total population). Other Factor: World War I	7.0	9.7	39.0%	3.81	4.71	23.6%	2,597	3,226	24.2%	63.2%
The Dust Bowl (2)	November 1933 to September 1936	The largest environmental disaster in U.S. history caused permanent migration of 500,000 people from the Midwest. Other Factor: Great Depression	9.2	16.0	73.6%	3.22	2.62	-18.6%	5,519	5,346	-3.1%	70.5%
Asian Flu Pandemic (2)	February 1957 to June 1958	70,000 deaths in U.S. Other Factors: USSR launched Sputnik, President Eisenhower suffered a stroke	44.9	45.2	0.7%	3.46	2.97	-14.2%	14,279	14,047	-1.6%	-0.9%
		Average		37.8%			-3.1%			6.5%		44.3%
		Median		39.0%			-14.2%			-1.6%		63.2%
		High		73.6%			23.6%			24.2%		70.5%
		Low		0.7%			-18.6%			-3.1%		-0.9%

(1) Monthly Prices on Stocks — Best Performance
(2) Year-End Prices on Real Estate — Worst Performance

"Veteran investors have found that major disasters tend to take place after the stock market has already given its clues that the rally is over."

Investor's Business Daily—July 2005

MAN-MADE TRAGEDIES

Trade embargoes, terrorism, shipwrecks, spaceship explosions, presidential assassinations, and political controversies. Except for war, these man-made situations have been the indelible "time stoppers" for people who lived through these times.

How have these events affected investors' actions?

In this section, 16 of the most significant man-made tragedies (11 sudden events and 5 protracted situations) that have occurred in America since the 1850s are examined in light of their short- and long-term effects on various types of investments.

Gas shortage lines of the 1970s

Alaska Pipeline 1976

Titanic

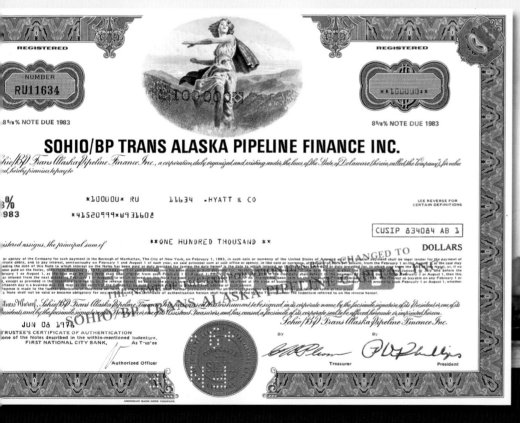

"The first panic of any importance was that of 1837. This panic had its origin in a misunderstanding between the United States Bank and President Jackson, whose election the officials of the bank opposed."

"No, sir, I'm sorry sir. Our oil comes from Texas."

U.S. Common Stocks with NYSE Volume

1967

4% Increase

Price of Oil

322% Increase

1973

25% Decrease

Franklin D. Roosevelt
with Saudi Prince,
1944 and 1970 embargo cartoons

"Sometimes I wonder what they do with the stuff."

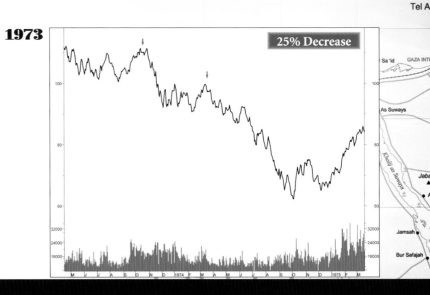

"A \$2 per barrel tariff imposed by President Ford on foreign crude oil
is an attempt to push prices high enough to force motorists to conserve fuel."
Time—July 21, 1975

178

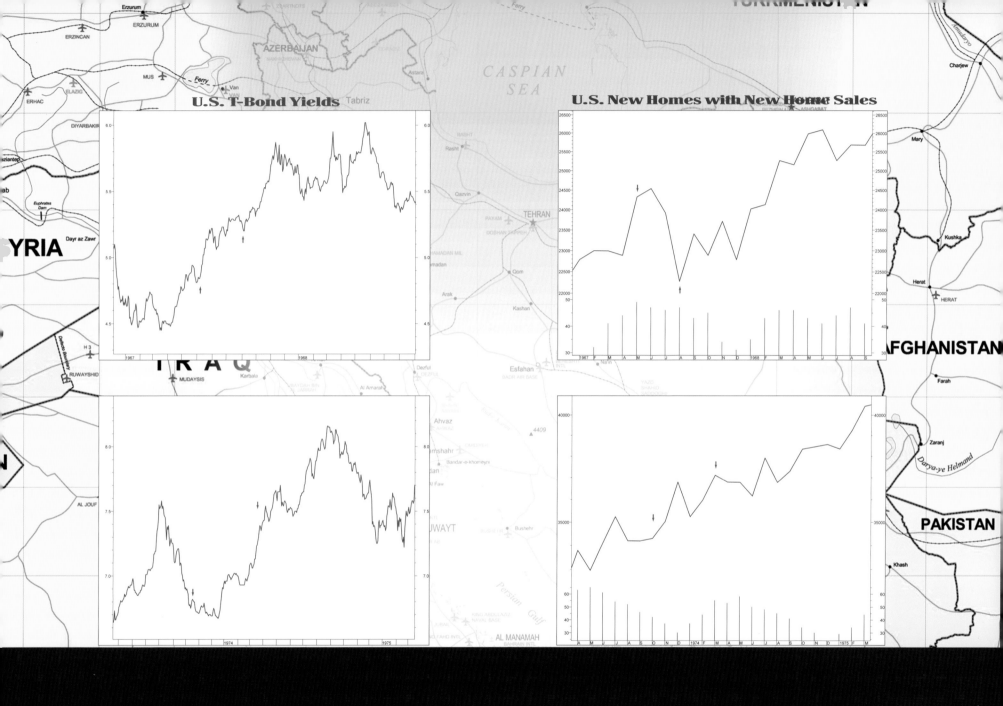

U.S. T-Bond Yields

U.S. New Homes with New Home Sales

"A few words from the unfailingly suave sheik (Yamani) could make
government officials shudder and cause stock markets from New York to New Delhi to fall."

TERRORISM ON WALL STREET

Wall Street 1920

World Trade Center 2001

U.S. Common Stocks with NYSE Volume

1-Year Change (19%)

1-Year Change (17%)

"Wall Street has repeatedly been a target for violence by the disaffected, but heretofore its response has been to grieve, shrug and move on, ultimately reaching new heights."

The Wall Street Journal—September 23, 2002

"A wagon with a red flag, indicating that it carried explosives,
and drawn by one horse had stopped at the curb close by J.P. Morgan's office."
NY Times—September 16, 1920

SHIPWRECKS

SS Central America Sinks 1857

U.S. Common Stocks with NYSE Volume

1-Year Change (10%)

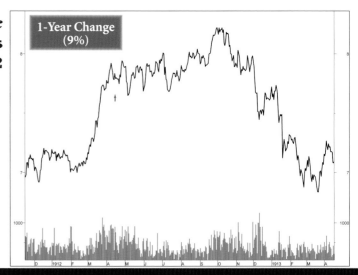

Titanic Sinks 1912

1-Year Change (9%)

International Mercantile Marine— owner of the *Titanic*

INTERNATIONAL MERCANTILE MARINE

100

16456

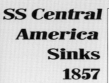

"The first-class passengers for *Titanic's* maiden voyage included some of the richest and most prominent people in the world."

Wikipedia.com—2008

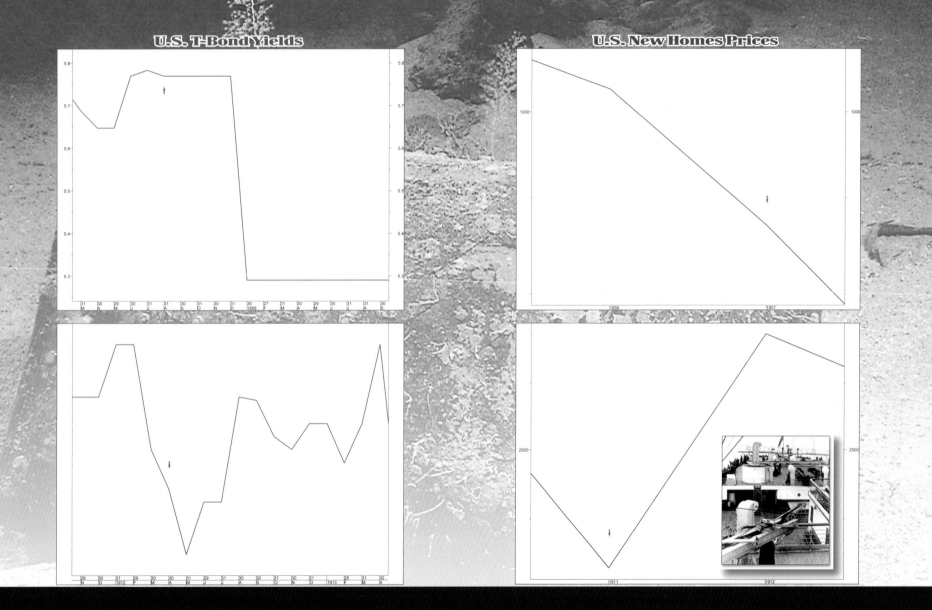

"But overspeculation, following the enormous production of gold,
and the abuses of credit in the promotion of new railroad and other companies,
together with tariff disturbances, brought on the panic of 1857."

Work of Wall Street, Pratt—1916

SPACE TRAVEL CALAMITIES

U.S. Common Stocks with NYSE Volume

U.S. T-Bond Yields

Challenger
1986

1-Year Change
33%

1-Year Change
33%

From a roll of
unprocessed film
recovered from wreckage
of space shuttle *Columbia*

Columbia
2003

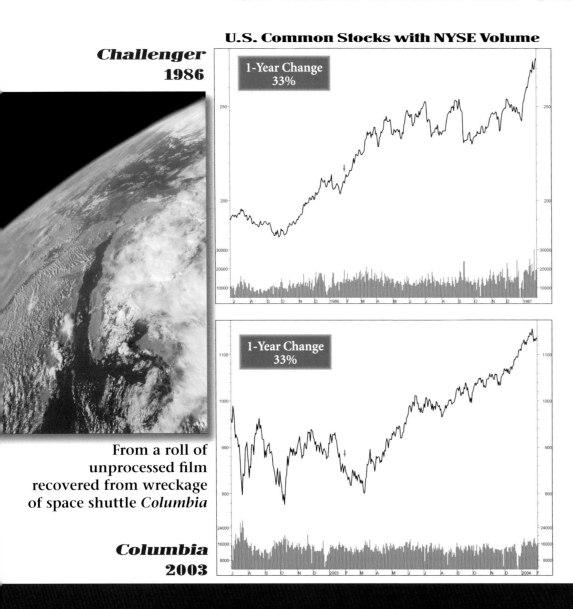

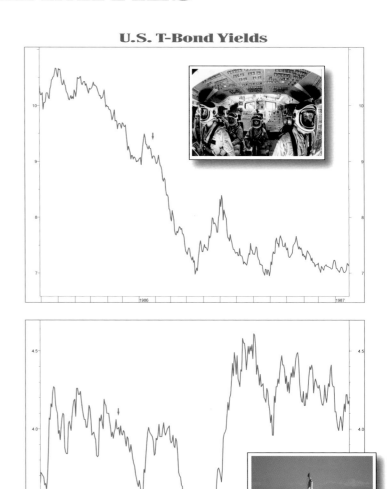

U.S. New Homes with New Home Sales

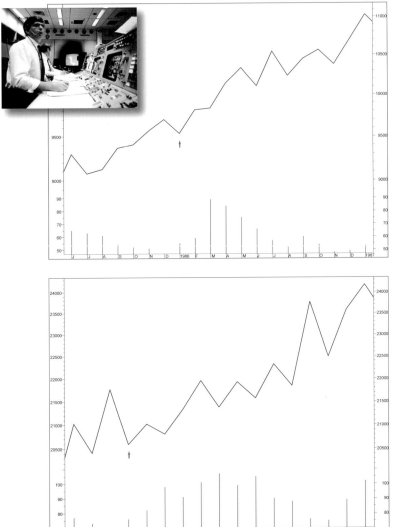

> "The second guessing will start soon enough. By Saturday night the whistle-blowers were already beginning to toot on the Internet and on the talking head shows, claiming they had predicted disaster for years."
>
> *Newsweek—February 10, 2003*

POLITICAL ASSASSINATIONS

U.S. Common Stocks

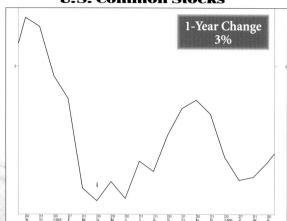

1-Year Change
3%

U.S. T-Bond Yields

U.S. New Home Prices

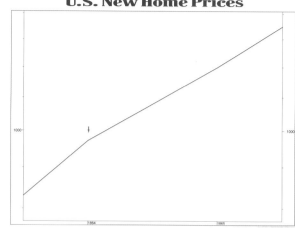

President Lincoln—1865

The Assassination
of President Lincoln at
Ford's Theatre, Washington, D.C.
April 14, 1865

"Stock market closed for over one week."
NYSE.com—2007

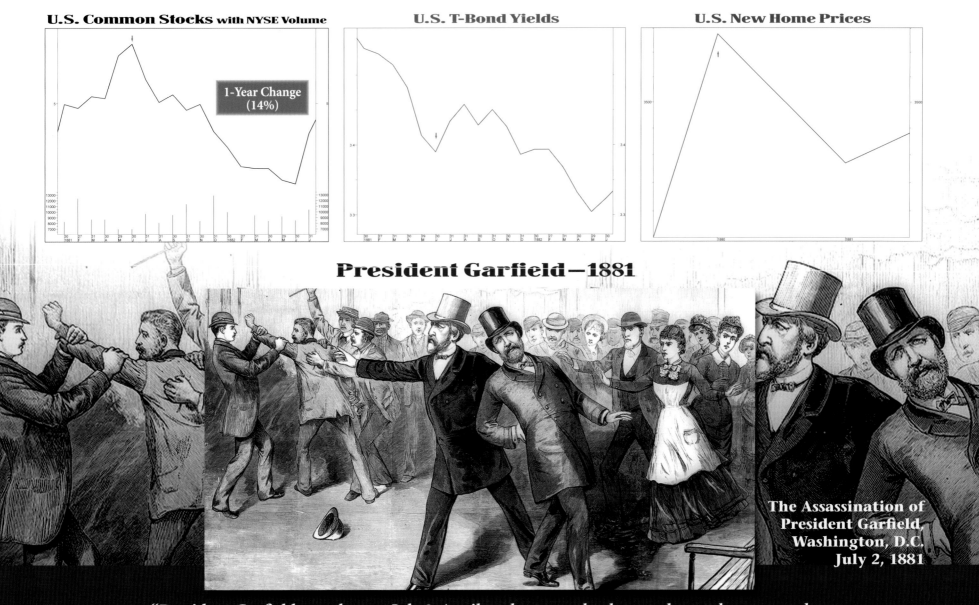

U.S. Common Stocks with NYSE Volume

1-Year Change
(14%)

U.S. T-Bond Yields

U.S. New Home Prices

President Garfield—1881

The Assassination of
President Garfield,
Washington, D.C.
July 2, 1881

"President Garfield was shot on July 2. A railroad rate war broke out almost the next week;
following which, the hot winds ruined the corn crop. All these occurrences were described,
as usual, as thunderclaps from a clear sky – then the markets collapsed."

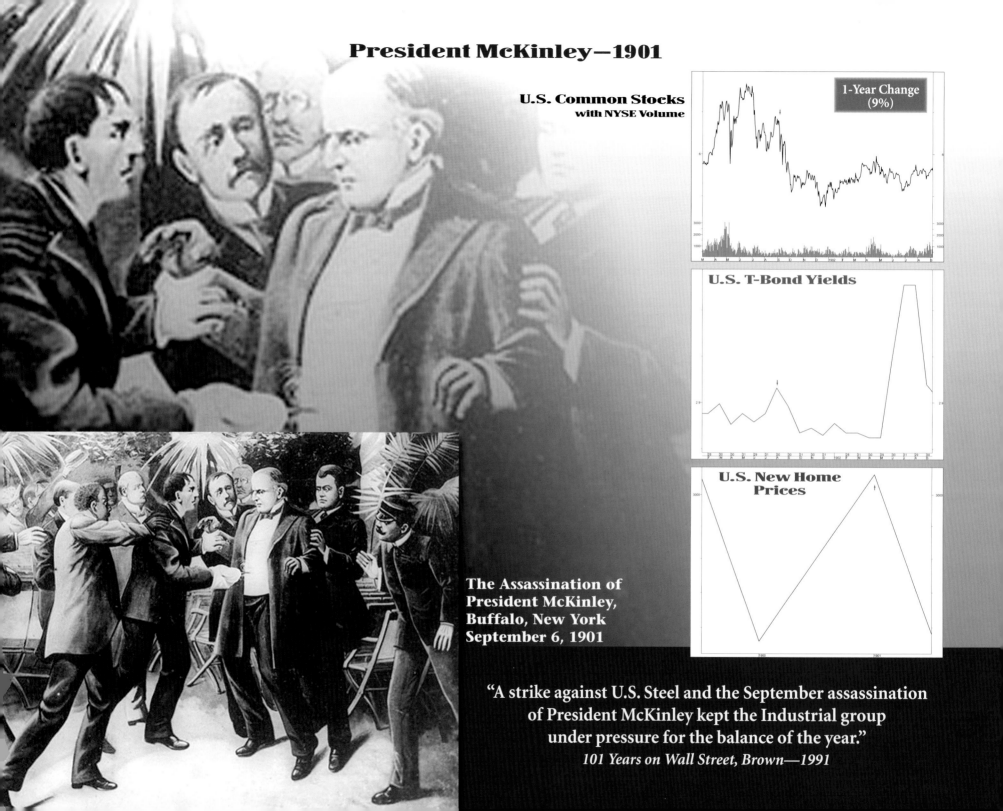

President McKinley—1901

U.S. Common Stocks
with NYSE Volume

1-Year Change (9%)

U.S. T-Bond Yields

U.S. New Home Prices

The Assassination of President McKinley, Buffalo, New York September 6, 1901

"A strike against U.S. Steel and the September assassination of President McKinley kept the Industrial group under pressure for the balance of the year."
101 Years on Wall Street, Brown—1991

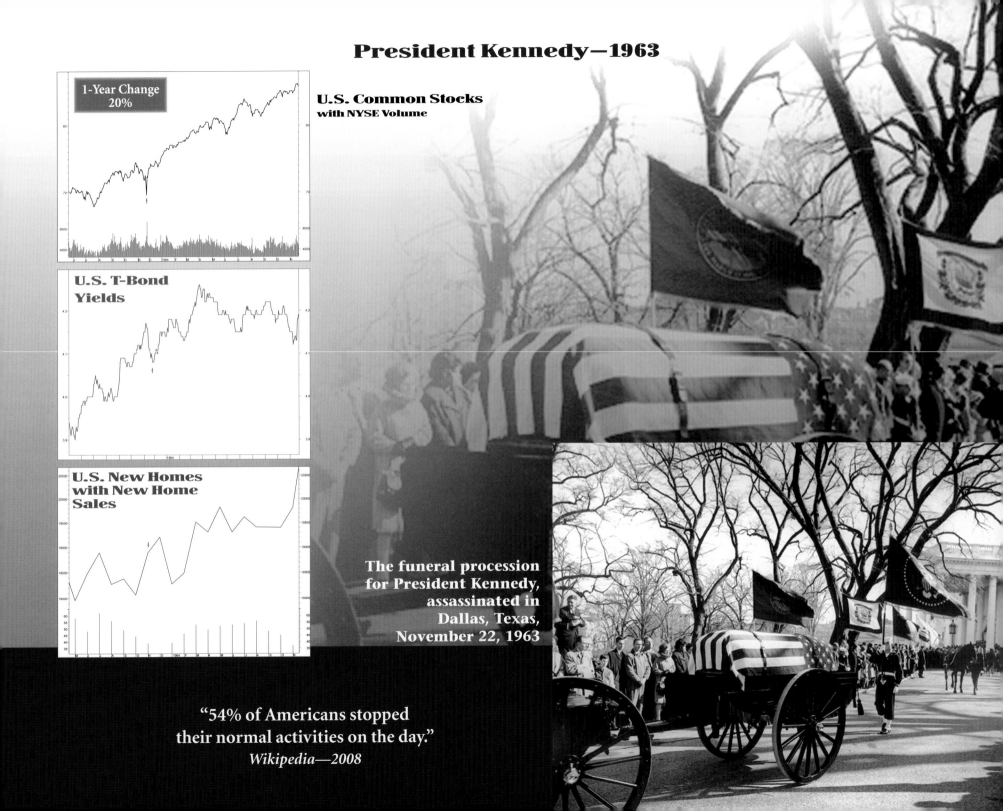

President Kennedy—1963

1-Year Change 20%

U.S. Common Stocks
with NYSE Volume

U.S. T-Bond Yields

U.S. New Homes with New Home Sales

The funeral procession for President Kennedy, assassinated in Dallas, Texas, November 22, 1963

"54% of Americans stopped their normal activities on the day."
Wikipedia—2008

WATERGATE/NIXON RESIGNATION–1973

U.S. Common Stocks with NYSE Volume

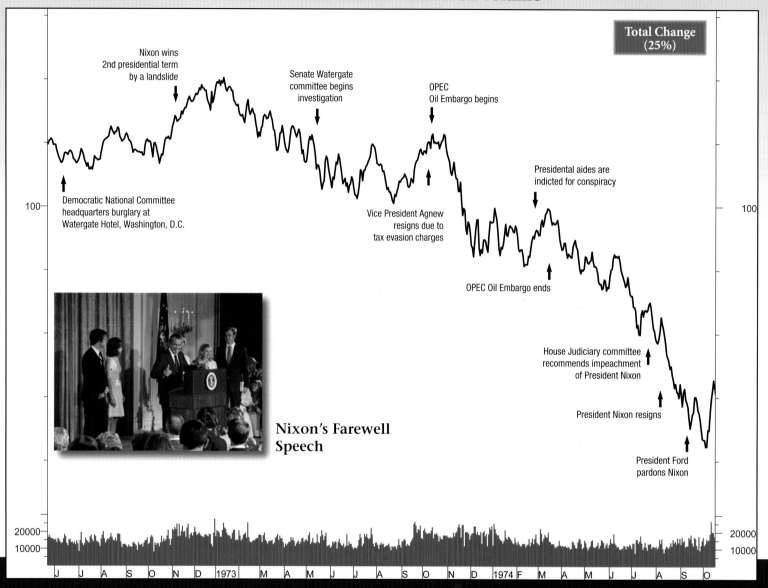

Total Change (25%)

Nixon wins 2nd presidential term by a landslide

Senate Watergate committee begins investigation

OPEC Oil Embargo begins

Presidental aides are indicted for conspiracy

Democratic National Committee headquarters burglary at Watergate Hotel, Washington, D.C.

100

Vice President Agnew resigns due to tax evasion charges

100

OPEC Oil Embargo ends

House Judiciary committee recommends impeachment of President Nixon

Nixon's Farewell Speech

President Nixon resigns

President Ford pardons Nixon

20000
10000

20000
10000

J J A S O N D 1973 M A M J J A S O N D 1974 F M A M J J A S O

"Through acts that made no sense,
discord would descend once again on a society
already weakened by ten years of upheaval over Vietnam."
Time—March 8, 1982

NF16618

COMMON STOCK

PAR VALUE $1.00

COMMON STOCK

PAR VALUE $1.00

PLAYBOY ENTERPRISES, INC.

INCORPORATED UNDER THE
— LAWS —
OF THE STATE
— OF —
DELAWARE

Playboy Enterprises certificate issued during Watergate Scandal

THIS CERTIFICATE IS TRANSFERABLE
— IN —
CHICAGO, ILLINOIS
OR IN
THE CITY OF NEW YORK

SEE REVERSE FOR
CERTAIN DEFINITIONS

U.S. T-Bond Yields

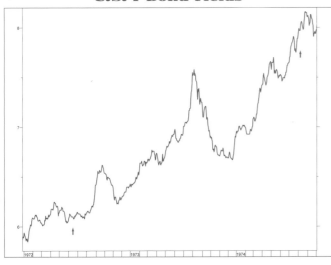

**Political
Scandals**
A timeless tradition

U.S. New Homes with New Home Sales

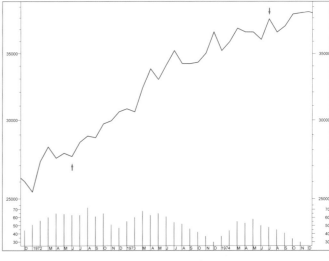

"It was very succinctly described by Mr. Gould in his testimony before the
Garfield Investigating Committee (into the President's role in the Gold Panic of 1869).
He said, 'The President (Grant) was an eager listener. The other gentlemen were discussing.
Some were in favor of Treasurer Boutwell's selling gold, and some were opposed to it.'"
Twenty-Eight Years in Wall Street, Clews—1887

PRESIDENT REAGAN SHOT–1981

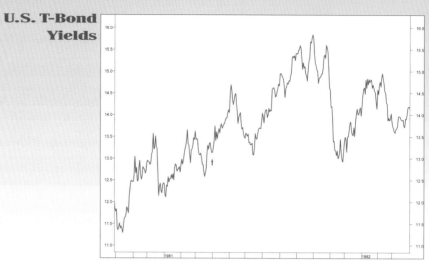

U.S. T-Bond Yields

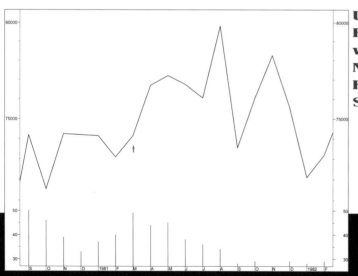

U.S. New Homes with New Home Sales

U.S. Common Stocks with NYSE Volume

1-Year Change (17%)

PRESIDENT CLINTON IMPEACHMENT TRIAL–1998

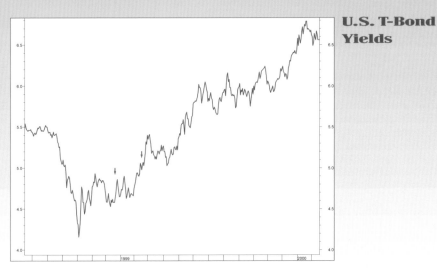

U.S. T-Bond Yields

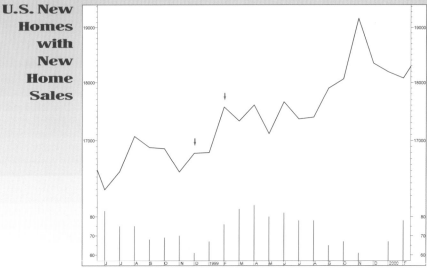

U.S. New Homes with New Home Sales

U.S. Common Stocks with NYSE Volume

1-Year Change
4%

"Elected men of the highest honor come out stained."
Bulls & Bears of New York, Smith—1875

BUSH/GORE ELECTION–2000

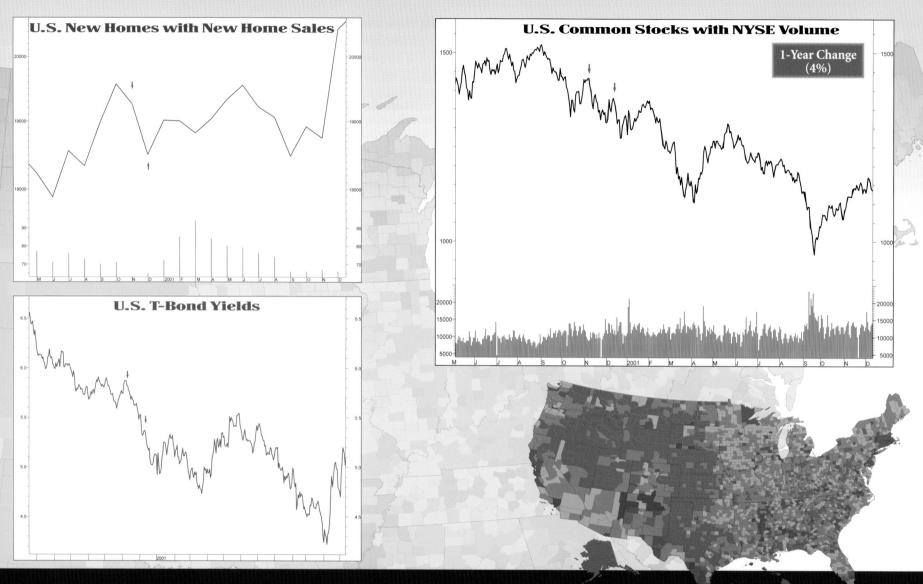

U.S. New Homes with New Home Sales

U.S. Common Stocks with NYSE Volume

1-Year Change
(4%)

U.S. T-Bond Yields

"A 1998 Report for the National Bureau of Standards recommends that punch card machines be eliminated due to frequent undervotes and recounting errors. Despite these warnings, states and localities did little or nothing; facing difficult budgetary choices, ensuring fair and accurate elections [were] viewed as less important than other priorities. At the same time, Congress took no action."

MAN-MADE DISASTERS SUMMARY

SINGLE EVENTS	Date	Description (What is it? What did it do?)	Common Stocks Price	1 Week After	% Chg	6 Months After	% Chg	1 Year After	% Chg	T-Bond (10 yr) Yields	6 Months After	% Chg	1 Year After	% Chg	Homes Prices	1 Year After	% Chg	Combined % Chg
Sinking of SS Central America (1, 2)	September 11 1857	Sank in hurricane off South Carolina en route to Wall Street with 15 tons of gold. Other Factor: Financial panic of 1857	1.5	na	na	1.5	0.0%	1.3	-10.1%	5.77	5.29	-8.3%	5.29	-8.3%	717	803	12.0%	1.9%
Lincoln Assassination (1, 2)	April 14 1865	Shot in Washington, D.C. theater and died next day, several members of Cabinet wounded, stock market closed more than a week. Other Factor: Civil War	2.6	na	na	2.9	9.1%	2.7	3.0%	5.59	5.59	0.0%	5.63	0.7%	972	1,200	23.5%	26.5%
Garfield Assassination (1, 2)	July 2 1881	Shot in Washington, D.C. railway station four months after taking office; died two months later.	5.3	na	na	4.9	-8.4%	4.6	-13.7%	3.39	3.39	0.0%	3.32	-2.1%	3,776	3,270	-13.4%	-27.1%
McKinley Assassination (2)	September 6 1901	Shot in Buffalo, N.Y. at Pan-American Exposition, died 8 days later.	6.4	6.2	-2.8%	5.7	-10.2%	5.8	-8.9%	2.92	2.87	-1.7%	3.03	3.8%	2,174	2,453	12.8%	3.9%
Titanic Sinking (2)	April 15 1912	Luxury ocean liner sank after hitting iceberg in North Atlantic; 1,517 people died (including many prominent business people).	7.8	7.8	-0.4%	8.1	4.1%	7.1	-9.0%	3.51	3.52	0.3%	3.52	0.3%	2,332	2,676	14.8%	5.7%
Wall Street Bombing (2)	September 16 1920	Foreign anarchists plant bomb in horse-drawn wagon at lunchtime in New York financial district; 38 killed, 400 injured.	7.7	7.6	-0.4%	6.6	-14.1%	6.2	-19.2%	5.67	5.27	-7.1%	5.12	-9.7%	4,027	4,489	11.5%	-7.7%
Kennedy Assassination (2)	November 22, 1963	Shot and killed in Dallas, Texas; NYSE closed immediately.	71.6	72.3	0.9%	80.7	12.7%	86.0	20.1%	4.10	4.20	2.4%	4.18	2.0%	18,065	19,816	9.7%	29.8%
Reagan Assassination Attempt	March 30, 1981	Shot and critically wounded in Washington, D.C.	134.6	135.5	0.6%	116.7	-13.3%	112.3	-16.6%	13.22	15.84	19.8%	14.19	7.3%	74,150	75,450	1.8%	-14.9%
Space Shuttle Challenger Explosion	January 28 1986	Spacecraft exploded shortly after launch, first astronauts killed since 1967.	206.4	211.8	2.6%	249.6	20.9%	275.4	33.4%	9.05	7.53	-16.8%	7.13	-21.2%	95,350	110,300	15.7%	49.1%
9/11 Attacks in NYC and Washington, D.C.	September 11 2001	Islamic terrorists hijacked airplanes and crashed them into World Trade Center and Pentagon; 2,993 killed, 2,000 injured; NYSE closed for one week.	1092.6	1033.8	-5.4%	1168.2	6.9%	909.5	-16.8%	4.84	5.32	9.9%	4.07	-15.9%	190,600	196,400	3.0%	-13.7%
Space Shuttle Columbia Explosion	February 1 2003	Spacecraft destroyed when re-entering earth's atmosphere. Other Factor: Al-Qaeda War	855.7	829.4	-3.1%	980.0	14.5%	1135.2	32.7%	4.00	4.44	11.0%	4.18	4.5%	205,950	235,800	14.5%	47.2%
		Average			-1.0%				-0.5%			0.9%		-3.5%			9.6%	9.1%

EXTENDED EVENTS	Date	Description (What is it? What did it do?)	Price	1 Week After	% Chg	6 Months After	% Chg	1 Year After	% Chg	Yields	6 Months After	% Chg	1 Year After	% Chg	Prices	1 Year After	% Chg	Combined % Chg
1967 Oil Embargo	June 6 to September 1 1967	OPEC limits oil supplies to Western countries supporting Israel in Six Day War. Other Factor: Vietnam War	89.79					93.7	4.3%	4.85			5.27	8.7%	24,327	22,270	-8.5%	-4.1%
Nixon Administration Scandals (Watergate)	June 15, 1972 to August 9 1974	Worst political scandal in U.S. history; resignation of both president and vice president in 1 year. Other Factors: Vietnam War, 1973 Oil Embargo	108.4					80.9	-25.4%	6.10			8.03	31.6%	27,779	37,919	36.5%	11.1%
1973 Oil Embargo	October 17 1973 to March 17 1974	OPEC halted all oil exports to countries militarily supporting Israel in the Yom Kippur War; oil prices rose from 75 cents to $12 a barrel. Other Factor: Vietnam War	110.2					98.1	-11.0%	6.82			7.23	6.0%	34,303	37,112	8.2%	-2.8%
President Clinton Impeachment Trial	December 19, 1998 to February 12 1999	Impeached by the House, acquitted by the Senate on charges of perjury and obstruction of justice. Other Factor: Dot Com Bubble	1188.0					1230.1	3.5%	4.58			5.06	10.5%	164,800	175,700	6.6%	10.2%
2000 Presidential Election (Bush and Gore)	November 7 to December 12 2000	Virtual tie in election required several vote recounts in Florida; Supreme Court stopped recounts and ruled in favor of Bush. Other Factor: Dot Com Bubble	1432.2					1371.2	-4.3%	5.87			5.36	-8.7%	195,700	185,050	-5.4%	-9.7%
		Average							-6.6%					9.6%			7.5%	0.9%

(1) Monthly Prices on Stocks — Best Performance
(2) Year-End Prices on Real Estate — Worst Performance

As the table shows, there have been various market reactions to these disasters. The common pattern is a knee-jerk correction averaging (1.0%), but within six months, stocks and real estate have appreciated well. The sinking of "gold ship" *SS Central America* with its 15 tons of gold bound for Wall Street triggered the Panic of 1857. Of the presidential tragedies, the McKinley assassination caused the worst short-term damage to the stock market.

"It was considered indispensable by the (Gold Panic of 1869) conspirators, for the consummation of their plans, that President Grant should be got out of the way by some means or other. Fortunately for him, and the honor of the nation, the plan succeeded without the necessity of offering him any violence."

WHICH DISASTER WREAKED THE MOST HAVOC ON INVESTORS?

The 1906 San Francisco Earthquake and Fire! But 9/11 had the greatest immediate impact on the stock market. Attacks on financial centers seem to be the most volatile, but the centers were also quick to recover. The combination of the Watergate political scandal and the 1973 Arab Oil Embargo caused damage to the stock market, yet home prices appreciated well.

NATIONAL DISASTER ≠ BEAR MARKET

"Down went the owners—greedy men whom hope of gain allured:
Oh, dry the starting tear, for they were heavily insured."
The Bab Ballads—1866

AMERICA'S PEACEFUL ACHIEVEMENTS

PANAMA CANAL

APOLLO MOON LANDINGS

TRANSCONTINENTAL RAILROAD
Completed May 10, 1869

Northern Pacific Railroad certificate—1883
signed by J.P. Morgan

Railroad certificate
signed by Jay Gould—1869

"The basis of all the discredit,
the embarrassments, the bankruptcies,
and the robberies of our railroad system
is thus laid at the inception of the enterprises."
Twenty-Eight Years in Wall Street, H. Clews—1887

IMPORTANT FACTS

• Considered by many the greatest American technological feat of the 19th century, some 1,777 miles of railroad were built through the Rocky Mountains and the Sierra Nevada.

• A national high-speed transportation system was created that accelerated the economic development, population growth, and military security of the American West.

• A scandal surrounded the awarding of $23 million of overbilled work.

• Estimated cost was $106 million (more than $500 billion in today's dollars).

• 38,000 acres of public land granted to Central Pacific and Union Pacific railroads.

• Other event—Fisk-Gould gold market scandal.

INVESTMENT PERFORMANCE

	Price	% Chg 6 months	% Chg 1 yr
Common Stocks ($)	$3.66	(6%)	2%
T-Bond Interest Rates (%)	5%	3%	3%
New Homes ($)	$1,380	na	(9%)

U.S. Common Stocks

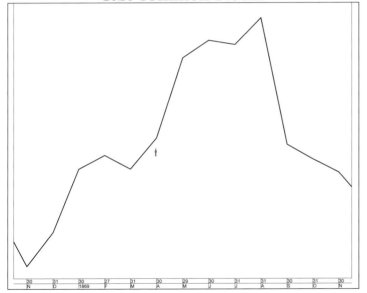

U.S. New Home Prices

U.S. T-Bond Yields

"The Crédit Mobilier scam was born out of a simple reality: in the 1860s,
the U.S. government wanted a transcontinental railroad more than investors did.
While a railroad across the Rockies had a glorious air to it,
the project also carried an enormous amount of risk, and risk is generally something investors prefer to avoid."
New Yorker Magazine—2003

PANAMA CANAL—Completed August 15, 1914

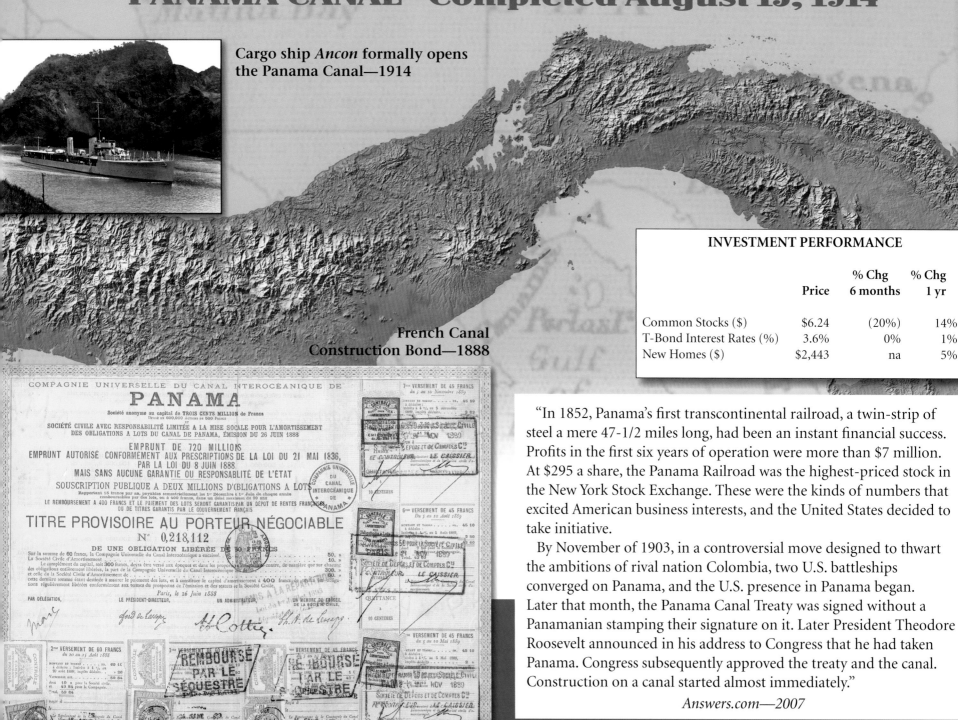

Cargo ship *Ancon* formally opens the Panama Canal—1914

French Canal Construction Bond—1888

INVESTMENT PERFORMANCE

	Price	% Chg 6 months	% Chg 1 yr
Common Stocks ($)	$6.24	(20%)	14%
T-Bond Interest Rates (%)	3.6%	0%	1%
New Homes ($)	$2,443	na	5%

"In 1852, Panama's first transcontinental railroad, a twin-strip of steel a mere 47-1/2 miles long, had been an instant financial success. Profits in the first six years of operation were more than $7 million. At $295 a share, the Panama Railroad was the highest-priced stock in the New York Stock Exchange. These were the kinds of numbers that excited American business interests, and the United States decided to take initiative.

By November of 1903, in a controversial move designed to thwart the ambitions of rival nation Colombia, two U.S. battleships converged on Panama, and the U.S. presence in Panama began. Later that month, the Panama Canal Treaty was signed without a Panamanian stamping their signature on it. Later President Theodore Roosevelt announced in his address to Congress that he had taken Panama. Congress subsequently approved the treaty and the canal. Construction on a canal started almost immediately."

Answers.com—2007

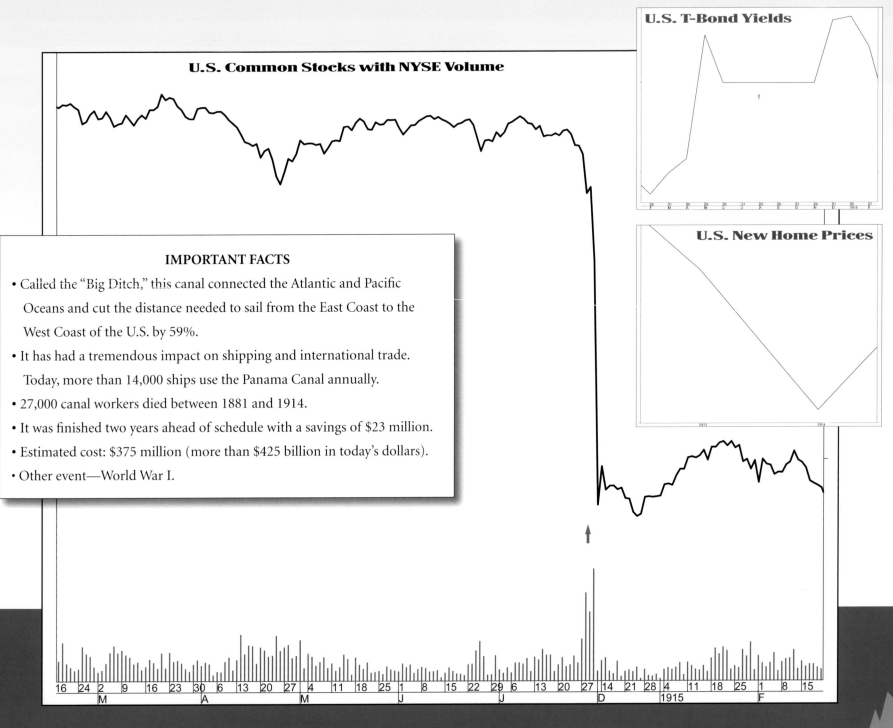

U.S. Common Stocks with NYSE Volume

U.S. T-Bond Yields

U.S. New Home Prices

IMPORTANT FACTS

• Called the "Big Ditch," this canal connected the Atlantic and Pacific
  Oceans and cut the distance needed to sail from the East Coast to the
  West Coast of the U.S. by 59%.

• It has had a tremendous impact on shipping and international trade.
  Today, more than 14,000 ships use the Panama Canal annually.

• 27,000 canal workers died between 1881 and 1914.

• It was finished two years ahead of schedule with a savings of $23 million.

• Estimated cost: $375 million (more than $425 billion in today's dollars).

• Other event—World War I.

HOOVER DAM – Completed October 26, 1936

"When the bills are paid and the turbines begin to produce electricity, the 'Six Companies' group will have turned a profit estimated at $7,000,000 and upward for all their work. This profit, which must be understood as a highly unofficial estimate, is the insurance premium the U.S. pays for efficiency. If the contractors spent all their money, botched the job, and went broke, the government might have to finish the dam to the tune of a great many millions. The U.S. is willing to pay a good profit for a good dam built rapidly."

Fortune Magazine—September 1933

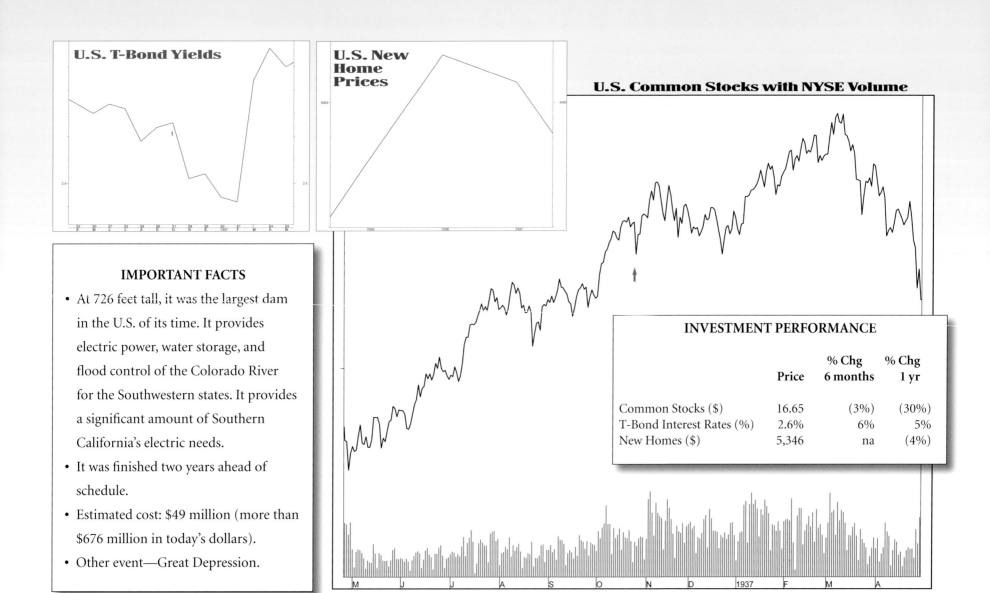

U.S. T-Bond Yields

U.S. New Home Prices

U.S. Common Stocks with NYSE Volume

IMPORTANT FACTS

- At 726 feet tall, it was the largest dam in the U.S. of its time. It provides electric power, water storage, and flood control of the Colorado River for the Southwestern states. It provides a significant amount of Southern California's electric needs.

- It was finished two years ahead of schedule.

- Estimated cost: $49 million (more than $676 million in today's dollars).

- Other event—Great Depression.

INVESTMENT PERFORMANCE

	Price	% Chg 6 months	% Chg 1 yr
Common Stocks ($)	16.65	(3%)	(30%)
T-Bond Interest Rates (%)	2.6%	6%	5%
New Homes ($)	5,346	na	(4%)

"Hoover's response to the stock market crash was to try and temper the effects of the financial panic on other sectors of the economy. This would be done primarily through the cooperation between business and labor, with the assistance of federal and local governments. These efforts were largely based on his experiences with the depression of 1921. In January, Hoover instituted a vigorous public works program which authorized $60 million to begin construction of the Hoover Dam, $75 million for road construction, and $500 million for public buildings."

Presidentialtimeline.org—2007

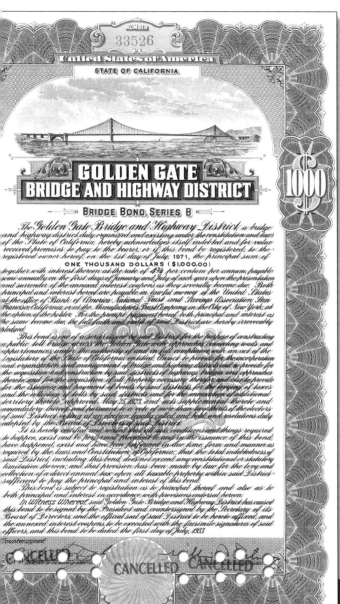

Bond used to pay for
Golden Gate Bridge—1933

"The construction budget at the time of voter approval was $30.1 million. However, the Golden Gate Bridge and Highway District was unable to sell the bonds until 1932, when the founder of San Francisco based Bank of America agreed on behalf of his bank to buy the entire project in order to help the local economy. The last of the construction bonds were retired in 1971, with $35 million and $38 million in interest payments financed only from bridge tolls."

Wikipedia.com—2007

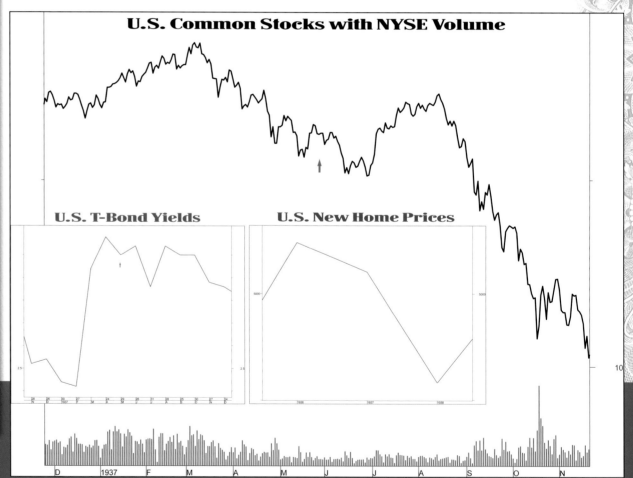

U.S. Common Stocks with NYSE Volume

U.S. T-Bond Yields

U.S. New Home Prices

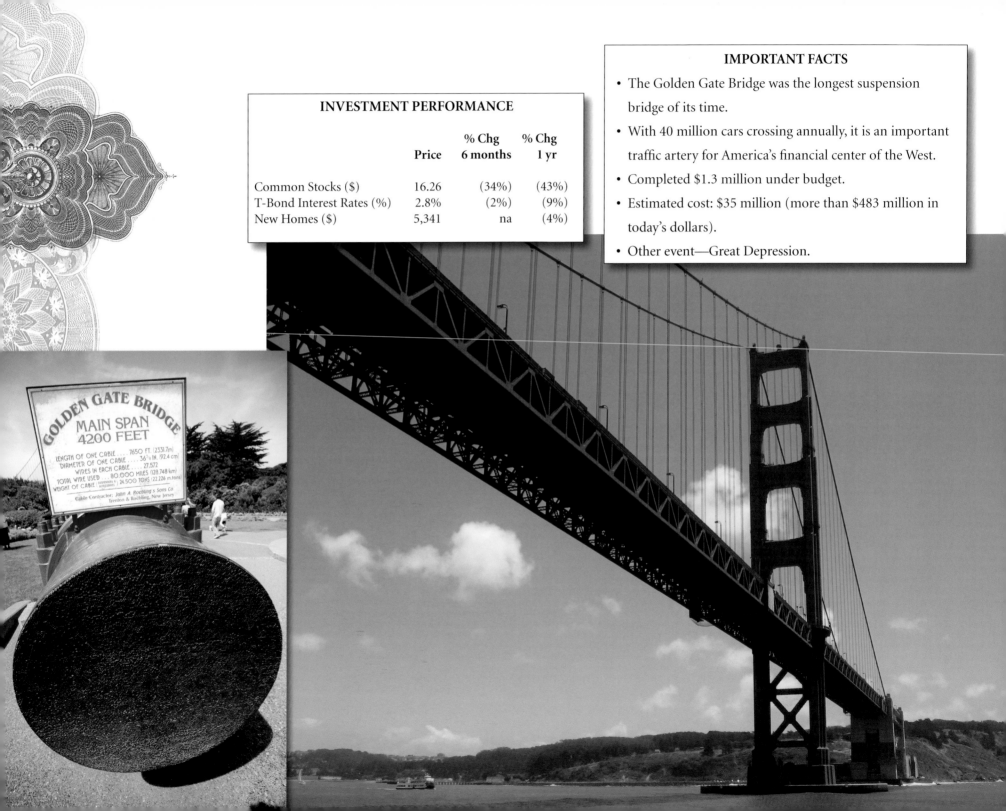

INVESTMENT PERFORMANCE

	Price	% Chg 6 months	% Chg 1 yr
Common Stocks ($)	16.26	(34%)	(43%)
T-Bond Interest Rates (%)	2.8%	(2%)	(9%)
New Homes ($)	5,341	na	(4%)

IMPORTANT FACTS

- The Golden Gate Bridge was the longest suspension bridge of its time.
- With 40 million cars crossing annually, it is an important traffic artery for America's financial center of the West.
- Completed $1.3 million under budget.
- Estimated cost: $35 million (more than $483 million in today's dollars).
- Other event—Great Depression.

GOLDEN GATE BRIDGE
MAIN SPAN
4200 FEET

LENGTH OF ONE CABLE . . . 7650 FT. (2331.7m)
DIAMETER OF ONE CABLE . . . 36⅜ IN. (92.4 cm)
WIRES IN EACH CABLE . . . 27,572
TOTAL WIRE USED . . . 80,000 MILES (128,748 km)
WEIGHT OF CABLE SUSPENDERS & ACCESSORIES . . . 24,500 TONS (22,226 m.tons)

Cable Contractor: John A. Roebling's Sons Co.
Trenton & Roebling, New Jersey

APOLLO 11 MOON LANDING – July 20, 1969

INVESTMENT PERFORMANCE

	Price	% Chg 6 months	% Chg 1 yr
Common Stocks ($)	93.52	(4%)	(17%)
T-Bond Interest Rates (%)	6.7%	16%	12%
New Homes ($)	27,541	na	(15%)

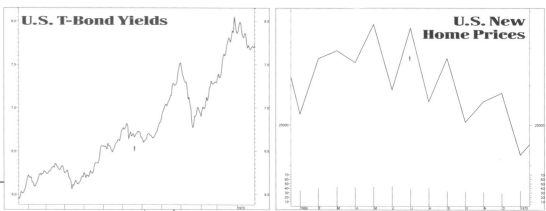

U.S. T-Bond Yields

U.S. New Home Prices

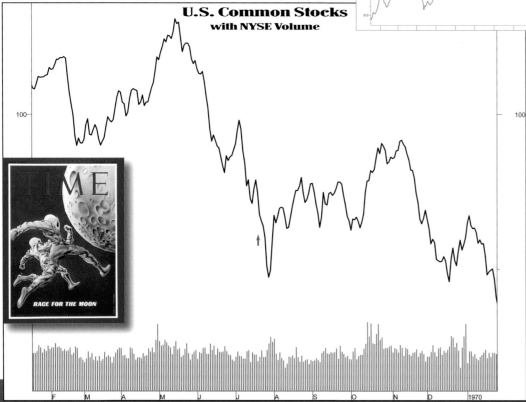

U.S. Common Stocks
with NYSE Volume

IMPORTANT FACTS

- It was the first of six lunar landings. A record achieved only by the U.S.

- It helped "jump start" a new age of technological innovation. Thousands of products and processes were developed during the Mercury, Gemini, and Apollo space programs.

- NYSE closed on July 21, 1969 for "National Day of Participation for Lunar Exploration."

- Kennedy's goal was exceeded with two moon landings by end of 1969.

- Estimated cost: $25 billion (more than $135 billion in today's dollars).

- Other event—Vietnam War.

"When John Kennedy first fixed U.S. sights on the moon in 1961,
he recognized it as a project of giant technological and economic proportions."
Newsweek—July 7, 1969

LESS
100 SHARES

No. M164338

IBM-made
computers
and
components
were used on all
U.S. spacecraft

LESS
THAN 100 SHARES

10 Shares

INTERNATIONAL BUSINESS MACHINES CORPORATION

*This certifi... 's not valid until countersigned by the Transfer Ag...
Witness the seal of the Corporation and the facsimile signatures of ...*

Dated F

Countersigned: International Business Machines Corporation, *Transfer Agent*

By P.K... *Transfer Clerk*

Registered: Morgan Guaranty Trust Company of New York, *Registrar*

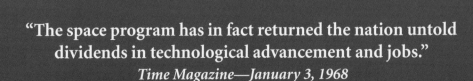

"The space program has in fact returned the nation untold
dividends in technological advancement and jobs."
Time Magazine—January 3, 1968

COLD WAR ENDED – December 31, 1991

IMPORTANT FACTS

- The 44-year nuclear standoff between the United States and the USSR ended peacefully with the Soviet Union dissolving into many countries and politically switching to a democratic structure.

- Largest benefits: Many military technologies transferred to private sector, large increases in worldwide trade between former adversaries, and the world economy primarily functioning by free-market capitalism.

- Estimated cost: $8 trillion.

- Other event—Recession.

"Just days after the dissolution of the Soviet Union, Boris Yeltsin resolved to embark on a program of radical economic reform, with the aim of restructuring Russia's economic system— converting the world's largest socialist planned economy into a market-oriented capitalist one."

Wikipedia.com—2007

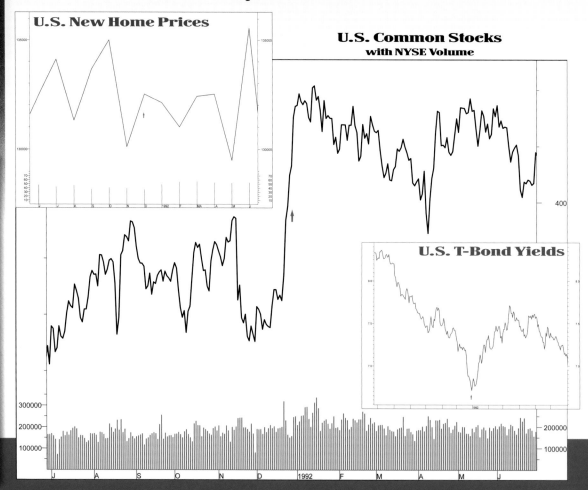

"We didn't win the Cold War, we were just a big bank that bankrupted a smaller bank because we had an arms race that wiped the Russians out."
Norman Mailer, Journalist—1996

"From 1949 to 1989, the top defense firms
outperformed the stock market by a huge margin.
An investor who held a portfolio of top defense stocks
during those four decades would have earned
2.4 times more than one who invested
an equal amount in a diversified portfolio."

Depression, War, and Cold War, R. Higgs—2006

INVESTMENT PERFORMANCE			
	Price	% Chg 6 months	% Chg 1 yr
Common Stocks ($)	417.1	(2%)	5%
T-Bond Interest Rates (%)	6.7%	6%	0%
New Homes ($)	132,500	na	3%

USSR
Government
Bond
early 1980s

Map of Iron Curtain

**Berlin Wall
photo by NATO**

PEACEFUL ACHIEVMENTS SUMMARY

The achievements listed below rank among the world's great accomplishments and America's mark on history. Though many of these endeavors were greeted by roaring crowds and ticker tape parades, stocks declined for six months following these events within an environment of raising interest rates and a mixed real estate market.

Sometimes the market's inverted logic is hard to understand. Take the years 1968 and 1969, and how investment markets reacted to them. By any measure, 1968 was a terrible year, with nationwide riots, political assassinations, and the realization that America was going to lose a war for the first time. Editorials of the time expressed the belief that our country was going to rip itself apart. Yet, through this turbulence, stocks and real estate increased 8% and 19% that year.

With a new popular president, the first troop withdrawals from Vietnam, and the crowning achievement of exceeding President Kennedy's goal of "landing a man on the moon before this decade is out," one would have thought that an improved American mood in 1969 would have translated into investment profits. Not the case! Both stocks and new homes suffered large loses and interest rates increased 27%.

Investors need to remember that history has repeatedly shown that what makes the cover of a magazine or a website's homepage isn't necessarily important to the financial markets.

EVENTS	DATE	DESCRIPTION (What is it? What did it do?)	Common Stocks Price	1 week After	% Chg	6 months Before	% Chg	6 months After	% Chg	1-Year After	% Chg	% Rates	6 months Before	% Chg	6 months After	% Chg	1-Year After	% Chg	Real Estate Prices	1-Year After	% Chg
Transcontinental Railroad Completed	5/10/1869	1,777 miles of railroad through West's mountain ranges linked all of the U.S. Considered by many the greatest technological feat of the 19th century. Other Factor—Fisk-Gould gold market scandal	3.66	na		3.26	-11%	3.44	-6%	3.72	2%	4.98	5.29	6%	5.12	3%	5.14	3%	1,380	1,254	-9%
Panama Canal Opens	8/15/1914	A 48-mile canal through Panama connected the Atlantic and Pacific Oceans and reduced the distance needed to travel from the East Coast to the West Coast of the U.S. by 59%. Other Factor—World War I	6.24	na		7.26	16%	4.98	-20%	7.10	14%	3.60	3.61	0%	3.60	0%	3.62	1%	2,443	2,560	5%
Hoover Dam Opens	10/26/1936	One of the largest dams in the U.S. A major factor for electric power, water storage, and flood control of the Colorado River for the fast-growing Southwestern states. Other Factor—Great Depression	16.65	17.17	3%	14.25	-14%	16.16	-3%	11.74	-30%	2.63	2.67	2%	2.79	6%	2.75	5%	5,346	5,144	-4%
Golden Gate Bridge Opens	5/27/1937	This bridge over San Francisco Bay was the longest suspension bridge of its time. It is an important traffic artery for America's financial center of the West. Other Factor—Great Depression	16.26	15.96	-2%	17.34	7%	10.67	-34%	9.28	-43%	2.75	2.51	-9%	2.69	-2%	2.51	-9%	5,341	5,144	-4%
Apollo 11 Moon Landing	7/20/1969	The first of six landings on the moon by human beings. It is widely recognized as one of the defining moments in human history. Other Factor—Vietnam War	93.52	90.21	-4%	101.69	9%	89.83	-4%	77.78	-17%	6.66	5.95	-11%	7.72	16%	7.45	12%	27,541	23,535	-15%
Cold War Ends	12/31/1991	The 44-year nuclear weapons standoff with the USSR ended peacefully with the Communist Soviet Union dissolving and placing most of the world under a free-market economy. Other Factor—Recession	417.10	418.00	0%	371.20	-11%	408.10	-2%	435.71	5%	6.71	8.26	23%	7.14	6%	6.68	-0%	132,500	136,100	3%
HISTORY SUMMARY																					
Best and Worst of Times!	1968 and 1969	1968: Tet Offensive (lost Vietnam War), assassination of Dr. Martin Luther King Jr. and Robert F. Kennedy	96.47							103.86	8%	5.70					6.21	9%	22,784	27,224	20%
		1969: Popular new president, troop withdrawals begin, exceed nation's moon landing goal	103.86							92.06	-11%	6.21					7.88	27%	27,224	25,801	-5%

Best Performance
Worst Performance

TICKER TAPE PARADE ≠ BULL MARKET

INVESTING THE HISTORICAL WAY

The focus of this book has been on the "big picture" of investing. This section focuses on putting this knowledge to work regardless of differing philosophies of investment selection (fundamental, technical, growth, value, etc.). In other words, the items discussed in the following pages are required for you to be a successful user of investment history, not a victim of it in the future!

Like an iceberg, the tip of investing is simply placing a buy or sell order. The real size and scale of the investment process should be a logical, consistent strategy tailor-made for the individual investor, which governs what, when, and how much to invest under a given set of historical circumstances.

A solid investment strategy requires the following:

Ken Winans, putting history to work in 1997!

SET REALISTIC GOALS and SENSIBLE ASSET ALLOCATIONS

A good game plan will more than likely lead to good results and that starts with setting a realistic long-term performance goal based on historical facts. Look at TABLE A—it provides average annual returns for seven different types of investments since 1850.

Notice that the words "quarterly performance" are nowhere to be found!

As the developer of market indexes (Winans International Preferred Stock Index (WIPSI)™ and Winans International Real Estate Index (WIREI)™), I know firsthand the pitfalls of managing portfolios based solely on quarterly comparisons to popular market benchmarks.

Ironically, many people who call themselves "long-term investors" blindly misuse these market indexes in quarterly head-to-head comparisons, and rapidly make asset allocation changes as if it were some kind of quarter horse race.

Worse yet, most investors don't know the basic assumptions used in calculating these indexes, and thus don't really know how best to use these marvelous tools.

For example, bond indexes are as "different as night and day" to stock market benchmarks and are not conducive to apples-to-apples comparisons. Unlike exchange-traded stocks, many of the investments used in bond indexes don't trade every day,

so price distortions within these fixed-income indexes can occur. It is also important to note that most bond indexes incorporate the interest payments only when they are paid, and not all the income that will be earned by the end of the year.

Because ignorance about index calculation methods can lead to false conclusions about true investment performance, it is wise to monitor several different types of indexes, from different sources, to reach realistic conclusions about an investment.

Remember, quarterly comparisons of investment performance with market benchmarks are not really useful to long-term investors, and should take a minimal role in the investment evaluation process.

TABLE A

Performance Summary Table (12/31/2007)							
	Average Annual Returns*					A $1 investment in 1900 is as of 12/31/2007	
	1850	1900	1950	1975	2000	Nominal	Inflation Adj.
GROWTH INVESTMENTS							
U.S. Common Stocks (+ Dividends)	11.1%	12.0%	12.9%	14.3%	2.7%	$24,508.00	$809.80
U.S. Homes (new, 40% Owner Equity)	7.9%	8.2%	10.6%	9.5%	6.1%	$313.20	$13.70
Commodities (20% Investor Equity)	4.5%	6.0%	5.6%	4.3%	14.4%	$8.00	$0.30
INCOME INVESTMENTS							
U.S. Preferred Stocks	na	7.4%	7.2%	11.2%	8.9%	$1,358.70	$42.20
U.S. Corporate Bonds	na	6.4%	7.2%	9.9%	6.6%	$589.20	$18.90
INTEREST AND INFLATION RATES							
10-Year T-Bonds	4.7%	4.8%	6.2%	7.4%	4.5%	$147.80	$5.10
3-Month T-Bills	4.2%	3.8%	5.0%	5.9%	3.0%	$56.60	$1.90
Inflation Rate	2.3%	3.1%	3.8%	4.5%	2.9%	na	na
* Investments purchased at beginning of year; no income reinvestment							

Time Frame Used for Goal Setting—Assuming no major changes in an investor's finances, it is common practice to set investment goals for a 5- to 10-year time horizon.

Realistically, most investors don't know enough about their future finances to establish a meaningful investment strategy beyond five years. This means that an investor who invests over the next 25 years will have five different five-year investment strategies. Like a long journey, where adjustments are made for direction and speed as more information is gathered during the trip, each new goal incorporates the success or failure of the previous investment campaigns.

Statistics to Use—One way to establish long-term performance goals is to take an investment's average annual return from different periods of time.

For example, TABLE A shows the total returns of U.S. common stocks over different time frames. By simply taking the average returns since 1900, a reasonable five-year benchmark for common stocks would be an average annual return of 10.5% (52.5% for a five-year total).

Asset Allocation (a.k.a. Investment Mix)—TABLE B shows performance projections based on different percentages of stocks and corporate bonds within a single portfolio.

An investor with $1,000,000 to invest faces several choices:

CAPITAL APPRECIATION (100% IN STOCKS)

- A 92% chance of achieving a 10.5% average annual return
- $105,000 in projected annual profits ($86,600 is expected from price appreciation and $18,400 from dividend income)

TABLE B

5-Year Portfolio Performance Goal and Asset Allocation Projections: 2007									Taxes	
Performance Since 1900				Average Annual Goal	Success Probabilities	Cumulative Goal Average		Beginning Amount	After-Tax LT Capital Gains Tax	Ordinary Income Tax
Growth Investments				10.5%	92%	52.5%				
Income Investments				7.5%	96%	37.5%		$1,000,000	15%	30%
Stock Amount	Stock Asset Allocation	Bond Amount	Bond Asset Allocation	Pretax Portfolio Goal	Portfolio Success Probabilities	Average Annual Return $	Capital Gains $	Income $	Capital Gains $	Income $
$1,000,000	100%	$0	0%	10.5%	92%	$105,000	$86,600	$18,400	$73,610	$12,880
$500,000	50%	$500,000	50%	9.0%	94%	$90,000	$52,500	$37,500	$44,625	$26,250
$0	0%	$1,000,000	100%	7.5%	96%	$75,000	$0	$75,000	$0	$52,500

NOTES
Investments bought 12/31 of the previous year.
Any realized profits qualify for long-term capital gains.
Commission costs not included.
Probabilities are based on the % of time for consecutive negative years.

BALANCED (50% STOCKS & 50% BONDS)

- A 94% chance of achieving a 9.0% average annual return
- $90,000 in projected annual profits ($52,500 is expected from price appreciation, and $37,500 from bond interest payments and stock dividends)

INCOME (100% IN BONDS)

- A 96% chance of achieving a 7.5% average annual return
- $75,000 in projected profits, with all income paid on a predetermined schedule ($552,500 after tax)
- All bonds have a pre-established value, if held to maturity date

To the novice investor who simply looks at the highest return possible, the choice is simple—invest in 100% common stocks—full speed ahead!

Hold it! Other factors need to be considered to meet ALL of an investor's expectations:

A need for greater certainty of return—Though it is common for the investment community to set an investor's asset allocation based mainly on age, an investor's personality and temperament have more to do with the investment mix of a portfolio than merely their seniority.

Many people, regardless of their education and background, simply can't handle high investment uncertainty and will panic and abandon a time-tested investment strategy at the first signs of trouble. Based on the 157-year historical fact that U.S. common stocks have negative years 28% of the time, bond investments (with predetermined interest payments, par values, and maturity dates) offer an attractive long-term investment choice to low-risk investors.

What type of portfolio profit is needed?— For investors who need to regularly withdraw funds from a portfolio, the type of investment profits is an important consideration.

In a portfolio 100% invested in stocks, most of the expected profits are in the form of capital gains that would require the selling of an investment or borrowing on margin for an investor to access the needed funds. Furthermore, because stocks historically have negative years 28% of the time, there would probably be instances when a stock investor would need to withdraw funds when his/her portfolio is at a temporary low point, thereby selling investments at less-than-opportune times.

On the other hand, a bond portfolio's profits are in the form of income that comes in at regular, predictable intervals and can be accessed without changing the portfolio's holdings.

Taxes—Historically, the government has treated profits generated by investments differently, in that interest income is typically taxed at a higher level than gains realized by selling a profitable investment (as seen in TABLE B).

This might require bonds to be kept in tax-deferred retirement accounts, or use some of the time-tested techniques to minimize taxes, such as using municipal bonds, tax loss selling, bond swaps, and amortizing premiums.

Investment strategy and tax planning need to go hand in hand for the best investment results!

Finally, it can be said that there is no such thing as a single best goal and asset allocation! What is important is to set a course of action that the investor can follow with confidence. Without a realistic expectation of performance, there cannot be the discipline required to take profits in an "easy money" bull market or aggressively purchase bargains during the financial carnage in a bear market.

EXECUTING THE INVESTMENT GAME PLAN

Once the five-year goal and asset allocation have been set, the job of constructing the portfolio begins.

Regardless of investment philosophy, investors must pay attention to the investment environment. This is the job of market analysis.

Buying new investments can be like trying to cross a busy intersection during rush hour in a new car you're not very familiar with—you need to pay real attention to the traffic signals to avoid an accident.

Market analysis has to answer one simple question: "Is it a bull or bear market?" When to buy (or sell) can be as important as what to buy (or sell), and market analysis provides insight about the current investing climate and possible economic threats in the near future.

Patience isn't often discussed in the investment process, because it doesn't generate fees and commissions. But it's important not to rush the construction of a portfolio when market conditions are not right, and investment prices don't meet the investor's buy parameters.

Take corporate income investments. They can vary in availability and valuation, and it can take up to 90 days to finish the portfolio construction process during normal economic conditions.

An analogy I find most useful in describing the first year of owning an income portfolio is building a new apartment building: (1) You have to pay to have the building built before rental income is received (e.g., transaction costs, accrued interest, etc.). (2) It takes time to find good tenants, so the building is usually not 100% occupied when completed (i.e., availability of income investments to purchase). (3) Because tenants will move in at different times, they pay rent at different times and amounts based on type of rental agreement (i.e., income investments pay different amounts of interest and dividends at various times).

Keep in mind that the performance clock starts ticking AFTER the portfolio construction phase, so don't start comparing the returns of a new portfolio to a goal until at least one full year after the portfolio is initially built or reconstructed!

Finally, investment discipline separates a truly successful investor from an individual who randomly puts in buy and sell orders based on "dinner party tips." Remember that investing doesn't have to be all or nothing, so be fully invested when your market analysis tools give you a green light.

Cartoon—1995

215

MONITORING AN INVESTMENT PORTFOLIO

Once a portfolio is constructed, it needs to be monitored and periodically evaluated. Reliable information is needed to properly monitor a portfolio. Unfortunately, today's investors have to deal with two significant problems:

- "Information overload" caused by a continuous stream of data that can be too short-term to be of any real use.
- Despite an abundance of timely information on stocks and commodities, there is a lack of such information on various types of bonds, preferred stocks, collectibles, and even real estate.

So, to properly monitor the health of a portfolio and evaluate its performance to the goals established, an investor has to obtain a report that answers the following questions:

General Issues

- Does it list the portfolio's five-year performance goal, and provide the annual and cumulative returns to show if the portfolio is on track with the established long-term goals?
- Does the report include all accounts the portfolio's assets are held in, as well as all annual deposits and withdrawals made by the investor?
- Does it show the targeted asset allocation versus actual allocation?
- Does it break down diversification by investment type, issuer, capitalization and industry, maturity, and agency ratings?
- Does it show position buy size versus the actual size of each investment in the portfolio to measure individual investment exposure for rebalancing purposes?
- Does it list the total amount of transaction activity?

Bonds and Preferred Stocks

- Does it show market value versus maturity value of the bond investments?
- Does it show a schedule of maturity and call dates, so reinvestment of proceeds can be planned?
- Does it show Average Annual Yield or Yield to Maturity for income estimation?

Leverage, Hedges, and Short Sales

- Does it show the amount of leverage and/or short sales being used, and the level of interest being paid on the margin?
- Does it show what percentage of the portfolio's market value is being hedged, and when the hedge expires?

Taxes and Costs

- Does it show the investor's annual taxes for income and capital gains?
- Does it show all portfolio-related costs (brokerage, advisory, sales loads, etc.) during the current year?

Remember, monitoring a portfolio involves more than simply checking the market value from a brokerage statement or website, and it is highly recommended that a portfolio be evaluated no more than quarterly and only when the investment markets are not open.

A Recommended Portfolio
in a Magazine of Wall Street—
1928

PORTFOLIO REBALANCING

Wall Street Roller Coaster
This can happen to any investment, anytime!

Investment portfolios are like plants in that they are constantly changing their size and shape. Growth is considered healthy, and there are times when they both need to be "pruned" to enhance future overall growth and prevent broken limbs from damaging the root system.

In the case of investment portfolios, periodic rebalancing involves selling part of a position that has grown much larger than the average-size investment, and reinvesting the proceeds into other investments to restore proper diversification to the portfolio.

If a portfolio is being monitored properly, then the larger positions should be easy to spot on a report. Rebalancing can be done in a logical, systematic fashion. For example, when a stock position becomes twice the size of an average-size position in the portfolio, it is reduced in size by 50%.

The key objective is to keep the portfolio properly diversified and minimize the risk of large positions harming the performance of the overall portfolio. Rotation is also done for tax reasons at year-end. If investors need capital losses to offset capital gains, then investments currently showing a loss are sold, with new investments bought immediately.

Though it is common to identify investments as core holdings, every investment should have a high price in which an investor is willing to realize significant profits by selling a portion of the position. Love your friends and family, but don't love your investments! Does the chart on this page look familiar? We have all witnessed star-performing investments tank in bear markets, in which high levels of profit evaporate quickly. Rebalancing will help to prevent this from happening.

As a final note, the process of creating an investment strategy, executing that strategy, monitoring the portfolio's progress, and rebalancing to keep the portfolio diversified is time-intensive, continuous work. Due to the time and knowledge required, many investors have elected to retain the services of a "money manager" or investment advisor to oversee the investment process. But the investor still needs to be actively involved in the important process of setting a realistic goal and periodically reviewing the portfolio in light of that goal.

Simply put, investor participation is required to be successful.

FINAL THOUGHTS

This landmark reference book has been designed to help an investor build and maintain a strong foundation based on historical financial facts. An investor can refer to *Investment Atlas* during a future calamity for clues to investment trends, or to find out the performance record of various types of investments (stocks, real estate, bonds, commodities, collectibles, and cash) over the past 200 years.

This book was broken into five sections:

There's Gold in Them Financial Hills!

This examined the spectacular growth of the U.S. economy and major developments of investing that have allowed investors, big and small, to amass wealth at rates never seen before in world history.

Time-Tested Investments

Here we studied the basic characteristics of six different types of investments since 1800. Unlike many investment books that view only one type of investment in a vacuum, this section included stocks, real estate, bonds, commodities, collectibles, and cash in combined studies. It showed that investors must follow the historical trends to know the advantages and disadvantages of these investments over time.

Market Cycles—From Easy Money to Crash Landings

This section examined major bull and bear markets since 1850, and demonstrated how the tools outlined in the "Time-Tested Investments" section can provide the reader with early clues as to the market's overall health.

Historical Events—Does Wall Street Care?

We studied the reactions of stocks, housing, and interest rates to various factors and scenarios that have continuously confronted investors throughout history, such as wars, disasters (natural and man-made), and the never-ending government actions (i.e., interest rates, taxes, and regulations) in reaction to these situations.

Investing the Historical Way

This demonstrated ways to practically use historical information in establishing a disciplined investment strategy: (1) Set reasonable goals. (2) Effectively build a portfolio. (3) Use proper ways to monitor an investment portfolio's progress. (4) Use proper investment rebalancing to improve the performance of a portfolio.

As a final thought, this book has demonstrated the power of history, and that investors' knowledge of history's trends can help them successfully navigate the investment world over time. But current events and economic cycles have a way of masking their historic roots, and investors suffering from hubris will once again claim that it's different this time during the next bull market. That is another historical fact we can count on!

Be a Profitable User of Investment History—Not a Victim of It!
Kenneth G. Winans—2008

APPENDIXES

DISCLAIMER

Past performance should not be taken as representative of future results. Kenneth G. Winans will not be liable for any loss or damage caused by readers' reliance on the contents of this book, which is for informational and educational purposes only, and should not be considered investment advice.

These investments are not suitable for everyone, and a professional advisor should be consulted about the merits of the investments listed in this book before investing.

The contents in this book were derived from data provided by third parties. Though these sources are considered reliable, Kenneth G. Winans does not guarantee or warrant the accuracy, adequacy, or completeness of the data used in this book.

The formulas and calculations used in this book are considered reliable and cannot be guaranteed. Changes can be made without notice.

All tax information provided in this book is for informational purposes only. Anything tax-related should be discussed with your accountant before it is used for tax purposes.

The amounts, percentages, and any reference to individual securities are for illustration purposes only and do not reflect actual performance and are not an endorsement of the company by Kenneth G. Winans.

Kenneth G. Winans and/or associates and/or employees may have an interest in the securities herein described and may make purchases or sales of these securities without advance notice and at any time.

The opinions expressed in this book are solely those of Kenneth G. Winans and not those of Winans International.

U.S. COMMON STOCK

Date	Total Return %	Total Return Index	Inflation Rate	Adjusted Total Return	Adjusted Total Return Index
		1.0			1.0
1850	25.3%	1.3	2.2%	23.2%	1.2
1851	4.6%	1.3	-2.1%	6.7%	1.3
1852	26.9%	1.7	1.1%	25.8%	1.7
1853	-5.8%	1.6	0.0%	-5.8%	1.6
1854	-20.5%	1.2	8.6%	-29.1%	1.1
1855	7.1%	1.3	3.0%	4.1%	1.1
1856	10.7%	1.5	-1.9%	12.6%	1.3
1857	-20.0%	1.2	2.9%	-22.9%	1.0
1858	21.0%	1.4	-5.7%	26.7%	1.3
1859	-3.2%	1.4	1.0%	-4.2%	1.2
1860	17.9%	1.6	0.0%	17.9%	1.4
1861	3.5%	1.7	6.0%	-2.5%	1.4
1862	61.2%	2.7	14.2%	47.1%	2.0
1863	43.5%	3.9	24.8%	18.7%	2.4
1864	12.5%	4.4	25.2%	-12.7%	2.1
1865	-2.4%	4.3	3.7%	-6.1%	2.0
1866	10.4%	4.7	-2.6%	13.0%	2.3
1867	8.0%	5.1	-6.8%	14.8%	2.6
1868	17.3%	6.0	-3.9%	21.3%	3.1
1869	8.3%	6.5	-4.1%	12.4%	3.5
1870	12.2%	7.3	-4.3%	16.5%	4.1
1871	13.2%	8.3	-6.4%	19.5%	4.9
1872	13.0%	9.3	0.0%	13.0%	5.5
1873	-6.2%	8.7	-2.0%	-4.2%	5.3
1874	9.9%	9.6	-4.9%	14.8%	6.1
1875	2.5%	9.9	-3.7%	6.2%	6.5
1876	-11.2%	8.7	-2.3%	-9.0%	5.9
1877	-4.0%	8.4	-2.3%	-1.6%	5.8
1878	11.6%	9.4	-4.8%	16.4%	6.7
1879	48.6%	13.9	0.0%	48.6%	10.0
1880	23.8%	17.2	2.5%	21.3%	12.1
1881	8.2%	18.6	0.0%	8.2%	13.1
1882	2.5%	19.1	0.0%	2.5%	13.5
1883	-2.8%	18.6	-1.6%	-1.2%	13.3
1884	-12.8%	16.2	-2.5%	-10.4%	11.9
1885	25.5%	20.3	-1.7%	27.2%	15.2
1886	12.7%	22.9	-2.6%	15.3%	17.5
1887	-2.1%	22.4	0.9%	-2.9%	17.0
1888	1.8%	22.8	0.0%	1.8%	17.3

Date	Total Return %	Total Return Index	Inflation Rate	Adjusted Total Return	Adjusted Total Return Index
1889	7.7%	24.6	-2.6%	10.3%	19.1
1890	-9.4%	22.3	-1.8%	-7.6%	17.6
1891	21.6%	27.1	0.0%	21.6%	21.4
1892	6.2%	28.8	0.0%	6.2%	22.8
1893	-15.5%	24.3	-0.9%	-14.5%	19.4
1894	2.4%	24.9	-4.6%	7.0%	20.8
1895	5.0%	26.2	-1.9%	6.9%	22.2
1896	5.6%	27.6	0.0%	5.5%	23.5
1897	26.4%	34.9	-1.0%	27.4%	29.9
1898	26.6%	44.2	0.0%	26.6%	37.9
1899	12.7%	49.8	0.0%	12.7%	42.7
1900	11.9%	55.7	1.0%	10.9%	47.3
1901	-4.2%	53.4	1.0%	-5.2%	44.9
1902	3.7%	55.3	1.0%	2.7%	46.1
1903	-19.5%	44.5	2.9%	-22.4%	35.8
1904	46.3%	65.2	0.9%	45.4%	52.0
1905	42.1%	92.6	-0.9%	43.0%	74.4
1906	2.2%	94.7	1.9%	0.3%	74.6
1907	-33.1%	63.3	4.6%	-37.8%	46.4
1908	52.4%	96.5	-1.8%	54.2%	71.6
1909	19.9%	116	-1.8%	21.7%	87.1
1910	-13.2%	100	4.6%	-17.7%	71.6
1911	5.5%	106	0.0%	5.5%	75.6
1912	12.9%	120	2.6%	10.2%	83.3
1913	-5.1%	113	1.7%	-6.9%	77.6
1914	-25.7%	84	0.8%	-26.6%	57.0
1915	87.5%	158	0.8%	86.6%	106
1916	1.8%	161	7.4%	-5.6%	100
1917	-14.5%	138	17.7%	-32.2%	68.1
1918	18.4%	163	17.7%	0.8%	68.6
1919	37.3%	223	15.0%	22.3%	83.8
1920	-27.1%	163	15.9%	-43.0%	47.7
1921	19.2%	194	-10.8%	30.0%	62.1
1922	28.7%	250	-6.5%	35.3%	84.0
1923	2.7%	257	2.0%	0.7%	84.6
1924	32.4%	340	0.0%	32.4%	112
1925	35.7%	461	2.9%	32.8%	149
1926	5.8%	488	0.5%	5.4%	157
1927	34.6%	657	-1.4%	36.0%	213
1928	42.6%	938	-1.4%	44.1%	307

Date	Total Return %	Total Return Index	Inflation Rate	Adjusted Total Return	Adjusted Total Return Index
1929	-8.0%	862	0.0%	-8.0%	282
1930	-24.0%	656	-2.4%	-21.5%	222
1931	-42.0%	380	-9.0%	-33.0%	148
1932	-9.1%	346	-10.4%	1.3%	150
1933	52.8%	528	-4.9%	57.7%	237
1934	-1.6%	519	3.2%	-4.9%	226
1935	46.5%	761	2.5%	44.0%	325
1936	33.1%	1,013	1.2%	31.9%	428
1937	-34.0%	669	3.6%	-37.6%	267
1938	29.7%	867	-1.7%	31.5%	351
1939	-0.5%	863	-1.8%	1.3%	356
1940	-9.8%	779	1.2%	-11.0%	317
1941	-11.2%	692	4.8%	-15.9%	267
1942	19.0%	823	10.8%	8.2%	288
1943	25.5%	1,034	6.2%	19.4%	344
1944	19.2%	1,232	1.5%	17.7%	406
1945	35.6%	1,671	2.4%	33.2%	540
1946	-8.0%	1,538	8.4%	-16.3%	452
1947	5.5%	1,623	14.6%	-9.1%	411
1948	5.6%	1,714	7.9%	-2.2%	402
1949	17.7%	2,017	-1.0%	18.7%	477
1950	29.9%	2,620	1.1%	28.8%	614
1951	23.0%	3,222	7.6%	15.3%	709
1952	17.6%	3,788	2.3%	15.3%	817
1953	-1.1%	3,745	1.0%	-2.1%	800
1954	51.1%	5,660	0.3%	50.8%	1,207
1955	31.0%	7,415	-0.3%	31.3%	1,585
1956	6.5%	7,898	1.6%	5.0%	1,663
1957	-10.4%	7,075	3.4%	-13.8%	1,434
1958	42.3%	10,065	3.0%	39.3%	1,997
1959	11.8%	11,251	0.6%	11.2%	2,221
1960	0.4%	11,299	1.7%	-1.3%	2,192
1961	26.5%	14,296	1.1%	25.4%	2,749
1962	-8.7%	13,051	1.1%	-9.8%	2,479
1963	22.4%	15,974	1.1%	21.3%	3,006
1964	16.3%	18,572	1.4%	14.9%	3,454
1965	12.3%	20,850	1.6%	10.6%	3,822
1966	-10.0%	18,767	2.9%	-12.9%	3,328
1967	23.6%	23,194	2.8%	20.8%	4,019
1968	10.9%	25,713	4.3%	6.6%	4,284

Date	Total Return %	Total Return Index	Inflation Rate	Adjusted Total Return	Adjusted Total Return Index
1969	-8.3%	23,589	5.3%	-13.6%	3,704
1970	3.6%	24,435	5.9%	-2.4%	3,617
1971	14.1%	27,877	4.3%	9.8%	3,970
1972	18.7%	33,103	3.3%	15.4%	4,583
1973	-13.3%	28,711	6.2%	-19.5%	3,691
1974	-24.0%	21,813	11.1%	-35.1%	2,394
1975	36.2%	29,702	9.0%	27.2%	3,045
1976	23.7%	36,756	5.8%	18.0%	3,593
1977	-5.8%	34,623	6.6%	-12.4%	3,147
1978	7.0%	37,033	7.6%	-0.6%	3,127
1979	18.5%	43,888	11.3%	7.2%	3,353
1980	31.2%	57,565	13.5%	17.7%	3,946
1981	-3.0%	55,825	10.4%	-13.4%	3,418
1982	20.0%	66,963	6.2%	13.8%	3,889
1983	21.7%	81,481	3.2%	18.5%	4,608
1984	5.9%	86,288	4.4%	1.5%	4,678
1985	29.6%	111,808	3.5%	26.0%	5,896
1986	18.3%	132,321	1.9%	16.5%	6,868
1987	5.4%	139,503	3.7%	1.8%	6,989
1988	16.0%	161,825	4.1%	11.9%	7,820
1989	30.5%	211,101	4.8%	25.6%	9,825
1990	-2.9%	205,065	5.4%	-8.2%	9,014
1991	28.7%	263,933	4.2%	24.5%	11,222
1992	7.5%	283,633	3.0%	4.5%	11,722
1993	9.6%	310,735	3.0%	6.6%	12,492
1994	1.4%	314,963	2.6%	-1.2%	12,337
1995	36.6%	430,273	2.8%	33.9%	16,514
1996	22.4%	526,498	3.0%	19.4%	19,718
1997	32.7%	698,699	2.4%	30.4%	25,704
1998	28.3%	896,221	1.5%	26.8%	32,582
1999	20.4%	1,079,283	2.2%	18.2%	38,517
2000	-9.6%	975,587	3.4%	-13.0%	33,515
2001	-11.8%	860,346	2.9%	-14.7%	28,597
2002	-21.5%	675,036	1.6%	-23.1%	21,986
2003	28.2%	865,200	2.0%	26.2%	27,742
2004	10.7%	957,721	3.5%	7.2%	29,732
2005	4.8%	1,003,822	3.5%	1.4%	30,134
2006	15.4%	1,158,496	2.0%	13.4%	34,184
2007	5.3%	1,220,360	4.2%	1.1%	34,560
Average	11.1%		2.3%	8.8%	
Median	10.6%		1.6%	8.2%	
High	87.5%		25.2%	86.6%	
Low	-42.0%		-10.8%	-43.0%	

223

U.S. PREFERRED STOCK

Date	Total Return %	Total Return Index	Inflation Rate	Adjusted Total Return	Adjusted Total Return Index
		1.00			1.00
1900	26.5%	1.26	1.0%	25.5%	1.25
1901	30.0%	1.64	1.0%	29.0%	1.62
1902	7.4%	1.76	1.0%	6.4%	1.72
1903	-11.0%	1.57	2.9%	-13.9%	1.48
1904	24.7%	1.96	0.9%	23.8%	1.84
1905	12.0%	2.19	-0.9%	12.9%	2.07
1906	-1.5%	2.16	1.9%	-3.4%	2.00
1907	-22.5%	1.68	4.6%	-27.1%	1.46
1908	37.3%	2.30	-1.8%	39.1%	2.03
1909	13.5%	2.61	-1.8%	15.3%	2.34
1910	-0.4%	2.60	4.6%	-5.0%	2.22
1911	6.7%	2.78	0.1%	6.6%	2.37
1912	5.9%	2.94	2.6%	3.3%	2.45
1913	2.6%	3.02	1.7%	0.9%	2.47
1914	6.8%	3.22	0.8%	6.0%	2.62
1915	12.8%	3.64	0.8%	11.9%	2.93
1916	7.8%	3.92	7.4%	0.4%	2.94
1917	-6.1%	3.68	17.7%	-23.7%	2.24
1918	13.9%	4.19	17.7%	-3.8%	2.16
1919	8.5%	4.55	15.0%	-6.5%	2.02
1920	-2.6%	4.44	15.9%	-18.5%	1.65
1921	15.0%	5.10	-10.8%	25.8%	2.07
1922	14.8%	5.86	-6.5%	21.4%	2.51
1923	3.7%	6.07	2.0%	1.7%	2.56
1924	9.4%	6.65	0.1%	9.3%	2.80
1925	8.3%	7.20	2.9%	5.3%	2.95
1926	9.0%	7.85	0.5%	8.5%	3.20
1927	10.6%	8.68	-1.4%	12.0%	3.58
1928	11.0%	9.63	-1.4%	12.5%	4.03
1929	6.1%	10.23	0.1%	6.0%	4.27

Date	Total Return %	Total Return Index	Inflation Rate	Adjusted Total Return	Adjusted Total Return Index
1930	5.6%	10.80	-2.4%	8.1%	4.62
1931	-10.8%	9.63	-9.0%	-1.8%	4.53
1932	8.4%	10.44	-10.4%	18.8%	5.38
1933	6.8%	11.15	-4.9%	11.7%	6.01
1934	22.5%	13.66	3.2%	19.3%	7.18
1935	17.0%	15.98	2.5%	14.5%	8.21
1936	8.1%	17.28	1.2%	6.9%	8.78
1937	0.0%	17.28	3.6%	-3.6%	8.47
1938	11.7%	19.31	-1.7%	13.4%	9.60
1939	5.1%	20.29	-1.8%	6.9%	10.26
1940	8.5%	22.01	1.2%	7.3%	11.01
1941	-1.3%	21.71	4.8%	-6.1%	10.34
1942	3.2%	22.40	10.0%	-6.8%	9.63
1943	6.1%	23.77	6.2%	-0.0%	9.63
1944	11.2%	26.44	1.5%	9.8%	10.57
1945	12.0%	29.62	2.4%	9.6%	11.59
1946	-1.5%	29.17	8.4%	-9.9%	10.44
1947	-4.6%	27.84	14.6%	-19.1%	8.44
1948	3.0%	28.69	7.9%	-4.8%	8.04
1949	11.2%	31.89	-1.0%	12.2%	9.02
1950	3.0%	32.84	1.1%	1.9%	9.19
1951	-6.1%	30.85	7.6%	-13.7%	7.93
1952	9.3%	33.72	2.3%	7.0%	8.49
1953	2.2%	34.45	1.0%	1.2%	8.59
1954	10.8%	38.18	0.3%	10.5%	9.50
1955	0.8%	38.47	-0.3%	1.1%	9.60
1956	-3.9%	36.97	1.6%	-5.5%	9.08
1957	4.5%	38.63	3.4%	1.1%	9.18
1958	0.2%	38.71	3.0%	-2.8%	8.92
1959	-1.2%	38.25	0.6%	-1.8%	8.76

Date	Total Return %	Total Return Index	Inflation Rate	Adjusted Total Return	Adjusted Total Return Index
1960	7.0%	40.92	1.7%	5.3%	9.23
1961	8.3%	44.34	1.1%	7.2%	9.89
1962	9.8%	48.70	1.1%	8.7%	10.75
1963	6.1%	51.65	1.1%	5.0%	11.29
1964	7.4%	55.49	1.4%	6.1%	11.97
1965	-2.0%	54.35	1.6%	-3.7%	11.53
1966	-9.8%	49.04	2.9%	-12.7%	10.07
1967	-6.6%	45.81	2.8%	-9.4%	9.12
1968	4.7%	47.98	4.3%	0.5%	9.16
1969	-10.1%	43.14	5.3%	-15.4%	7.75
1970	10.9%	47.85	5.9%	5.0%	8.14
1971	8.7%	52.03	4.3%	4.4%	8.50
1972	4.8%	54.52	3.3%	1.5%	8.63
1973	-5.4%	51.58	6.2%	-11.6%	7.63
1974	-3.0%	50.03	11.1%	-14.1%	6.55
1975	13.2%	56.63	9.0%	4.2%	6.83
1976	21.7%	68.93	5.8%	16.0%	7.91
1977	3.4%	71.27	6.6%	-3.2%	7.66
1978	-3.5%	68.79	7.6%	-11.1%	6.81
1979	-4.5%	65.68	11.3%	-15.8%	5.74
1980	-6.9%	61.12	13.5%	-20.4%	4.56
1981	7.2%	65.54	10.4%	-3.1%	4.42
1982	35.1%	88.52	6.2%	28.9%	5.70
1983	12.3%	99.42	3.2%	9.1%	6.22
1984	15.5%	114.79	4.4%	11.1%	6.91
1985	25.7%	144.28	3.5%	22.2%	8.44
1986	40.9%	203.31	1.9%	39.0%	11.73
1987	-1.9%	199.38	3.7%	-5.6%	11.08
1988	8.8%	216.93	4.1%	4.7%	11.60
1989	19.4%	259.01	4.8%	14.6%	13.29

Date	Total Return %	Total Return Index	Inflation Rate	Adjusted Total Return	Adjusted Total Return Index
1990	6.9%	276.93	5.4%	1.5%	13.49
1991	21.5%	336.60	4.2%	17.3%	15.83
1992	12.9%	379.98	3.0%	9.9%	17.39
1993	17.6%	446.72	3.0%	14.6%	19.93
1994	-9.5%	404.44	2.6%	-12.1%	17.52
1995	24.6%	504.08	2.8%	21.9%	21.36
1996	7.4%	541.14	3.0%	4.4%	22.29
1997	22.3%	661.65	2.4%	19.9%	26.73
1998	16.6%	771.23	1.5%	15.1%	30.76
1999	-8.5%	705.58	2.2%	-10.7%	27.46
2000	9.5%	772.89	3.4%	6.2%	29.15
2001	18.9%	918.82	2.9%	16.0%	33.82
2002	13.9%	1046.23	1.6%	12.3%	37.98
2003	16.8%	1221.57	2.0%	14.8%	43.59
2004	11.1%	1356.94	3.5%	7.6%	46.88
2005	2.0%	1383.70	3.5%	-1.5%	46.18
2006	8.6%	1502.34	2.0%	6.6%	49.23
2007	-9.6%	1358.66	4.2%	-13.8%	42.44
Average	7.4%		3.1%	4.3%	
Median	7.4%		2.7%	5.3%	
High	40.9%		17.7%	39.1%	
Low	-22.5%		-10.8%	-27.1%	

U.S. HOME PRICES (60% LEVERAGE)

Date	Total Return %	Total Return Index	Inflation Rate	Adjusted Total Return	Adjusted Total Return Index
		1.00			1
1850	17.3%	1.17	2.2%	15.1%	1.15
1851	16.9%	1.37	-2.1%	19.0%	1.37
1852	33.7%	1.83	1.1%	32.6%	1.82
1853	19.4%	2.19	0.0%	19.4%	2.17
1854	-20.6%	1.74	8.6%	-29.2%	1.54
1855	-39.4%	1.05	3.0%	-42.4%	0.89
1856	-11.0%	0.94	-1.9%	-9.1%	0.80
1857	-24.6%	0.71	2.9%	-27.5%	0.58
1858	-28.1%	0.51	-5.7%	-22.4%	0.45
1859	19.2%	0.61	1.0%	18.2%	0.53
1860	-27.5%	0.44	0.0%	-27.5%	0.39
1861	-25.7%	0.33	6.0%	-31.7%	0.26
1862	32.7%	0.43	14.2%	18.5%	0.31
1863	8.8%	0.47	24.8%	-16.0%	0.26
1864	59.4%	0.75	25.2%	34.2%	0.35
1865	37.5%	1.03	3.7%	33.8%	0.47
1866	42.1%	1.47	-2.6%	44.7%	0.68
1867	14.9%	1.68	-6.8%	21.7%	0.83
1868	-26.7%	1.23	-3.9%	-22.8%	0.64
1869	-14.6%	1.05	-4.1%	-10.5%	0.58
1870	-6.0%	0.99	-4.3%	-1.7%	0.57
1871	8.9%	1.08	-6.4%	15.3%	0.65
1872	-16.6%	0.90	0.0%	-16.6%	0.54
1873	-53.4%	0.42	-2.0%	-51.3%	0.26
1874	38.1%	0.58	-4.9%	42.9%	0.38
1875	22.9%	0.71	-3.7%	26.6%	0.48
1876	8.8%	0.77	-2.3%	11.0%	0.53
1877	-33.9%	0.51	-2.3%	-31.6%	0.36
1878	105.7%	1.05	-4.8%	110.4%	0.76
1879	98.4%	2.09	0.0%	98.4%	1.52
1880	91.7%	4.00	2.5%	89.2%	2.87
1881	-21.4%	3.14	0.0%	-21.5%	2.25
1882	11.0%	3.49	0.0%	11.0%	2.50
1883	-43.9%	1.96	-1.6%	-42.3%	1.44
1884	-19.1%	1.58	-2.5%	-16.6%	1.20
1885	-10.8%	1.41	-1.7%	-9.1%	1.09
1886	23.7%	1.75	-2.6%	26.3%	1.38
1887	-21.5%	1.37	0.9%	-22.4%	1.07
1888	-34.1%	0.90	0.0%	-34.1%	0.71
1889	15.8%	1.05	-2.6%	18.4%	0.84

Date	Total Return %	Total Return Index	Inflation Rate	Adjusted Total Return	Adjusted Total Return Index
1890	9.1%	1.14	-1.8%	10.9%	0.93
1891	-10.0%	1.03	0.0%	-10.0%	0.84
1892	0.8%	1.04	0.0%	0.8%	0.84
1893	-1.5%	1.02	-0.9%	-0.6%	0.84
1894	14.0%	1.16	-4.6%	18.6%	0.99
1895	28.9%	1.50	-1.9%	30.9%	1.30
1896	-24.8%	1.13	0.0%	-24.9%	0.98
1897	16.0%	1.31	-1.0%	17.0%	1.14
1898	37.9%	1.80	0.0%	37.9%	1.58
1899	62.9%	2.94	0.0%	62.9%	2.57
1900	-47.1%	1.55	1.0%	-48.1%	1.33
1901	31.5%	2.04	1.0%	30.5%	1.74
1902	-46.5%	1.09	1.0%	-47.5%	0.91
1903	20.5%	1.32	2.9%	17.6%	1.07
1904	35.0%	1.78	0.9%	34.0%	1.44
1905	32.5%	2.35	-0.9%	33.4%	1.92
1906	-30.4%	1.64	1.9%	-32.3%	1.30
1907	-24.8%	1.23	4.6%	-29.4%	0.92
1908	-16.5%	1.03	-1.8%	-14.7%	0.78
1909	47.5%	1.52	-1.8%	49.3%	1.17
1910	-14.4%	1.30	4.6%	-19.0%	0.95
1911	-16.8%	1.08	0.0%	-16.8%	0.79
1912	23.6%	1.34	2.6%	21.0%	0.95
1913	-6.0%	1.26	1.7%	-7.7%	0.88
1914	-8.2%	1.15	0.8%	-9.0%	0.80
1915	7.7%	1.24	0.8%	6.8%	0.85
1916	19.9%	1.49	7.4%	12.5%	0.96
1917	-15.7%	1.25	17.7%	-33.4%	0.64
1918	-14.3%	1.08	17.7%	-31.9%	0.44
1919	58.2%	1.70	15.0%	43.2%	0.62
1920	39.7%	2.38	15.9%	23.8%	0.77
1921	18.4%	2.81	-10.8%	29.2%	1.00
1922	7.9%	3.04	-6.5%	14.5%	1.14
1923	7.8%	3.27	2.0%	5.8%	1.21
1924	-0.5%	3.26	0.0%	-0.5%	1.20
1925	5.0%	3.42	2.9%	2.1%	1.23
1926	32.1%	4.52	0.5%	31.6%	1.62
1927	7.7%	4.87	-1.4%	9.1%	1.76
1928	30.5%	6.35	-1.4%	31.9%	2.33
1929	-5.3%	6.02	0.0%	-5.3%	2.20

Date	Total Return %	Total Return Index	Inflation Rate	Adjusted Total Return	Adjusted Total Return Index
1930	-17.5%	4.96	-2.4%	-15.1%	1.87
1931	-16.6%	4.14	-9.0%	-7.6%	1.73
1932	-69.8%	1.25	-10.4%	-59.4%	0.70
1933	106.7%	2.58	-4.9%	111.6%	1.49
1934	-45.7%	1.40	3.2%	-48.9%	0.76
1935	26.7%	1.78	2.5%	24.2%	0.94
1936	26.0%	2.24	1.2%	24.8%	1.17
1937	-6.0%	2.10	3.6%	-9.7%	1.06
1938	-21.5%	1.65	-1.7%	-19.8%	0.85
1939	19.6%	1.97	-1.8%	21.3%	1.03
1940	-16.3%	1.65	1.2%	-17.5%	0.85
1941	-14.0%	1.42	4.8%	-18.7%	0.69
1942	-2.5%	1.39	10.8%	-13.3%	0.60
1943	-15.0%	1.18	6.2%	-21.2%	0.47
1944	2.0%	1.20	1.5%	0.6%	0.48
1945	-15.7%	1.01	2.4%	-18.1%	0.39
1946	36.6%	1.38	8.4%	28.3%	0.50
1947	33.1%	1.84	14.6%	18.5%	0.59
1948	42.1%	2.62	7.9%	34.2%	0.80
1949	23.9%	3.24	-1.0%	24.9%	0.99
1950	-22.3%	2.52	1.1%	-23.3%	0.76
1951	61.2%	4.06	7.6%	53.5%	1.17
1952	-8.0%	3.73	2.3%	-10.3%	1.05
1953	21.2%	4.52	1.0%	20.3%	1.26
1954	16.1%	5.25	0.3%	15.7%	1.46
1955	34.8%	7.08	-0.3%	35.2%	1.98
1956	25.4%	8.88	1.6%	23.8%	2.45
1957	13.4%	10.07	3.4%	10.0%	2.69
1958	-14.8%	8.58	3.0%	-17.7%	2.21
1959	3.4%	8.87	0.6%	2.8%	2.28
1960	23.3%	10.94	1.7%	21.6%	2.77
1961	9.2%	11.95	1.1%	8.1%	2.99
1962	11.8%	13.36	1.1%	10.7%	3.31
1963	4.6%	13.98	1.1%	3.5%	3.43
1964	19.7%	16.73	1.4%	18.3%	4.06
1965	-5.4%	15.83	1.6%	-7.0%	3.77
1966	11.0%	17.57	2.9%	8.1%	4.08
1967	3.7%	18.22	2.8%	0.9%	4.11
1968	31.2%	23.90	4.3%	26.9%	5.22
1969	-8.4%	21.90	5.3%	-13.7%	4.50

Date	Total Return %	Total Return Index	Inflation Rate	Adjusted Total Return	Adjusted Total Return Index
1970	-17.9%	17.98	5.9%	-23.8%	3.43
1971	21.7%	21.88	4.3%	17.4%	4.03
1972	28.0%	28.01	3.3%	24.7%	5.02
1973	32.5%	37.11	6.2%	26.3%	6.34
1974	7.7%	39.97	11.1%	-3.4%	6.13
1975	22.5%	48.99	9.0%	13.6%	6.96
1976	15.5%	56.56	5.8%	9.7%	7.64
1977	22.9%	69.50	6.6%	16.3%	8.88
1978	24.7%	86.64	7.6%	17.1%	10.39
1979	8.5%	94.04	11.3%	-2.7%	10.11
1980	17.1%	110.09	13.5%	3.6%	10.47
1981	3.0%	113.41	10.4%	-7.3%	9.70
1982	7.6%	122.05	6.2%	1.5%	9.84
1983	9.3%	133.40	3.2%	6.1%	10.44
1984	6.7%	142.31	4.4%	2.3%	10.68
1985	17.8%	167.61	3.5%	14.2%	12.20
1986	16.4%	195.12	1.9%	14.6%	13.98
1987	25.5%	244.89	3.7%	21.8%	17.03
1988	13.4%	277.59	4.1%	9.2%	18.61
1989	6.4%	295.44	4.8%	1.6%	18.91
1990	0.5%	296.96	5.4%	-4.9%	17.99
1991	-8.8%	270.87	4.2%	-13.0%	15.65
1992	4.3%	282.64	3.0%	1.3%	15.86
1993	-0.5%	281.32	3.0%	-3.5%	15.31
1994	13.7%	319.79	2.6%	11.1%	17.01
1995	5.2%	336.46	2.8%	2.5%	17.42
1996	6.6%	358.59	3.0%	3.6%	18.05
1997	2.5%	367.64	2.4%	0.2%	18.09
1998	7.0%	393.43	1.5%	5.5%	19.08
1999	14.8%	451.73	2.2%	12.6%	21.49
2000	1.4%	458.03	3.4%	-2.0%	21.06
2001	16.8%	534.86	2.9%	13.9%	23.99
2002	10.4%	590.32	1.6%	8.8%	26.10
2003	5.3%	621.77	2.0%	3.3%	26.97
2004	22.8%	763.29	3.5%	19.2%	32.16
2005	4.6%	798.70	3.5%	1.2%	32.54
2006	5.4%	841.72	2.0%	3.4%	33.65
2007	-17.6%	693.64	4.2%	-21.8%	26.30
Average	7.9%		2.3%	5.7%	
Median	7.8%		1.6%	5.6%	
High	106.7%		25.2%	111.6%	
Low	-69.8%		-10.8%	-59.4%	

U.S. HOME PRICES (0%LEVERAGE)

Date	Total Return %	Total Return Index	Inflation Rate	Adjusted Total Return	Adjusted Total Return Index
		1.00			1
1850	10.8%	1.11	2.2%	8.6%	1.09
1851	10.5%	1.22	-2.1%	12.7%	1.22
1852	21.1%	1.48	1.1%	20.0%	1.47
1853	12.1%	1.66	0.0%	12.1%	1.65
1854	-12.8%	1.45	8.6%	-21.4%	1.29
1855	-24.6%	1.09	3.0%	-27.6%	0.94
1856	-6.9%	1.02	-1.9%	-5.0%	0.89
1857	-15.4%	0.86	2.9%	-18.3%	0.73
1858	-17.6%	0.71	-5.7%	-11.9%	0.64
1859	12.0%	0.79	1.0%	11.0%	0.71
1860	-17.2%	0.66	0.0%	-17.2%	0.59
1861	-16.1%	0.55	6.0%	-22.1%	0.46
1862	20.4%	0.66	14.2%	6.3%	0.49
1863	5.5%	0.70	24.8%	-19.3%	0.39
1864	37.1%	0.96	25.2%	11.9%	0.44
1865	23.5%	1.19	3.7%	19.8%	0.53
1866	26.3%	1.50	-2.6%	28.9%	0.68
1867	9.3%	1.64	-6.8%	16.1%	0.79
1868	-16.7%	1.36	-3.9%	-12.8%	0.69
1869	-9.1%	1.24	-4.1%	-5.0%	0.65
1870	-3.7%	1.19	-4.3%	0.5%	0.66
1871	5.6%	1.26	-6.4%	11.9%	0.74
1872	-10.4%	1.13	0.0%	-10.4%	0.66
1873	-33.4%	0.75	-2.0%	-31.3%	0.45
1874	23.8%	0.93	-4.9%	28.6%	0.58
1875	14.3%	1.07	-3.7%	18.0%	0.69
1876	5.5%	1.12	-2.3%	7.7%	0.74
1877	-21.2%	0.89	-2.3%	-18.9%	0.60
1878	66.0%	1.47	-4.8%	70.8%	1.03
1879	61.5%	2.37	0.0%	61.5%	1.66
1880	57.3%	3.73	2.5%	54.8%	2.56
1881	-13.4%	3.23	0.0%	-13.4%	2.22
1882	6.9%	3.46	0.0%	6.9%	2.37
1883	-27.4%	2.51	-1.6%	-25.8%	1.76
1884	-11.9%	2.21	-2.5%	-9.4%	1.59
1885	-6.8%	2.06	-1.7%	-5.1%	1.51
1886	14.8%	2.37	-2.6%	17.4%	1.78
1887	-13.5%	2.05	0.9%	-14.3%	1.52
1888	-21.3%	1.61	0.0%	-21.3%	1.20

Date	Total Return %	Total Return Index	Inflation Rate	Adjusted Total Return	Adjusted Total Return Index
1889	9.9%	1.77	-2.6%	12.5%	1.35
1890	5.7%	1.87	-1.8%	7.5%	1.45
1891	-6.2%	1.75	0.0%	-6.2%	1.36
1892	0.5%	1.76	0.0%	0.5%	1.37
1893	-1.0%	1.75	-0.9%	-0.0%	1.36
1894	8.7%	1.90	-4.6%	13.4%	1.55
1895	18.1%	2.24	-1.9%	20.0%	1.86
1896	-15.5%	1.89	0.0%	-15.5%	1.57
1897	10.0%	2.08	-1.0%	11.0%	1.74
1898	23.7%	2.58	0.0%	23.7%	2.15
1899	39.3%	3.59	0.0%	39.3%	3.00
1900	-29.4%	2.53	1.0%	-30.4%	2.09
1901	19.7%	3.03	1.0%	18.7%	2.48
1902	-29.1%	2.15	1.0%	-30.1%	1.73
1903	12.8%	2.43	2.9%	9.9%	1.90
1904	21.9%	2.96	0.9%	20.9%	2.30
1905	20.3%	3.56	-0.9%	21.2%	2.79
1906	-19.0%	2.88	1.9%	-20.9%	2.21
1907	-15.5%	2.44	4.6%	-20.1%	1.76
1908	-10.3%	2.18	-1.8%	-8.5%	1.61
1909	29.7%	2.83	-1.8%	31.5%	2.12
1910	-9.0%	2.58	4.6%	-13.6%	1.83
1911	-10.5%	2.31	0.0%	-10.5%	1.64
1912	14.8%	2.65	2.6%	12.1%	1.84
1913	-3.8%	2.55	1.7%	-5.5%	1.74
1914	-5.1%	2.42	0.8%	-6.0%	1.63
1915	4.8%	2.53	0.8%	4.0%	1.70
1916	12.5%	2.85	7.4%	5.0%	1.78
1917	-9.8%	2.57	17.7%	-27.5%	1.29
1918	-8.9%	2.34	17.7%	-26.6%	0.95
1919	36.4%	3.19	15.0%	21.4%	1.15
1920	24.8%	3.98	15.9%	8.9%	1.26
1921	11.5%	4.44	-10.8%	22.3%	1.54
1922	4.9%	4.66	-6.5%	11.5%	1.71
1923	4.9%	4.89	2.0%	2.9%	1.76
1924	-0.3%	4.87	0.0%	-0.3%	1.76
1925	3.1%	5.03	2.9%	0.2%	1.76
1926	20.1%	6.03	0.5%	19.6%	2.10
1927	4.8%	6.32	-1.4%	6.2%	2.23
1928	19.1%	7.53	-1.4%	20.5%	2.69

Date	Total Return %	Total Return Index	Inflation Rate	Adjusted Total Return	Adjusted Total Return Index
1929	-3.3%	7.28	0.0%	-3.3%	2.60
1930	-10.9%	6.48	-2.4%	-8.5%	2.38
1931	-10.4%	5.81	-9.0%	-1.4%	2.35
1932	-43.6%	3.27	-10.4%	-33.2%	1.57
1933	66.7%	5.46	-4.9%	71.6%	2.69
1934	-28.6%	3.90	3.2%	-31.8%	1.84
1935	16.7%	4.55	2.5%	14.2%	2.10
1936	16.2%	5.29	1.2%	15.0%	2.41
1937	-3.8%	5.09	3.6%	-7.4%	2.23
1938	-13.5%	4.40	-1.7%	-11.7%	1.97
1939	12.2%	4.94	-1.8%	14.0%	2.25
1940	-10.2%	4.44	1.2%	-11.4%	1.99
1941	-8.7%	4.05	4.8%	-13.5%	1.72
1942	-1.5%	3.99	10.8%	-12.3%	1.51
1943	-9.4%	3.61	6.2%	-15.5%	1.28
1944	1.3%	3.66	1.5%	-0.2%	1.27
1945	-9.8%	3.30	2.4%	-12.2%	1.12
1946	22.9%	4.06	8.4%	14.5%	1.28
1947	20.7%	4.90	14.6%	6.1%	1.36
1948	26.3%	6.18	7.9%	18.4%	1.61
1949	14.9%	7.11	-1.0%	16.0%	1.87
1950	-13.9%	6.12	1.1%	-15.0%	1.59
1951	38.2%	8.45	7.6%	30.6%	2.07
1952	-5.0%	8.03	2.3%	-7.3%	1.92
1953	13.3%	9.10	1.0%	12.3%	2.16
1954	10.0%	10.01	0.3%	9.7%	2.37
1955	21.8%	12.19	-0.3%	22.1%	2.89
1956	15.9%	14.12	1.6%	14.3%	3.30
1957	8.4%	15.31	3.4%	5.0%	3.47
1958	-9.2%	13.89	3.0%	-12.2%	3.05
1959	2.1%	14.19	0.6%	1.5%	3.09
1960	14.6%	16.26	1.7%	12.8%	3.49
1961	5.8%	17.19	1.1%	4.6%	3.65
1962	7.4%	18.46	1.1%	6.3%	3.88
1963	2.9%	18.99	1.1%	1.8%	3.95
1964	12.3%	21.33	1.4%	10.9%	4.38
1965	-3.4%	20.61	1.6%	-5.0%	4.16
1966	6.9%	22.03	2.9%	3.9%	4.33
1967	2.3%	22.54	2.8%	-0.5%	4.30
1968	19.5%	26.93	4.3%	15.2%	4.96
1969	-5.2%	25.52	5.3%	-10.5%	4.44
1970	-11.2%	22.66	5.9%	-17.1%	3.68

Date	Total Return %	Total Return Index	Inflation Rate	Adjusted Total Return	Adjusted Total Return Index
1971	13.6%	25.74	4.3%	9.3%	4.02
1972	17.5%	30.25	3.3%	14.2%	4.59
1973	20.3%	36.39	6.2%	14.1%	5.24
1974	4.8%	38.15	11.1%	-6.3%	4.91
1975	14.1%	43.52	9.0%	5.1%	5.16
1976	9.7%	47.73	5.8%	3.9%	5.36
1977	14.3%	54.55	6.6%	7.7%	5.77
1978	15.4%	62.96	7.6%	7.8%	6.22
1979	5.3%	66.32	11.3%	-5.9%	5.85
1980	10.7%	73.39	13.5%	-2.8%	5.69
1981	1.9%	74.78	10.4%	-8.5%	5.21
1982	4.8%	78.34	6.2%	-1.4%	5.13
1983	5.8%	82.89	3.2%	2.6%	5.27
1984	4.2%	86.35	4.4%	-0.2%	5.26
1985	11.1%	95.94	3.5%	7.6%	5.66
1986	10.3%	105.79	1.9%	8.4%	6.13
1987	15.9%	122.65	3.7%	12.3%	6.88
1988	8.3%	132.89	4.1%	4.2%	7.17
1989	4.0%	138.23	4.8%	-0.8%	7.12
1990	0.3%	138.67	5.4%	-5.1%	6.76
1991	-5.5%	131.06	4.2%	-9.7%	6.10
1992	2.7%	134.62	3.0%	-0.3%	6.08
1993	-0.3%	134.22	3.0%	-3.3%	5.88
1994	8.5%	145.70	2.6%	5.9%	6.23
1995	3.3%	150.45	2.8%	0.5%	6.26
1996	4.1%	156.63	3.0%	1.1%	6.34
1997	1.6%	159.10	2.4%	-0.8%	6.29
1998	4.4%	166.07	1.5%	2.9%	6.47
1999	9.3%	181.45	2.2%	7.1%	6.92
2000	0.9%	183.04	3.4%	-2.5%	6.75
2001	10.5%	202.23	2.9%	7.6%	7.26
2002	6.5%	215.33	1.6%	4.9%	7.62
2003	3.3%	222.50	2.0%	1.3%	7.72
2004	14.2%	254.15	3.5%	10.7%	8.55
2005	2.9%	261.52	3.5%	-0.6%	8.50
2006	3.4%	270.33	2.0%	1.4%	8.62
2007	-11.0%	240.60	4.2%	-15.2%	7.31
Average	4.9%		2.3%	2.7%	
Median	4.9%		1.6%	2.7%	
High	66.7%		25.2%	71.6%	
Low	-43.6%		-10.8%	-33.2%	

229

U.S. CORPORATE BONDS

Date	Total Return %	Total Return Index	Inflation Rate	Adjusted Total Return	Adjusted Total Return Index
		1.00			1.00
1863	7.8%	1.08	24.8%	-17.0%	0.83
1864	2.9%	1.11	25.2%	-22.3%	0.64
1865	-3.3%	1.07	3.7%	-7.0%	0.60
1866	13.1%	1.21	-2.6%	15.6%	0.69
1867	8.0%	1.31	-6.8%	14.8%	0.80
1868	10.5%	1.45	-3.9%	14.4%	0.91
1869	4.5%	1.51	-4.1%	8.6%	0.99
1870	14.6%	1.73	-4.3%	18.8%	1.18
1871	11.9%	1.94	-6.4%	18.3%	1.39
1872	7.4%	2.08	0.0%	7.4%	1.49
1873	6.1%	2.21	-2.0%	8.2%	1.62
1874	15.0%	2.54	-4.9%	19.9%	1.94
1875	12.2%	2.85	-3.7%	15.8%	2.24
1876	9.3%	3.12	-2.3%	11.6%	2.50
1877	7.1%	3.34	-2.3%	9.4%	2.74
1878	7.2%	3.58	-4.8%	12.0%	3.07
1879	9.9%	3.93	0.0%	9.8%	3.37
1880	10.4%	4.34	2.5%	7.9%	3.64
1881	4.2%	4.52	0.0%	4.2%	3.79
1882	5.3%	4.76	0.0%	5.3%	3.99
1883	6.2%	5.06	-1.6%	7.8%	4.30
1884	4.9%	5.31	-2.5%	7.3%	4.62
1885	17.4%	6.23	-1.7%	19.1%	5.50
1886	8.1%	6.73	-2.6%	10.7%	6.08
1887	0.1%	6.73	0.9%	-0.8%	6.03
1888	7.6%	7.25	0.0%	7.6%	6.49
1889	5.5%	7.65	-2.6%	8.2%	7.02
1890	-1.1%	7.57	-1.8%	0.7%	7.08
1891	10.0%	8.32	0.0%	9.9%	7.78
1892	8.4%	9.02	0.0%	8.4%	8.43
1893	3.9%	9.37	-0.9%	4.8%	8.83
1894	11.0%	10.40	-4.6%	15.6%	10.22
1895	3.5%	10.76	-1.9%	5.5%	10.77
1896	3.2%	11.11	0.0%	3.2%	11.12
1897	10.8%	12.31	-1.0%	11.8%	12.43
1898	12.7%	13.88	0.0%	12.7%	14.01
1899	2.4%	14.21	0.0%	2.4%	14.35

Date	Total Return %	Total Return Index	Inflation Rate	Adjusted Total Return	Adjusted Total Return Index
1900	10.8%	15.75	1.0%	9.8%	15.75
1901	9.2%	17.19	1.0%	8.2%	17.04
1902	2.5%	17.62	1.0%	1.5%	17.30
1903	-4.5%	16.82	2.9%	-7.4%	16.02
1904	17.7%	19.79	0.9%	16.7%	18.69
1905	4.4%	20.67	-0.9%	5.4%	19.70
1906	2.3%	21.14	1.9%	0.4%	19.77
1907	-5.1%	20.07	4.6%	-9.7%	17.85
1908	15.3%	23.14	-1.8%	17.0%	20.90
1909	5.3%	24.35	-1.8%	7.1%	22.37
1910	2.7%	25.00	4.6%	-1.9%	21.94
1911	4.9%	26.24	0.0%	4.9%	23.02
1912	2.3%	26.84	2.6%	-0.3%	22.95
1913	-0.2%	26.79	1.7%	-1.9%	22.51
1914	-1.0%	26.53	0.8%	-1.8%	22.10
1915	12.9%	29.95	0.8%	12.1%	24.77
1916	6.1%	31.77	7.4%	-1.4%	24.43
1917	-7.7%	29.31	17.7%	-25.4%	18.22
1918	9.3%	32.02	17.7%	-8.4%	16.69
1919	-2.0%	31.37	15.0%	-17.0%	13.85
1920	0.0%	31.39	15.9%	-15.9%	11.64
1921	17.6%	36.91	-10.8%	28.4%	14.96
1922	11.9%	41.29	-6.5%	18.4%	17.71
1923	2.5%	42.33	2.0%	0.5%	17.80
1924	9.9%	46.52	0.0%	9.9%	19.56
1925	7.8%	50.15	2.9%	4.9%	20.51
1926	8.3%	54.33	0.5%	7.9%	22.12
1927	8.2%	58.77	-1.4%	9.6%	24.25
1928	1.3%	59.52	-1.4%	2.7%	24.91
1929	2.6%	61.04	0.0%	2.5%	25.54
1930	6.6%	65.06	-2.4%	9.0%	27.84
1931	-13.5%	56.29	-9.0%	-4.5%	26.60
1932	7.5%	60.50	-10.4%	17.9%	31.36
1933	17.9%	71.31	-4.9%	22.8%	38.50
1934	19.2%	85.02	3.2%	16.0%	44.66
1935	7.8%	91.66	2.5%	5.3%	47.04
1936	11.5%	102.20	1.2%	10.3%	51.87
1937	-8.0%	94.07	3.6%	-11.6%	45.87

Date	Total Return %	Total Return Index	Inflation Rate	Adjusted Total Return	Adjusted Total Return Index
1938	2.5%	96.44	-1.7%	4.3%	47.83
1939	5.1%	101.40	-1.8%	6.9%	51.14
1940	6.6%	108.10	1.2%	5.4%	53.90
1941	2.8%	111.10	4.8%	-2.0%	52.83
1942	8.7%	120.73	10.8%	-2.1%	51.70
1943	12.2%	135.44	6.2%	6.0%	54.83
1944	13.1%	153.13	1.5%	11.6%	61.19
1945	6.5%	163.03	2.4%	4.1%	63.69
1946	-1.2%	161.06	8.4%	-9.6%	57.59
1947	-3.3%	155.67	14.6%	-17.9%	47.26
1948	6.0%	165.04	7.9%	-1.8%	46.39
1949	6.1%	175.14	-1.0%	7.2%	49.71
1950	5.0%	183.91	1.1%	4.0%	51.67
1951	-2.6%	179.09	7.6%	-10.3%	46.37
1952	5.8%	189.40	2.3%	3.5%	47.99
1953	1.9%	192.99	1.0%	0.9%	48.45
1954	7.3%	207.04	0.3%	7.0%	51.82
1955	0.4%	207.88	-0.3%	0.7%	52.20
1956	-5.2%	197.13	1.6%	-6.7%	48.68
1957	2.1%	201.28	3.4%	-1.3%	48.06
1958	3.2%	207.80	3.0%	0.3%	48.19
1959	-1.5%	204.59	0.6%	-2.1%	47.16
1960	10.4%	225.94	1.7%	8.7%	51.27
1961	3.9%	234.82	1.1%	2.8%	52.71
1962	9.9%	258.10	1.1%	8.8%	57.34
1963	5.5%	272.41	1.1%	4.4%	59.89
1964	6.0%	288.84	1.4%	4.7%	62.68
1965	1.6%	293.42	1.6%	-0.0%	62.66
1966	-2.2%	287.06	2.9%	-5.1%	59.47
1967	-2.0%	281.41	2.8%	-4.8%	56.61
1968	5.7%	297.52	4.3%	1.5%	57.44
1969	-1.0%	294.53	5.3%	-6.3%	53.83
1970	9.2%	321.69	5.9%	3.3%	55.59
1971	15.0%	369.88	4.3%	10.7%	61.53
1972	10.1%	407.12	3.3%	6.8%	65.68
1973	4.7%	426.37	6.2%	-1.5%	64.72
1974	-0.7%	423.23	11.1%	-11.8%	57.05
1975	14.3%	483.94	9.0%	5.4%	60.11

Date	Total Return %	Total Return Index	Inflation Rate	Adjusted Total Return	Adjusted Total Return Index
1976	24.7%	603.30	5.8%	18.9%	71.48
1977	5.6%	636.94	6.6%	-1.0%	70.73
1978	1.2%	644.66	7.6%	-6.4%	66.22
1979	-4.0%	618.57	11.3%	-15.3%	56.07
1980	-2.3%	604.64	13.5%	-15.7%	47.25
1981	2.5%	620.03	10.4%	-7.8%	43.56
1982	38.5%	858.56	6.2%	32.3%	57.63
1983	10.5%	948.91	3.2%	7.3%	61.85
1984	16.6%	1,106.04	4.4%	12.2%	69.39
1985	27.9%	1,414.25	3.5%	24.3%	86.26
1986	22.1%	1,726.91	1.9%	20.2%	103.73
1987	2.1%	1,763.45	3.7%	-1.5%	102.13
1988	12.5%	1,983.38	4.1%	8.4%	110.66
1989	14.9%	2,279.51	4.8%	10.1%	121.86
1990	7.8%	2,456.76	5.4%	2.4%	124.77
1991	17.5%	2,887.62	4.2%	13.3%	141.38
1992	13.5%	3,277.55	3.0%	10.5%	156.22
1993	8.3%	3,548.37	3.0%	5.3%	164.47
1994	-4.2%	3,398.91	2.6%	-6.8%	153.27
1995	20.7%	4,103.87	2.8%	18.0%	180.83
1996	5.3%	4,323.34	3.0%	2.4%	185.14
1997	9.7%	4,743.96	2.4%	7.4%	198.81
1998	9.6%	5,200.82	1.5%	8.1%	214.95
1999	-3.2%	5,032.24	2.2%	-5.5%	203.23
2000	9.4%	5,504.38	3.4%	6.0%	215.43
2001	10.7%	6,090.61	2.9%	7.8%	232.21
2002	10.3%	6,718.02	1.6%	8.7%	252.47
2003	8.9%	7,317.38	2.0%	6.9%	269.97
2004	5.0%	7,681.87	3.5%	1.5%	273.91
2005	0.8%	7,744.76	3.5%	-2.6%	266.67
2006	3.2%	7,991.05	2.0%	1.2%	269.90
2007	4.8%	8,375.12	4.2%	0.6%	271.43
Average	6.7%		2.3%	4.4%	
Median	6.1%		1.6%	5.3%	
High	38.5%		25.2%	32.3%	
Low	-13.5%		-10.8%	-25.4%	

10-YEAR U.S. TREASURY BOND YIELDS

Date	Total Return %	Total Return Index	Inflation Rate	Adjusted Total Return	Adjusted Total Return Index
		1.00			1.00
1850	5.3%	1.05	2.2%	3.1%	1.03
1851	5.2%	1.11	-2.1%	7.3%	1.11
1852	5.0%	1.16	1.1%	3.9%	1.15
1853	5.0%	1.22	0.0%	5.0%	1.21
1854	5.6%	1.29	8.6%	-3.0%	1.17
1855	5.5%	1.36	3.0%	2.5%	1.20
1856	5.7%	1.44	-1.9%	7.6%	1.29
1857	5.8%	1.52	2.9%	2.8%	1.33
1858	5.3%	1.60	-5.7%	11.0%	1.47
1859	5.5%	1.69	1.0%	4.5%	1.54
1860	5.9%	1.79	0.0%	5.9%	1.63
1861	6.6%	1.91	6.0%	0.6%	1.64
1862	5.8%	2.02	14.2%	-8.4%	1.50
1863	5.5%	2.13	24.8%	-19.3%	1.21
1864	5.2%	2.24	25.2%	-20.0%	0.97
1865	5.6%	2.36	3.7%	1.9%	0.99
1866	5.4%	2.49	-2.6%	7.9%	1.07
1867	5.4%	2.62	-6.8%	12.2%	1.20
1868	5.2%	2.76	-3.9%	9.2%	1.31
1869	5.1%	2.90	-4.1%	9.2%	1.43
1870	5.3%	3.05	-4.3%	9.6%	1.56
1871	5.1%	3.21	-6.4%	11.5%	1.74
1872	5.4%	3.38	0.0%	5.4%	1.84
1873	5.4%	3.56	-2.0%	7.4%	1.97
1874	5.3%	3.75	-4.9%	10.2%	2.17
1875	5.1%	3.95	-3.7%	8.8%	2.36
1876	5.3%	4.15	-2.3%	7.6%	2.54
1877	5.4%	4.38	-2.3%	7.8%	2.74
1878	4.0%	4.56	-4.8%	8.7%	2.98
1879	3.9%	4.73	0.0%	3.9%	3.10
1880	3.6%	4.90	2.5%	1.1%	3.13
1881	3.4%	5.07	0.0%	3.4%	3.23
1882	3.3%	5.24	0.0%	3.3%	3.34
1883	3.2%	5.40	-1.6%	4.9%	3.50
1884	3.3%	5.58	-2.5%	5.7%	3.70
1885	3.2%	5.76	-1.7%	4.9%	3.89
1886	3.1%	5.94	-2.6%	5.7%	4.11
1887	3.2%	6.13	0.9%	2.3%	4.20
1888	3.1%	6.32	0.0%	3.1%	4.33
1889	3.1%	6.52	-2.6%	5.8%	4.58
1890	3.3%	6.73	-1.8%	5.1%	4.82
1891	3.4%	6.96	0.0%	3.4%	4.98

Date	Total Return %	Total Return Index	Inflation Rate	Adjusted Total Return	Adjusted Total Return Index
1892	3.5%	7.21	0.0%	3.5%	5.16
1893	3.5%	7.46	-0.9%	4.4%	5.38
1894	3.5%	7.72	-4.6%	8.1%	5.82
1895	3.3%	7.97	-1.9%	5.3%	6.12
1896	3.3%	8.24	0.0%	3.3%	6.33
1897	3.1%	8.49	-1.0%	4.1%	6.59
1898	3.1%	8.76	0.0%	3.1%	6.79
1899	3.0%	9.02	0.0%	3.0%	6.99
1900	2.9%	9.28	1.0%	1.9%	7.13
1901	2.9%	9.55	1.0%	1.9%	7.26
1902	3.0%	9.83	1.0%	2.0%	7.40
1903	3.0%	10.12	2.9%	0.1%	7.41
1904	3.1%	10.43	0.9%	2.1%	7.57
1905	3.1%	10.75	-0.9%	4.0%	7.87
1906	3.1%	11.08	1.9%	1.2%	7.96
1907	3.4%	11.45	4.6%	-1.3%	7.86
1908	3.3%	11.83	-1.8%	5.0%	8.26
1909	3.4%	12.24	-1.8%	5.2%	8.69
1910	3.5%	12.66	4.6%	-1.1%	8.59
1911	3.5%	13.11	0.0%	3.5%	8.89
1912	3.5%	13.57	2.6%	0.9%	8.97
1913	3.6%	14.05	1.7%	1.9%	9.14
1914	3.6%	14.56	0.8%	2.8%	9.40
1915	3.6%	15.09	0.8%	2.8%	9.66
1916	3.6%	15.63	7.4%	-3.8%	9.29
1917	3.8%	16.23	17.7%	-13.9%	8.00
1918	3.7%	16.84	17.7%	-13.9%	6.89
1919	4.9%	17.67	15.0%	-10.1%	6.19
1920	5.4%	18.62	15.9%	-10.5%	5.54
1921	4.5%	19.45	-10.8%	15.3%	6.39
1922	4.3%	20.29	-6.5%	10.9%	7.08
1923	4.4%	21.18	2.0%	2.4%	7.25
1924	4.0%	22.02	0.0%	4.0%	7.53
1925	3.8%	22.85	2.9%	0.9%	7.60
1926	3.6%	23.67	0.5%	3.1%	7.83
1927	3.2%	24.42	-1.4%	4.6%	8.19
1928	3.5%	25.26	-1.4%	4.9%	8.59
1929	3.4%	26.11	0.0%	3.4%	8.88
1930	3.2%	26.95	-2.4%	5.7%	9.38
1931	3.9%	28.01	-9.0%	12.9%	10.60
1932	3.4%	28.95	-10.4%	13.8%	12.06
1933	3.5%	29.97	-4.9%	8.4%	13.08
1934	3.0%	30.86	3.2%	-0.2%	13.04

Date	Total Return %	Total Return Index	Inflation Rate	Adjusted Total Return	Adjusted Total Return Index
1935	2.8%	31.73	2.5%	0.3%	13.09
1936	2.5%	32.53	1.2%	1.3%	13.26
1937	2.7%	33.41	3.6%	-0.9%	13.13
1938	2.5%	34.23	-1.7%	4.2%	13.69
1939	2.3%	35.02	-1.8%	4.1%	14.25
1940	1.9%	35.68	1.2%	0.7%	14.34
1941	2.1%	36.42	4.8%	-2.7%	13.96
1942	2.1%	37.19	10.8%	-8.7%	12.74
1943	2.1%	37.97	6.2%	-4.0%	12.23
1944	2.1%	38.77	1.5%	0.7%	12.31
1945	1.7%	39.42	2.4%	-0.7%	12.22
1946	1.8%	40.14	8.4%	-6.6%	11.42
1947	2.2%	41.01	14.6%	-12.4%	10.00
1948	2.1%	41.88	7.9%	-5.8%	9.43
1949	1.8%	42.64	-1.0%	2.8%	9.70
1950	2.2%	43.56	1.1%	1.1%	9.81
1951	2.5%	44.66	7.6%	-5.1%	9.30
1952	2.5%	45.78	2.3%	0.3%	9.33
1953	2.6%	46.97	1.0%	1.6%	9.48
1954	2.5%	48.15	0.3%	2.2%	9.69
1955	3.0%	49.57	-0.3%	3.3%	10.01
1956	3.6%	51.35	1.6%	2.0%	10.21
1957	3.2%	53.00	3.4%	-0.2%	10.19
1958	3.9%	55.05	3.0%	0.9%	10.28
1959	4.7%	57.63	0.6%	4.1%	10.70
1960	3.8%	59.84	1.7%	2.1%	10.93
1961	4.1%	62.27	1.1%	2.9%	11.25
1962	3.9%	64.67	1.1%	2.7%	11.56
1963	4.1%	67.35	1.1%	3.0%	11.91
1964	4.2%	70.18	1.4%	2.8%	12.25
1965	4.7%	73.45	1.6%	3.0%	12.62
1966	4.6%	76.85	2.9%	1.7%	12.84
1967	5.7%	81.23	2.8%	2.9%	13.20
1968	6.2%	86.24	4.3%	1.9%	13.45
1969	7.9%	93.03	5.3%	2.6%	13.80
1970	6.5%	99.08	5.9%	0.6%	13.88
1971	5.9%	104.92	4.3%	1.6%	14.10
1972	6.4%	111.64	3.3%	3.1%	14.54
1973	6.9%	119.34	6.2%	0.7%	14.64
1974	7.4%	128.18	11.1%	-3.7%	14.09
1975	7.8%	138.12	9.0%	-1.2%	13.92
1976	6.8%	147.53	5.8%	1.1%	14.07
1977	7.8%	159.01	6.6%	1.2%	14.23

Date	Total Return %	Total Return Index	Inflation Rate	Adjusted Total Return	Adjusted Total Return Index
1978	9.2%	173.56	7.6%	1.6%	14.46
1979	10.3%	191.48	11.3%	-1.0%	14.32
1980	12.4%	215.29	13.5%	-1.1%	14.17
1981	14.0%	245.38	10.4%	3.6%	14.68
1982	10.4%	270.80	6.2%	4.2%	15.30
1983	11.8%	302.81	3.2%	8.6%	16.61
1984	11.6%	337.79	4.4%	7.2%	17.81
1985	9.0%	368.19	3.5%	5.5%	18.78
1986	7.2%	394.81	1.9%	5.4%	19.79
1987	8.8%	429.67	3.7%	5.2%	20.81
1988	9.1%	468.94	4.1%	5.0%	21.86
1989	7.9%	506.13	4.8%	3.1%	22.54
1990	8.1%	547.02	5.4%	2.7%	23.14
1991	6.7%	583.73	4.2%	2.5%	23.72
1992	6.7%	622.84	3.0%	3.7%	24.60
1993	5.8%	659.15	3.0%	2.9%	25.30
1994	7.8%	710.83	2.6%	5.2%	26.62
1995	5.6%	750.49	2.8%	2.8%	27.37
1996	6.4%	798.75	3.0%	3.5%	28.32
1997	5.8%	844.68	2.4%	3.4%	29.29
1998	4.7%	883.96	1.5%	3.1%	30.21
1999	6.5%	940.97	2.2%	4.2%	31.49
2000	5.1%	989.15	3.4%	1.7%	32.03
2001	5.1%	1,039.30	2.9%	2.2%	32.74
2002	3.8%	1,079.10	1.6%	2.3%	33.48
2003	4.3%	1,125.18	2.0%	2.3%	34.24
2004	4.2%	1,172.89	3.5%	0.7%	34.49
2005	4.4%	1,224.38	3.5%	0.9%	34.81
2006	4.7%	1,281.92	2.0%	2.7%	35.76
2007	4.0%	1,333.59	4.2%	-0.2%	35.68
Average	4.7%		2.3%	2.4%	
Median	4.0%		1.6%	2.9%	
High	14.0%		25.2%	15.3%	
Low	1.7%		-10.8%	-20.0%	

U.S. GOVERNMENT ACTIONS and INVESTMENTS

Beginning of Year	President	House Speaker	Investment Taxes				Short-Term Interest Rates			Investments			
			Individual Income Tax	% Chg	Capital Gains Tax	% Chg	Fed Chairman	Fed Funds Rate	% Chg	Common Stocks	% Chg	Real Estate	% Chg
1913	Wilson (D)	Clark (D)	15		7		Hamlin	3.00		7		2,586	
1914	Wilson (D)	Clark (D)	15	0%	7	0%	Hamlin	3.00	0%	5	-31%	2,452	-5%
1915	Wilson (D)	Clark (D)	15	0%	7	0%	Hamlin	3.00	0%	9	82%	2,570	5%
1916	Wilson (D)	Clark (D)	15	0%	7	0%	Harding	3.00	0%	8	-4%	2,891	12%
1917	Wilson (D)	Clark (D)	67	347%	7	0%	Harding	3.00	0%	7	-22%	2,607	-10%
1918	Harding (R)	Clark (D)	77	15%	7	0%	Harding	4.00	33%	7	11%	2,375	-9%
1919	Harding (R)	Clark (D)	73	-5%	7	0%	Harding	4.75	19%	9	30%	3,239	36%
1920	Harding (R)	Gillett (R)	73	0%	7	0%	Harding	7.00	47%	6	-33%	4,043	25%
1921	Harding (R)	Gillett (R)	73	0%	12.5	79%	Harding	4.50	-36%	7	13%	4,506	11%
1922	Harding (R)	Gillett (R)	58	-21%	12.5	0%	Harding	4.00	-11%	9	22%	4,730	5%
1923	Harding (R)	Gillett (R)	44	-24%	12.5	0%	Crissinger	4.50	13%	8	-3%	4,959	5%
1924	Harding (R)	Gillett (R)	46	5%	12.5	0%	Crissinger	3.00	-33%	11	26%	4,946	-0%
1925	Coolidge (R)	Gillett (R)	25	-46%	12.5	0%	Crissinger	3.50	17%	14	30%	5,101	3%
1926	Coolidge (R)	Longworth (R)	25	0%	12.5	0%	Crissinger	4.00	14%	14	0%	6,124	20%
1927	Coolidge (R)	Longworth (R)	25	0%	12.5	0%	Crissinger	4.00	0%	18	29%	6,418	5%
1928	Coolidge (R)	Longworth (R)	25	0%	12.5	0%	Young	5.00	25%	24	38%	7,642	19%
1929	Hoover (R)	Longworth (R)	24	-4%	12.5	0%	Young	4.50	-10%	21	-12%	7,387	-3%
1930	Hoover (R)	Longworth (R)	25	4%	12.5	0%	Young	2.00	-56%	15	-29%	6,579	-11%
1931	Hoover (R)	Longworth (R)	25	0%	12.5	0%	Meyer	3.50	75%	8	-47%	5,898	-10%
1932	Hoover (R)	Garner (D)	63	152%	12.5	0%	Meyer	2.50	-29%	7	-15%	3,324	-44%
1933	F. Roosevelt (D)	Garner (D)	63	0%	12.5	0%	Meyer	2.00	-20%	10	47%	5,541	67%
1934	F. Roosevelt (D)	Rainey (D)	63	0%	32	156%	Eccles	1.50	-25%	10	-6%	3,958	-29%
1935	F. Roosevelt (D)	Byrns (D)	63	0%	32	0%	Eccles	1.50	0%	13	41%	4,617	17%
1936	F. Roosevelt (D)	Byrns (D)	78	24%	39	22%	Eccles	1.50	0%	17	28%	5,367	16%
1937	F. Roosevelt (D)	Bankhead (D)	78	0%	39	0%	Eccles	1.00	-33%	11	-39%	5,164	-4%
1938	F. Roosevelt (D)	Bankhead (D)	78	0%	30	-23%	Eccles	1.00	0%	13	25%	4,470	-13%
1939	F. Roosevelt (D)	Bankhead (D)	78	0%	30	0%	Eccles	1.00	0%	13	-5%	5,016	12%
1940	F. Roosevelt (D)	Bankhead (D)	78	0%	30	0%	Eccles	1.00	0%	11	-15%	4,506	-10%
1941	F. Roosevelt (D)	Rayburn (D)	80	3%	30	0%	Eccles	1.00	0%	9	-18%	4,112	-9%
1942	F. Roosevelt (D)	Rayburn (D)	88	10%	25	-17%	Eccles	0.50	-50%	10	12%	4,049	-2%
1943	F. Roosevelt (D)	Rayburn (D)	88	0%	25	0%	Eccles	0.50	0%	12	19%	3,669	-9%
1944	F. Roosevelt (D)	Rayburn (D)	94	7%	25	0%	Eccles	0.50	0%	13	14%	3,715	1%
1945	F. Roosevelt (D)	Rayburn (D)	94	0%	25	0%	Eccles	0.50	0%	17	31%	3,350	-10%
1946	Truman (D)	Rayburn (D)	86	-9%	25	0%	Eccles	0.50	0%	15	-12%	4,117	23%
1947	Truman (D)	Rayburn (D)	86	0%	25	0%	Eccles	1.00	100%	15	0%	4,970	21%
1948	Truman (D)	Martin (R)	82	-5%	25	0%	Eccles	1.50	50%	15	-1%	6,277	26%
1949	Truman (D)	Martin (R)	82	0%	25	0%	McCabe	1.50	0%	17	10%	7,214	15%
1950	Truman (D)	Rayburn (D)	84	2%	25	0%	McCabe	1.75	17%	20	22%	6,209	-14%
1951	Truman (D)	Rayburn (D)	91	8%	25	0%	McCabe	1.75	0%	24	16%	8,582	38%
1952	Truman (D)	Rayburn (D)	91	0%	25	0%	Martin	1.75	0%	27	12%	8,151	-5%
1953	Eisenhower (R)	Rayburn (D)	91	0%	25	0%	Martin	2.00	14%	25	-7%	9,233	13%
1954	Eisenhower (R)	Martin (R)	91	0%	25	0%	Martin	1.28	-36%	36	45%	10,160	10%
1955	Eisenhower (R)	Martin (R)	91	0%	25	0%	Martin	2.48	94%	46	26%	12,373	22%
1956	Eisenhower (R)	Rayburn (D)	91	0%	25	0%	Martin	2.94	19%	47	3%	14,335	16%
1957	Eisenhower (R)	Rayburn (D)	91	0%	25	0%	Martin	2.98	1%	40	-14%	15,534	8%
1958	Eisenhower (R)	Rayburn (D)	91	0%	25	0%	Martin	2.42	-19%	55	38%	14,102	-9%
1959	Eisenhower (R)	Rayburn (D)	91	0%	25	0%	Martin	3.99	65%	60	8%	14,401	2%
1960	Eisenhower (R)	Rayburn (D)	91	0%	25	0%	Martin	1.98	-50%	58	-3%	16,498	15%
1961	Kennedy (D)	Rayburn (D)	91	0%	25	0%	Martin	2.33	18%	72	23%	17,449	6%
1962	Kennedy (D)	McCormack (D)	91	0%	25	0%	Martin	2.93	26%	63	-12%	18,737	7%
1963	Kennedy (D))	McCormack (D)	91	0%	25	0%	Martin	3.38	15%	75	19%	19,278	3%